Health Care Finance and Economics

Steven R. Eastaugh, ScD

Professor
Department of Health Service Management and Leadership
School of Public Health and Health Service
School of Business and Public Management
George Washington University
Washington, DC

JONES AND BARTLETT PUBLISHERS
Sudbury, Massachusetts
BOSTON   TORONTO   LONDON   SINGAPORE

World Headquarters
Jones and Bartlett Publishers
40 Tall Pine Drive
Sudbury, MA 01776
978-443-5000
info@jbpub.com
www.jbpub.com

Jones and Bartlett Publishers
International
Barb House, Barb Mews
London W6 7PA
UK

Jones and Bartlett Publishers Canada
2406 Nikanna Road
Mississauga, ON L5C 2W6
CANADA

Library of Congress Cataloging-in-Publication Data
Eastaugh, Steven R., 1952–
  Health care finance and economics / Steven R. Eastaugh.
    p. cm.
  Includes bibliographical references and index.
  ISBN 0-7637-3146-3
    1. Medical economics. I. Title.

RA410.E267 2002
338.4'33621—dc21

2003047494

Publisher: Michael Brown
Production Manager: Amy Rose
Associate Production Editor: Renée Sekerak
Associate Editor: Chambers Moore
Associate Marketing Manager: Joy Stark-Vancs
Manufacturing Buyer: Therese Bräuer
Composition: AnnMarie Lemoine
Text Design: Dartmouth Publishing, Inc.
Cover Design: Kristin Ohlin
Printing and Binding: Malloy Incorporated
Cover Printing: Malloy Incorporated

Printed in the United States of America
07 06 05 04 03   10 9 8 7 6 5 4 3 2 1

*This book is dedicated
to my ten-year-old son,
Robert*

Dr. Steven R. Eastaugh is professor of Health Finance and Economics at the George Washington University and an internationally acclaimed speaker, consultant, and change agent. He is a graduate of Harvard School of Public Health, Harvard's John F. Kennedy School of Government, Harvard Economics Department, and has a Doctor of Science in Public Health from Johns Hopkins School of Public Health. His research areas include capital budgeting, financial ratio analysis, profitability and liquidity, as well as cost benefit and cost effectiveness. He is the author of seven books and 109 journal articles.

In his quarter century of teaching, he has trained and inspired over three thousand healthcare managers and leaders in the U.S. and around the world. He is the winner of numerous awards, including the American College of Healthcare Executives Edgar Hayhow Award for "Best health care article of the year." Dr. Eastaugh has also conducted Health Services Research in 29 countries. Dr. Eastaugh formerly taught at Cornell University and was senior staff health economist at the National Academy of Sciences.

When not working, Steve is a devoted father, scuba diver, and painter.

Contents

10 Debt Financing and Capital Structure   **223**

Preface

In terms of health care, what Americans want is nearly impossible—unlimited access to the best care at affordable prices. Health care has priced itself into the public eye by assuming an increasing proportion of the American economy. Resources are limited, which is why understanding finance and economics, the science of the allocation of scarce resources, is vital to healthcare managers and providers.

The reader will develop admiration for (1) what a manager can do to enhance productivity, market strategy, quality, and profitability; (2) what a financial manager can do to manage capital structure, investment decisions, and financial decisions; (3) what healthcare managers and providers can do to enhance access, promote managed care, and learn from technology assessment studies; and (4) what a payer can do to buy prudently yet preserve the biomedical capacity of the nation.

In preparing this book, I intentionally have cast a wide net to include both healthcare managers and providers. I anticipate that this wide audience is more interested in a synthesis of currently available study results and potential policy ramifications than in new research methods. The reader should come away with a better understanding of the financial management and health economics literature and a renewed appreciation of the fact that the behavior of consumers and providers is only partially understood at this time.

Chapters 1 and 2 offer an introduction to the current health industry financial perspective. Chapter 3 shifts the focus to how we pay the doctor. Chapters 4 and 5 shift the focus to productivity enhancement programs and gainsharing incentive programs. Chapters 6 and 7 discuss cost-effectiveness and cost-benefit analysis. Chapter 8 shifts the focus to marketing and pricing. Chapters 9 and 10 outline financing and investment decisions. Chapter 11 examines various future issues in and alternatives to health care.

Health Care Finance and Economics contains more than 400 references; however, because not everything worth knowing is published in the journals, I use a second source of information. For 25 years I have accumulated, through management consulting work, firsthand accounts of ways to improve economic efficiency, productivity, quality, and access. As an economist, I grew tired of sterile econometric measurement of a cost function and wanted to jump into the tougher task of cutting costs while enhancing service quality. Such real-world experience helps improve the text by reporting success and failure (authors seldom advertise failures in journals). In this era of bare-bones reimbursement, learning from our failures and the failures of the competition will become increasingly important for managers.

Finally, I acknowledge the invaluable assistance of Tom Davy, DrPH(c), FACHE in the preparation of this text. I have also depended on the assistance of others in writing this book, including Bernie Horak, PhD, FACHE, David Dranove, PhD, James Begun, Duncan Neuhauser, PhD, FACHE, and Ruth Hanft.

Chapter 1

Economic Incentives and Fund Flows

Our past solutions are our current problems.

– Duncan Neuhauser

Demands are infinite, whereas the resources are finite, regardless of whether the care is funded through health insurance or from public funds. The marketplace system encourages demand and diversity, whereas the controlled system leads to uniformity, rationing, and possibly mediocrity.

– John Lister

▶ **Critical points in this chapter:**

- Different delivery models in American health care

- Economies of scale and efficiency

- Discounting and net present value

- Types of risk

Healthcare costs are very much in the public eye. The health sector accounts for almost 15 percent of the American economy. Government mandates health benefit packages, making premiums more costly, thus increasing the number of uninsured citizens. As a result, state and national programs designed to reduce the number of uninsured Americans have the opposite effect. We pay to build 600,000 hospital beds and then complain because we have too many acute care beds and hospital-based specialists. We pay tens of billions of dollars for hospital-based graduate medical education and then complain that there are too many specialists. We offer no funding for primary care graduate medical education and wonder why we do not have enough primary care physicians. U.S. health care frequently finances the frivolous, while underfunding the necessary, such as care for the poor and emergency departments. The United States' past "solutions" are current problems in today's health policy.

Economists have long studied supply curves and demand curves in the healthcare industry. A supply curve is a graphic representation of the relationship between the market price of a good or service and the quantity supplied (the higher the price of a good or service, the more will be supplied). A demand curve is a graphic representation of the relationship between the price of a good or service and the quantity demanded (the lower the price of a good or service, the higher the demand).

From a bird's eye view, healthcare executives need to pay more attention to the basics of supply and demand. Emergency medicine is a good example. The current problem with emergency department overcrowding does not result from any increase in patient volume. Large, well-run managed care systems are doing a better job of keeping their patients away from the expensive emergency department (ED). However, some badly managed HMOs underprovide service and end up sending insured patients to the ED due to their inability to receive a "convenient" primary care appointment from their HMO.

The root problem, however, is that the number of available EDs has been cut back. Between 1994 and 2001, some 546 EDs were closed, including 172 in rural areas (Eastaugh 2002). Emergency departments are flooded for three reasons. First, emergency departments have smaller staffs (thanks to the nursing shortage, which is exacerbated by the additional stress of working in an overcrowded facility). Second, EDs are filled with soon-to-be-inpatients who sit in observation units for 24 to 48 hours because hospital beds are unavailable. The ED must treat more patients with a higher intensity because the supply of hospital beds is limited. In the last eight years, we have closed 114,000 hospital beds, thus creating more work for the emergency departments. Third, even in a "health care as a private good" model, emergency medicine in America has become a public good. This has resulted from the withering of the American medical safety net, the legal requirements to (COBRA, the Consolidated Omnibus Budget Reconciliation Act of 1996 and EMTALA, the Emergency Medical Treatment and Active Labor Act) and the current reality of disaster preparation and response.

The credo of a hospital's chief financial officer is that cash makes the world go round. In the current bare-bones reimbursement climate, everything is a major pruning opportunity. Healthcare managers have an increased willingness to divest, close, or otherwise downsize product lines that generate a financial loss. The emergency department is seen as a financial weak spot because indigent patients and poorly reimbursed Medicaid patients enter the door through the ED. If a hospital closes its ED, it reduces its potential financial losses.

The nation's EDs should work to improve their efficiency despite the obstacles they face. However, in contrast to the business sector of health care, EDs are very limited in their ability to raise prices to improve their financial position. The new ambulatory patient classification (APC) system severely limits the EDs' ability to generate higher revenues. The APC crises are unilaterally set by the government, so the prices are set low. Emergency medicine is increasingly squeezed by a declining supply of EDs, regulation of prices, managed care, and staffing shortages. This strengthens the argument for a national health plan as outlined by the American Hospital Association (2002) or at least for greater funding to neighborhood clinics and small local community hospitals, including emergency departments.

Economic transfers of patients (the transfer of a patient to another facility to avoid financial burden) are on the rise even while socially responsible physicians cry out that care for the poor is incumbent upon society. The pressures to transfer come jointly from medical staff and hospitals concerned with their own profit margins. Emergency physicians treat large numbers of nonacute patients who cannot afford a private physician. Because these visits are irregular, care is fragmented, time-consuming, and costly. The ED is not a model for efficient continuity of care. Moreover, emergency medicine training programs do not equip emergency physicians to treat chronic stable medical conditions such as hypertension and diabetes. A hytertensive cerebral bleed or hyperosmolar coma is managed with more confidence than a high blood pressure of 180/100 or a glucose of 340. Trained to "assume the worst," ED staff use expensive laboratory and radiological studies to examine patients with moderate symptoms because the emergency patient is defined as "high risk." The use of highly trained staff, expensive equipment, and high administrative overhead makes ED care at least twice as expensive as comparable care rendered in an office setting.

Some analysts have suggested hospital-based HMOs for the poor as a second-best alternative to passage of a national health plan. In practice, such halfway solutions have not worked. In Washington, DC and Massachusetts, the creation of hospital-based managed care systems has created another layer of red tape and bureaucracy, without substantial improvement in access for the uninsured. Just as "necessity is the mother of invention," the corollary is also true: A lack of necessity can impede innovation. Physicians need to balance their defensive medicine practices with cost-effective decision making, adjusting levels of care to the actual patient needs. The results would be good economics and good medicine.

Emergency Medicine as a Public Good

As stated earlier, even if we are to consider health care a private good in the United States, we should consider emergency medicine a public good. Emergency departments do much more than provide episodic care. Federal law requires that they provide health care to all who present themselves, regardless of their ability to pay. As such, EDs have become the primary health-care safety net in this country. We must end our national cognitive dissonance in requiring EDs to provide treatment without compensation.

In recent years, emergency medicine has come under great pressure due to disaster planning and response. Emergency departments of both public and private hospitals play an increasingly important, and often uncompensated, role in local disaster response.

Hospital cost accountants are on the side of providers, seeking money for their value, while HMO and government accountants seek value for their money. Such HMOs would revel in a $1600 expense they did not have to pay. For every $1600 underbill, however, there often exists a $1600 double bill in the form of a second hospital repeating the workup of the first hospital following an economic transfer. The elimination of repeat workups is one more argument for the passage of a universal national health program.

Despite several federal and state laws, pressures for "economic transfers" are strong. Consider a simple example. An uninsured diabetic shows up at your ED with a glucose of 750 and a pH of 7.17, and his family physician is contacted. The family physician says the patient has not paid for his last seven visits and he should be transferred to the city hospital. The ED physician will insist that the patient is too sick to transfer, but the family doctor says: "Give him insulin and an amp of bicarbonate, call him stable, and transfer him to the hospital for the poor." The Consolidated Omnibus Reconciliation Act (COBRA) gives ammunition to emergency physicians who may be pressed to transfer indigent patients. The threat of legal and monetary sanction makes good care economically desirable even for those patients who do not pay. Laws can be passed to discourage economic transfers, but they do not eliminate the problem. When a transfer is considered primarily for economic reasons, there are no expected medical benefits to justify the risks to the patient. Patients may decompensate or even die in transfer; delays in treatment occur; tests and radiographs frequently are repeated at the receiving institution.

Some hospital executives behave like "seagull" managers towards emergency medicine — swooping in, screeching, picking on ethical physicians, and then closing the ED or flying off. We must prevent emergency medicine from being a big "loser" in the market transformation of U.S. health care. For the uninsured, the ED is the physician of last resort. Will society solve this problem in the near future? Health care in the United States is still treated as a privilege and not as a right. As with any privilege, there are those who can afford it those who cannot. Until the U.S. political process is ready to make health care a right for all, including explicit public acceptance of the massive administrative cost of such an action, all changes will be only temporary fixes. Low payment rates and the resulting financial pressures have blurred the distinction between health care as a necessary service and health care as a business. Healthcare firms that cannot keep financially solvent will surely fail, as would any other business with unsound financing. But for those hospitals tempted to manage costs by refusing care to those who cannot pay, the COBRA laws have created a counteractive fiscal incentive to not dump the uninsured patient.

We must not confuse bad management with destiny. Alternative delivery systems and new criteria for reimbursement are needed to provide efficient care for non-urgent ED patients so that optimal resources are available to treat truly urgent patients. Emergency physicians should be able to "do what is best for the patient" and still be a partner in maintaining the economic viability of the hospital. Emergency physicians sometimes overuse costly lab tests and radiology studies in the name of defensive medicine. The ED is an inefficient setting for primary care of chronic stable patients. Do not blame the patients: Those lacking access to private care have only the emergency departments.

Tension exists between the HMOs' desire to provide treatment at the lowest cost and the EDs' desire to expedite patient care without engendering risk or liability. In order to control unnecessary hospital visits, for example, most prepaid health plans screen patients before allowing them to seek care in EDs. At this time, the military health system, 34 states, and Washington, DC have adopted a "reasonable lay person definition of emergency care." This law requires managed care and other health insurance plans to pay for emergency care based on what a reasonable layperson might consider an emergency prospectively, rather than on what the insurance company might consider an emergency retrospectively (for example, chest pain that turned out to be excess gas or heartburn). Not all states have adopted this law yet. Patients and doctors often do not agree on what constitutes a medical emergency. Although ethical and compassionate "gatekeeper" physicians try to cap internal costs to the managed care system, they are in reality placing increased economic and physical burdens on their enrollees.

Coverage Reform and Charity Care

Managers get little sympathy from the public concerning stories of unpaid hospital bills. Many analysts have pointed out that the terms *uncompensated* or *indigent* care lump both charity care and debt into a single category. It is hard to get accurate national estimates of the percentage of debt resulting from people financially incapable of paying their bills, in contrast to the percentage of people unwilling (because they are dissatisfied) to pay some portion of their bills. In affluent suburban markets, less than 10 percent of debt might be charity care, whereas in low-income areas debt is 95 percent charity care. In 2001, hospitals provided an estimated $9.8 billion of charity care and accumulated an estimated $19 billion of debt. Although $28 billion of free care to the poor might seem an insignificant amount in macroeconomic terms for a nation that spends over $30 billion per week on health care, it represents an ethical and financial problem for one-third of hospitals (Office of National Cost Estimates 2002). The best way to communicate with the public is to talk of people not covered by health insurance rather than in terms of unpaid bills.

Almost 39 million Americans lack health insurance. The United States has the largest number of uninsured citizens in the world. South Africa passed national health insurance reform in 1997, and South Korea passed national health insurance in the spring of 1989. The United States is the only industrial nation in the world that does not treat health care as a basic human right. Americans must bring together all major provider groups, consumer groups, and payers groups that will unite behind the cause of equity and equality despite providers resisting attempts to institute change. An example is the failure of the Clinton Reform Plan in 1993. Improved equity in health care would help enhance the productivity and output of our nation.

Integrated Systems

Payers are tired of fragmentation; they want to deal with one organization, not dozens of billing centers and different organizations. Approximately 170 integrated health systems (IHS) contain 3,800 hospitals and control 85 percent of the acute medical care expenses (9.1 percent of the 2002 Gross Domestic Product of our economy, or GDP). Hospitals, rather than physicians or managed care corporations, have been the primary driving force for two-thirds of the IHSs. The transformation from a fragmented independent system to an integrated one is intended to raise the effectiveness and efficiency of services; to negotiate and deliver care under managed care contracts; and to appropriately align the incentives of hospitals, physicians, and other providers (chapters 4 and 11 deal with incentive system design).

An IHS must face seven basic issues:

- Unified governance and an enrolled population for which the system is responsible;
- A shared mission among all participants that calls for eliminating unnecessary redundancy, improving quality and efficiency, and containing costs;
- Formal sharing of capital among providers;

- Seamless delivery of care with joint-equity ownership in or contracts among the healthcare delivery components, including acute care, physicians, long-term care, home care, and managed care;
- Fiscally rational aligned incentives for providers and patients so that all parties make optimal use of the IHS;
- Systemwide electronic sharing of medical, clinical, and financial data; and
- Systemwide contracts with payers under which the system accepts significant financial risk.

The IHS methods that prove most effective in these seven areas will come to dominate the healthcare marketplace in the future.

Why is the mature IHS slow to develop in some markets? The answer relates to a basic law of physical chemistry — the item in short supply drives the system (and acts as the rate-limiting step to growth). To have only 80 or 90 percent of what is necessary puts the IHS at the mercy of the missing resources needed to flesh out a comprehensive, one-step, full-service system. Competition from a supplier can also keep an IHS immature. A managed care-sponsored IHS can have a sufficient volume of enrollees, such that the second area IHS (provider-sponsored) becomes a competitor with their supplier (the dominant managed care firm). Classic competition models do not work well when the competitor is the supplier. In the new marketplace, the old answers and the old questions are both suspect.

Are HMOs Growing in Market Power?

In 2002, the 10 biggest publicly traded HMOs sat on $20 billion in cash. HMO-sponsored IHSs can come to dominate the provider-sponsored IHSs because they have cash, volume, and better economies of scale. Some physicians in HMOs may wish to go on salary or retire ("take the cash on the stump and run"). Teaching hospitals are increasingly sponsoring the IHS strategy. IHSs are increasing being paid under risk-based payment systems. Global capitation is the most comprehensive form of risk payment. Under less than full global capitation, some carve-outs are allowed for special services, such as cardiac surgery and mental health. Under global capitation, the risk of profit or loss rests fully with the volume providers. The larger IHS with larger patient volume better spreads the medical risk. Larger IHSs have less risk. With the maturation of an IHS comes greater physician support for disease management, outcomes-based medicine, and population-based medicine. The primary-secondary-tertiary providers increasingly try, in the words of the AMA (American Marketing Association), to place patients in more cost-effective channels of service distribution. We will discuss marketing and pricing in chapter 8 and risk and return in chapters 9 and 10.

The youngest IHSs often emerge as a supply-side response to physician hospital organizations (PHO). PHOs have a number of weaknesses. First, PHOs have not been willing to restrict membership to cost-effective practitioners. Second, PHOs do not require exclusive commitments from physicians; physicians contract with the HMOs directly or through other groups, so the PHO lacks any effective contracting leverage. PHOs also let every physician on a medical staff become members. Third, physicians on multiple hospital staffs can spread their loyalty to the point that hospitals do not have strict loyalty from PHO physicians. Fourth, PHOs are not effective organizations because the physicians work from independent practices, and the hospitals are separate entities. This means that PHOs are nothing more than joint marketing devices with no relation to real integrated health care. The PHOs have no effect on the cost structure of either hospital or physicians' services.

By contrast, mature (10 years and older) IHSs are very selective about with whom they do business. The mature IHS aligns provider incentives to foster cost-effective clinical decision making. Higher quality care tends to cost less because resources are not wasted on correcting mistakes. It also assumes and manages risk (full-time global capitation contracts). Quality outcomes are measured and new efficiencies are constantly introduced. Consumers benefit from one-stop shopping and lower premiums. In seeking competitive advantage, the mature IHS goes beyond insurance to direct delivery and ownership of the system. Such IHS plans buy hospitals, merge to create single integrated structures, and build or buy primary care networks.

The mature IHS emphasizes four basic themes. First, for accountants and managers, all elements of the system become cost centers, so cost shifting and code creep (upcoding) are games of the past. Second, the IHS focuses on measuring value and controlling utilization through continuous quality improvement. Third, mature IHSs emphasize wellness and prevention so that payments to hospitals and specialists are minimized. Last, the IHS works to develop comprehensive coordination so that patients can benefit from one-stop shopping, and the medical staff morale stays high.

In 2002, almost 88 percent of private-sector workers at a business with 20 or more employees were covered by managed care plans such as HMOs and preferred provider organizations (PPO), according to a study by A. Foster Higgins and Co. (2002), a benefits consulting firm. This demonstrates an increase from 49 percent in 1992. The fraction of Americans in traditional indemnity plans declined from 73 percent in 1988 to 18 percent in 2002, according to Blue Cross (2003). PPOs increased from 10 percent of the market share in 1988 to 63 percent in 2002. HMOs increased from 17 percent of market share to 30 percent in 2002. The various types of managed care plans are listed in **Table 1-1**. New point-of-service (POS) managed care systems, which allow enrollees to go outside the usual listed panel of providers if they pay 20 percent to 30 percent of the bill (the total charges being higher than usual because no discounts were negotiated with the health plan) covered 1.1 percent of Americans in 2002.

Scale Economies

Larger for-profit HMOs have good balance sheets with large amounts of cash, highly valued stock that they can use as cash to make acquisitions and grow, and highly sophisticated marketing teams. Larger firms have better production efficiency and better spread the medical insurance risk over a larger population.

Size also might be an issue for both nonprofit and for-profit HMOs. Three points have come out of previous research (Eastaugh 1993): (1) an optimal size for communication and early fiscal survival is 80,000 enrollees; (2) to survive, an HMO should achieve a critical mass of 80,000 enrollees in five years; and (3) if the HMO is too large, it should be subdivided into smaller segments. (Kaiser Oakland subdivided into decentralized segments of 80,000 enrollees each, and thus provides better communication with the medical staff). Future research should consider long-run average cost curves and a more traditional economic analysis; for example, optimal size soon might be 100,000 enrollees. Survivor analysis and market share statistics provide only indirect evidence.

As the nation moves into more of a managed care environment, productivity and utilization patterns improve. Consider the situation if we use the 10 largest HMOs as a benchmark. If 98 percent of all Americans were in large managed care plans, we would need 36,000 fewer generalists and 178,000 fewer specialists. Instead of expanding the number of primary care physicians by 196,000 over three decades, the nation might need only 200,000 more primary care physicians if the healthcare system becomes as efficient as the 10 largest HMOs.

Table 1–1 Managed Care Product Comparisons				
	Role of PCP	Patient Cost Sharing	Access to Specialists	Out-of-Network Coverage
Closed Panel HMO	Member required to select a PCP	Minimal co-payment for office visit; 100 percent hospital coverage	Must have referral from PCP for coverage	No
EPO	Member not required to select a PCP; PCP does not function as a gatekeeper	Minimal co-payment for office visit; 100 percent hospital coverage	Permits direct access to network providers	No
Open Access HMO	Member required to select a PCP; PCP functions as a gatekeeper, managing and coordinating care and authorizing visits to specialists	Higher co-payments when self-referring to a specialist	Permits self referral to a network specialist with higher co-payments	No
POS plan	Member required to select a PCP; PCP functions as a gatekeeper, managing and coordinating care and authorization visits for in-network coverage	Minimal co-payments for in-network care; higher co-payment and deductible for out-of-network coverage	Must have referral from PCP for in-network coverage; permits direct access to network providers with higher co-payments	Yes

(continues)

	Role of PCP	Patient Cost Sharing	Access to Specialists	Out-of-Network Coverage
Open Access PPO	Member not required to select a PCP; PCP does not function as a gatekeeper	Minimal co-payment in network; coinsurance and deductible for out-of-network coverage	Permits direct access to network providers	Yes

Taste for Managed Care

Government and the general public have brought up concerns over the quality of HMO service, but HMOs appear to be performing quality control adequately, according to Interstudy (2002). Consumers are also concerned with the time, cost, and restrictions of choice associated with HMO care. From the patient perspective, access to specialty referrals might pose a problem. Referrals are less of a problem for consumers in large staff- or group-model HMOs, where patients can simply walk down the hall to the specialist's office. However, in an IPA-model HMO, the consumer often has to travel to a different office building. A second potential problem involves consumer expectations. Some consumers unrealistically expect a plastic surgeon to treat every cut and specialists to address every minor complaint. This segment of the market would be wise to avoid enrolling in HMOs. Moreover, any HMO that caters to such whims either must go out of business or find specialists willing to work for $40 per hour.

Rural communities are less likely to be served by HMOs, presumably because of the lack of critical mass (volume) of potential enrollees, but this generality is not true of all rural communities. For example, some rural areas have active business coalitions that have fueled the development of HMOs with sufficient initial start-up resources and promotional campaigns. HMOs offer certain rural areas the opportunity to retain resources and patients within the community. The percentage of rural communities served by HMOs has been on the increase. An estimated 28 percent of counties with fewer than 10,000 residents had HMOs in 2002 (up from only 4 percent in 1980); 41 percent of rural counties with 10,000 to 49,999 residents had HMOs in 2002 (up from 11 percent in 1980). Virtually 100 percent of urban communities had one or more HMOs available in 2002 (Interstudy 2002).

HMO physicians are concerned with the mechanism by which holdout risk pools are distributed. The physicians have full knowledge of the fee schedule or age-adjusted capitation rate of reimbursement from the HMO plan, but the risk pool can be handled a number of ways. Each clinician might have a referral fund to ensure that he or she does his or her work and does not shunt it off to other physicians (does not over-refer). Deficits in the referral fund might be covered with a 20 percent across-the-board holdout risk pool (because the HMO physician cannot be held to blame for this "unexpected" event), but the HMO would pay 40 percent to 60 percent of any hospital-fund surplus to the physicians. Even HMOs without explicit risk pools or withholds offer some incentive to hold costs down. For example, a prepaid group practice HMO like Harvard Pilgrim might budget physician bonus pay at 5.5 percent of salaries, but depending on cost-control effectiveness, the bonus might vary from 0 percent to 10.5 percent of salaries. The decision to issue bonus pay is decentralized for a large three-tiered HMO like HIP of Greater New York, which contracts with 12 physicians groups and 46 hospitals.

HMO physicians seem increasingly willing to accept fixed flat fees and practice guidelines. Increasingly, physicians are being paid a flat fee for each patient no matter how much care is given, providing a financial incentive to give less care. In 1990, 35 percent of HMO physicians were paid flat fees; by 2002, it was 73 percent. Practice guidelines that suggest treatments for various illnesses have become more prevalent. In 1990, 31 organizations had published 700 sets of guidelines. Today, 82 organizations have issued 2,600 sets, and 95 percent have written practice guidelines (American Association of Health Plans 2002).

The style of medicine may differ in newer, less financially solvent HMOs, as compared to older, larger, more established HMOs. In large HMOs, where risks are widely shared and capital investment has been largely amortized, there may be no more denial of beneficial care than under a fee-for-service payment system. There is an obvious incentive for all HMOs to curtail non-beneficial care, but there is a presumption that weak HMOs might succumb to financial incentives and shave the costs of some beneficial care. There is no hard evidence in this area, but Medicare is attempting to improve rates to avoid "moral hazard" (Luft 1999). The style of medicine practiced in HMOs might reduce expenditures by 15 to 25 percent, principally through a 25 to 40 percent reduction in hospital admissions.

Rate Setting

Wrightson (1998) provided an excellent survey of HMO rate-setting methods and the technical issues behind the ongoing rancorous debate among employers, providers, and HMOs over the ways to determine premiums and prices paid to providers. Fiscal risk to the HMO is higher for community rating than for Kaiser's adjusted community rating (by patient class, which allows individual groups to have different rates depending on their composition by age, sex, marital status, and industry). However, patient case-mix risk is minimized through experience rating, which sets premiums that reflect the cost experience of the particular group enrolled, or through group-specific rating.

Most HMOs reduce risk by purchasing reinsurance from a large third party for catastrophic expenses; for example, insuring payment of 75 percent of hospital expenses in excess of $25,000 for one patient in a year. Sometimes reinsurance is purchased on an aggregate rather than a catastrophic basis, insuring total HMO costs in excess of 115 percent of annual revenue. Because HMO revenues are fixed, prospective control of costs and management of risk exposure are high priorities for the capitation plan performance (Eastaugh 1998).

Quality is an important issue in picking a health plan, and individuals can ask their employers for comparative data called the Health Plan Employer Data and Information Set (HEDIS). For example, the data show that in 1997 more than 91 percent of Kaiser plan members received first-trimester prenatal care, compared to only 80 percent for Aetna U.S. Health Care (the second largest plan, with 4.9 million enrollees). Florida data show marked selection biases with respect to HMO enrollment and disenrollment (Morgan, Vernig, Devito, and Persily 1999). Over four years the rate of inpatient services used in the HMO-enrollment group during the year before enrollment was 66 percent of the rate of that of the fee-for-service group, whereas the rate in the HMO-disenrollment group after disenrollment was 180 percent of that of the fee-for-service group.

Consumers are also highly interested in out-of-pocket costs. PPOs tend to have the highest premiums because they have the least control over provider behavior. POS plans start to deselect (reduce the number of) specialists and implement tougher utilization controls. HMOs have the lowest premiums, and staff model HMOs have the lowest usage of hospitals and specialists. The market trends seem to suggest that the PPOs and POSs are halfway on the road to HMOs, and that many HMOs are on the road to full-risk global capitation contracts.

Will HMOs Evolve or Wither?

Cassandra saw the future of HMOs and it did not work. Traditional HMOs do lots of utilization review and preauthorization of high-cost care, such as that for hospitals and specialists. This paperwork hassle is totally eliminated under total risk capitation (TRC, sometimes called global capitation). Under TRC, an IHS is paid per member per month (PMPM) for both hospital and physician care. This results in the HMO passing all risk to the providers. Only well-organized IHSs can be successful under global capitation. For specialists who do not adjust their behavior and time costs and join a mature IHS, the word *capitation* sounds like what was done to the aristocracy during the French Revolution. Specialists working without the benefits of a strong IHS will lose the "heads" of their practices — their patient base. As former U.S. Public Health Service Surgeon General C. Everett Koop pointed out, some 180,000 U.S. specialists should be retrained as generalists to deliver basic primary care.

Scandals in the HMO industry, although few, have made "managed care" less than consumer-friendly in the media (reports on "managed care" or "managed care through managed cost-HMO to patient: drop dead"). HMOs also have an image problem with physician specialists, because they hire fewer specialists and have a shortage of primary care physicians. Patients dislike the reduced average duration of visit time. The average time of a patient visit has declined from 15 minutes to 8 minutes in the last decade. Some HMO physicians see 60 patients per day.

If HMOs do not evolve into TRC systems, they might make the ultimate cost sacrifice by simply closing down. HMOs could be replaced by direct contracting. Physician groups and hospitals in Detroit, Michigan, and New Mexico already are beginning to eliminate the managed care middleman, internalize cost-control functions, and contract directly, with more than 75 percent of their net cost savings from provider discounts. If the providers cannot discount any more, over half the administrative fees can be trimmed by eliminating the HMO middleman. HMOs could eventually go the way of the old-line indemnity insurance companies and wither out of business by 2015.

Consumer Demand and Technology

Although the explosion in health insurance coverage during the past 40 years is the single most important factor in the increased demand for medical care, other factors have had influences as well. Growth in the population and increases in the average life span have contributed to the demand for medical care: The fastest growing age group is the 65-and-older category whose per capita expenditures on health care are four times those of adults aged 19 to 64. In addition, many innovations in medical technology are extremely expensive and increase the demand for medical care in multiplicative fashion. According to the Office of National Cost Estimates (2002), physicians represent 18.5 percent of the health economy, or nearly $302 billion (chapter 3 addresses physician payment options).

Medical technology has moved into the public eye as a culprit in rising healthcare costs. However, there is a wide range of options about whether technology is, on balance, a major or minor source of rising costs. Technology can sometimes be cost-decreasing, although this is less frequently the case in the medical field. Most economists question whether technology accounts for even one-third of the cost inflation problem. However, it is clear that new medical technology creates new patient demand.

Clinicians, for example, have an incomplete understanding of life-cycle costing, product maturity, and development. Some physicians find technology a convenient bogeyman to blame for increasing healthcare costs. If technology and demanding patients are tagged as 75 percent of the cost-control problem, then organized medicine proceeds to lobby for higher fee schedules and claims that its members, as professionals, are not getting enough money for their value. Advocates for either price competition or tight fee schedules reverse the perspective and ask if consumers are getting enough value for their money. Readers of this text are encouraged to come to believe that consumers and third-party payers need better-funded, high-quality assessments of the costs, risks, and benefits of medical technology. The argument that technology cannot be evaluated because it presents a "moving target," constantly improving and efficiently circumscribing the indicators of clinical usage, is not to be believed. Careful analysis is especially needed in those gray areas where technology attempts to improve quality-adjusted life years (QALY) without extending life expectancy.

Some medical technologies, such as visualizing gallstones with ultrasound and crushing them with lithotripsy, appear cost-decreasing. This is also clearly quality-enhancing to the patient in comparison to traditional exploratory surgery. Unfortunately, the public is not well versed in life-cycle costing or the risks of old-style invasive medicine (with iatrogenic infections and prolonged lengths of stay). The media tend to focus excessive attention on capital outlays rather than on long-run cost-benefit trade-offs and cost-effectiveness. The public reads that magnetic resonance imaging (MRI) technology costs one to two million dollars more than traditional X-ray equipment, or that IBM is bringing a $20 million compact synchrotron to market, and concludes that healthcare costs must be 90 percent technology-driven. This is simply not true. Much of the administrative technology that hospitals have added since 1984 is cost-decreasing in pharmacy or nursing. For example, you will learn about staffing patterns in chapter 5.

The low-price items (costing under $400) are what we need to monitor the most. The need for more cost-effective clinical decision-making is clear when one considers the burden of an inflation in demand and cost in medical tests and procedures. In 2001 dollars, the nation annually spends $12 billion on 480 million blood cholesterol tests; $8 billion on 305 million urinalysis tests; $11 billion on 156 million sequential multiple analyzer tests; $5 billion on 158 million blood counts; $6.1 billion on 60 million chest X-rays; $4.8 billion on 38 million ultrasound exams (for pregnancy and for heart and gall-bladder problems); $3.4 billion for 36 millions annual electrocardiograms; $3.3 billion on 31 million endoscopy exams; and $3.6 billion for 8.6 million stress/treadmill tests. Utilization review and prior-certification programs have done little to slow the inflation in demand and cost for these tests and procedures. Media coverage has helped foster the explosion in patient demand for repeat cholesterol tests. One could speculate that adoption of Medicare physician fee schedules in 1998 for certain procedures, such as endoscopy, held down volume for those procedures. Even smaller expenditures, such as Pap tests, are a $1.6 billion item with 44 million performed annually. Ultimately, education based on the evolution of cost-effective preferred practice patterns is the number-one tool we have to control physicians' ordering habits. In looking at changing practice style in medicine, monetary present value issues must be considered.

The size and scope of the U.S. health economy is outlined in **Table 1–2**. In 2002 we spent $589.6 billion in the hospital sector, but only $57 billion on public health, health promotion, and health education. Hospitals, physicians, and other professionals will require $1,332 billion in spending by

2007. Two federal programs, Medicare and Medicaid, will represent $717 billion of the health sector by 2007. By 2011, the country will be spending $56 billion per week on the health sector.

Net Present Value Analysis: Discounting

The uneven distribution of costs and benefits over time poses the analyst little conceptual difficulty. One simply reduces the stream of future costs and benefits to net present value by discounting. The most common rationale for discounting social programs to present value reflects the uncertainty of the future: A benefit in hand is worth two in the future. In contrast, health economists have downplayed the business sector rationale for discounting, which is the time value of money. In the business sector, uncertainty is always incorporated in the equation through the use of decision trees.

Most studies offer a sensitivity analysis of the impact of discounting based on cost per year of life saved: $31,300 for heart transplants discounted at 10 percent (but $27,200 if they are discounted at 5 percent), or $50,600 for liver transplants discounted at 10 percent (but $44,000 if they are discounted at 5 percent). A discounted rate of 10 percent produces a discount factor of 0.3855 after 10 years and a discount factor of 0.0085 after 50 years. In other words, benefits accruing a decade from now are worth just less than 2/5 of today's comparable accruing benefits; benefits accruing 50 years from now are worth 1/85 as much as comparable benefits accruing today.

The discount rate is designed to reflect the opportunity cost of postponing benefits or costs over an uncertain future. Economists posit that the yield on private investment can be properly regarded as the appropriate opportunity yield for public investment only if the subjective cost of risk-bearing is the same for the average taxpayer as it is for the private investor. The benchmarks should be a function of the source of financing; private consumption has a higher discount rate than public investment. The discount rate most frequently used is 10 percent. Opportunity cost principles argue for a high discount rate. The true cost of a healthcare investment is the return that could have been achieved if the resources had gone elsewhere in the private sector. The relevant comparison is not the expected rate of return but the expected rate of return net of the subjective costs of risk bearing. The corporate discount rate is obviously overinflated because it includes both a risk premium and a markup for corporate taxes. To achieve equivalent after-tax investor

Table 1–2 National Health Expenditures (NHE), by Source of Funds and Amounts: Selected Calendar Years 1988 – 2011					
Source of funds	**1988**	**1993**	**2002**	**2007**	**2011**
NHE, billions	$558.1	$888.1	$1,545.9	$2,174.9	$2,815.8
Private funds	331.7	497.7	848.7	1,191.8	1,500.2
Out-of-pocket payments	118.9	146.9	226.9	311.0	395.6
Private health insurance	174.9	298.1	537.3	766.9	966.1
Public funds	226.4	390.4	697.1	983.0	1,315.7
Federal	154.1	274.4	484.1	669.8	890.5
Medicare	89.0	148.3	259.3	344.3	450.1
Medicaid	31.0	76.8	143.5	216.0	301.5
Other federal	34.1	49.3	81.3	109.5	138.9
State and local	72.3	116.0	213.0	313.2	425.2
Medicaid	24.1	44.8	103.3	156.8	220.3
Other state and local	48.2	71.1	109.7	156.4	204.9
Expenditures					
Professional services	$176.3	$280.7	$495.8*	$700.3	$906.2
Nursing homes and home healthcare	48.9	87.6	143.7	189.0	237.2
Home healthcare	8.4	21.9	39.9	55.4	70.8
Nursing home care	40.5	65.7	103.8	133.6	166.4
Retail outlet sales of medical products	58.7	87.5	216.8	350.7	498.7
Prescription drugs	30.6	51.3	160.9	289.9	433.9
Other medical products	28.1	36.2	55.9	70.9	84.9
Government public health activities	15.5	27.2	57.4	90.9	120.9
Investment (research, construction)	22.7	31.8	48.9	67.6	88.0
Hospital care	209.4	320.0	476.1*	631.5	774.5

Source: ONCE (2002)

* Hospital care, including professional services, was $589.6 billion in 2002

earnings, a corporation must offer stockholders an 8 percent return (that is an 8 percent before-tax gross return) to compete with a riskless municipal bond returning 5 percent. Operationally, the second choice, government borrowing rates (currently the Federal Office of Management and Budget, or OMB's, discount rate is 6 percent), serves as the upper boundary over time. The most prudent course of action is to perform a sensitivity analysis of the net present value under a range of discount rates. If a sensitivity analysis can demonstrate that selection of a discount rate does not affect the recommendation, then the tenuousness of the assumption will not be a source of concern.

Defining Types of Efficiency

An attempt to lower costs without reducing the quality or intensity of care is an attempt to improve efficiency. Efficiency can be identified in three forms: technical, economic, and allocative. *Technical efficiency* refers to the relationship between input and output, regardless of cost. If one can reduce the amount of input and still produce the same output, then maximum technical efficiency has been achieved. In a hospital context, for example, inputs might be full-time equivalent (FTE) employees, and outputs would be days of care. *Economic efficiency* refers to the relationship between inputs and costs. A day of care provided at the minimum possible cost and input creates economic efficiency. *Allocative efficiency* in health care involves determining from among which inputs the allocation of resources would be least costly for achieving an improved level of output (health status). A health production function is necessary to describe the relationship between combinations of inputs and the resulting outputs. Chapters 4 and 5 in this volume address improved levels of health output produced using different combinations of inputs. The reader should be careful to differentiate production functions from the production possibility curve (a similarly labeled concept), which describes the trade-off among different outputs from a given set of resources. The following sections consider the effects of pricing policies and capacity (size, equipment) decisions on efficiency.

In considering what happens to the level of output as the level of input increases, we are addressing the issue of economies of scale. If output grows at the same rate that inputs are increased, then there are constant returns to scale (per-unit costs are the same at any given level of output). If output increases at a rate greater than inputs are increased, then there are increasing returns to scale (per-unit costs decrease at high levels of output). Economies of scale are shallow (11–14 percent) in the hospital industry compared to other industries (60–95 percent) (Eastaugh 1998).

Paperwork Cost Management

Do hospitals need to spend one-fifth of our funds on administration? And cannot a more efficient system that includes 34 million uninsured adults and five million uninsured children be built? Expanding hospital access and trimming paperwork are the two major issues facing the medical sector. Administrative costs related to the industry can be reduced dramatically by implementing a nationwide electronic date interchange (EDI) system. Estimates suggest that such a system could trim one-third from the $310 billion spent annually in the United States on healthcare administrative costs by automating 11 transactions traditionally performed manually (Eastaugh 1998). The greatest potential for cost savings lies in the electronic conversion of enrollments, submissions, and payments. Numerous case studies show that employing EDI or Internet systems can save millions of dollars in administrative healthcare costs, which are estimated to account for 22 percent of healthcare spending. For example, a New Jersey study found that $980 million in annual administrative healthcare cost could be saved by the state's healthcare industry if hospitals, physicians, and payers employed EDI technology.

The benefits of EDI technology are numerous. A paper-based claim that takes 20 minutes to process manually takes only 40 seconds to process electronically. EDI systems decrease the number of claims rejected one or more times by 30 percent. Waiting time for reimbursement declines by 70 percent, thus improving cash flow. In one state, 16 hospitals, 52 physicians groups, and the nine largest insurance carriers in an 11-county region implemented EDI systems for the following transactions: enrollments, claims submission, payments and remittance, scheduling, eligibility verification, prescription ordering, claims inquiry, referral authorization, test orders and results, materials management, and coordination of benefits (Eastaugh 1995). Cost savings have been substantial, trimming costs by 30 percent since 1995.

Health services delivery is emerging as a market-driven industry. The Department of Health and Human Services seems to be moving in the direction of more competition through competitive bidding and capitation contracts. Healthcare payers should work to devise a bidding scheme that manages cost reduction without harming quality. The last chapter of this text suggests a quality-enhancing bidding system.

In the following chapters, various aspects of efficiency, equity, and service quality are considered in detail. Chapter 2 outlines a number of recent examples of standard costing, facility specialization, and product-line selection strategy. Capital budget decisions are driven by net present value (NPV), the present value of the cash inflows minus the present value of the cash outflows. Zero value for NPV means a project's cash inflows are just sufficient to return the capital invested in the project and provide investors with their required rates of return on that invested capital. If a project has a negative NPV, its cash inflows are insufficient to compensate the firm for the capital invested, so the project is unprofitable and acceptance would erode the financial status of the firm. If a project has a positive NPV, it is generating excess cash flows. These excess cash flows can be used for modernization, reinvestment in the firm, or to pay financial returns to investors.

> ### ▶ Summary Points:
>
> * Health care is a large part of the U.S. economy.
>
> * The U.S. healthcare "system" is financially and technically fragmented but can unify politically when it feels threatened.
>
> * Healthcare costs are affected by many factors.
>
> * One of these factors is "unfunded mandates" — The government requires someone to provide a good or service but does not reimburse the provider for the provision of said good or service.

> ### Research and Discussion Questions:
>
> * What are "public goods"? What are "private goods"?
>
> * Is health care a public or private good?
>
> * Is it fair to require hospital emergency departments to provide unreimbursed care?
>
> * How do the terms we use shape our beliefs (for example, charity care and debt both being considered uncompensated care)?

References

A. Foster Higgins and Co. 2002. Trends in employee health care coverage, New York, NY.

American Association of Health Plans. 2002. *Patterns in HMO enrollment* (11th ed.). Washington, DC: American Association of Health Plans.

American College of Emergency Physicians Policy. 2002. *www.acep.org*.

American Hospital Association. 2002. Finding common ground for expanded health coverage to the uninsured. *http://www.ahapolicyforum.org/policyresources/CoverageUniversalA1120.sap*.

Blue Cross. 2003. Trends in insurance coverage (press release). Washington, DC: Blue Cross.

Eastaugh, S. 1993. *Health economics: Efficiency, quality, and equity*. Westport, CT: Auburn House.

Eastaugh, S. 1995. Nationwide EDI system can trim administrative costs by $73 billion. *Healthcare Financial Management* 49(6): 45–47.

Eastaugh, S. 1998. *Health care finance*. Gaithersburg, MD: Aspen.

Eastaugh, S. 2002. Hospital costs and specialization. *JH Care Finance* 28(1): 61–72.

Interstudy. 2002. *The Interstudy competitive edge, part III: Regional market analysis*. Minneapolis, MN: Interstudy.

Jaklevic, M.C. 2001. Hospital weighted down. *Modern Healthcare 2001* 31(36): 69–72.

Kaiser Family Foundation. 2002. Employer health benefits 2002 annual survey.

Lister, J. 1998. National Health Service. *New England Journal of Medicine* 318(22): 1473.

Luft, H. 1999. Potential methods to reduce risk selection. *Inquiry* 32(11): 23–32.

Morgan, R., Vernig, B., Devito, C., Persily, N. 1999. The Medicare HMO Revolving Door. *New England Journal of Medicine* 337(3): 169–175.

Office of National Cost Estimates. 2002. *Trends in health care spending.* Washington, DC: U.S. Government Printing Office.

Weiner, J., and Dobson, A. 1997. Risk-adjusted Medicare capitation rates using ambulatory and inpatient diagnoses. *Health Care Financing Review* 17(3): 77–98.

Wrightson, C. 1998. *HMO rate setting and financial strategy.* Ann Arbor, MI: HAP Press.

Chapter 2

Product-Line Specialization and Standard Costing: Selection, Risk, and Return

Because of little expense, a small leak will sink a great ship.

– Benjamin Franklin

It is futile to attempt to eliminate risk, and questionable to try to minimize it. But it is essential that specialization and diversification risks taken be the right risks.

– Peter Drucker

Specialization helps trim cost and improve service quality.

– Malcolm Baldridge

▶ **Critical points in this chapter:**

• Risk analysis

• Market forces

• Specialization

Once upon a time we lived in a nearly risk-free world of cost reimbursement in which something ventured was always something gained. Now we live in a risky world where failure is allowed, smart risks are rewarded, and timidity is not a viable strategy. Getting a piece of the cash flow requires resilience, patience, and realistic financial feasibility analysis of risk and return. The typical new venture goes through a five-step cycle:

1. Develop a good idea for cost-effective quality healthcare delivery.
2. Write a coherent business plan for expansion.
3. Attract the capital to roll up and buy out the competition.
4. Improve the efficiency of the production process.
5. Reap the economies of scale and productivity gains of the new consolidated firm.

Investors are increasingly attracted to the healthcare sector because of the proliferation of inefficient providers and the high degree of fragmentation in the marketplace. The five-stage process described above (in which an investor forms a platform model company and rolls up the competition) has been used in U.S. business for two decades. Risk analysis involves objective risks and harder-to-quantify subjective risks. If projections suggest that under a wide range of possible assumptions, the venture will have good profitability and a positive net present value (NPV), then the feasibility analysis is robust, and investor confidence will be high. The better the feasibility results, the better the risk classification for the venture. Capital infusion typically comes from three sources:

1. Internal funding (retained earnings and debt)
2. Venture capital
3. Publicly traded securities (stock)

One cannot fool the marketplace. At any given point in time, all stocks in an equivalent risk class are priced to offer the same expected rate of return. This is a basic definition for equilibrium in any well-functioning capital market. The cash flow to owners of the stock comes in the form of cash dividends and capital gains (or losses).

Nonprofits utilize the same financial philosophy, instead of venture capital. The nonprofit ethic of the century is best summarized by the Catholic Hospital Association slogan: "No margin, no mission." Social benefits to the community are best produced if you follow the dictum of Benjamin Franklin: "Beware leaks of all sorts, in both revenues and expenses." In summary, a successful firm knows that its success depends on its knowledge of risk: What it knows and how quickly it can learn new approaches.

Product-Line Selection

The healthcare marketplace has become increasing risky because there is a widening spread of possible outcomes. The measure of spread is the standard deviation (or variance). Risk has two components: unique risk (specific to the individual organization), and marketwide industry risk (changes in Medicare payment policies). Healthcare strategic planners can eliminate unique risk by diversifying their business ventures, but they cannot eliminate market risk.

Mathematical principles applied to investment portfolios also can be applied to a portfolio of departments of strategic business units within an organization. The ideal business investment would have a high expected return and a low standard deviation. Businesses that offer the highest expected return for a given standard deviation are labeled efficient. That is, at the margin, each business is working equally hard. If one business has a greater marginal effort or overall risk than another, it must have a proportionately greater expected financial return.

A healthcare organization may want to deploy capital over a mix of ventures to yield the highest NPV. However, forecasting revenues, expenses, and NPV is an imperfect process. One way to forecast a venture's risk is to estimate the NPV for scenarios involving optimum, average, and poor performance, and multiply the NPV for each scenario (i) by the probability estimate (P) that the scenario will occur. By adding the results of these scenarios together, an expected monetary value (EMV) for the project is obtained (see **Table 2-1**).

A full mathematical simulation called quadratic programming can quantify the EMV for a very large number of i scenarios. In practice, quadratic programming has multiple optimal solutions, but all alternatives are efficient. The degree to which healthcare organizations adjust their new-venture investment cycles will vary according to organizational size, ownership, financial status, and risk tolerance (Eastaugh 2000).

Table 2-1 Expected Monetary Value (EMV) Calculation			
Scenario (i)	NPV	Probability(P)	NPV x P
High Estimate	$562,000	0.20	$112,400
Middle Estimate	310,000	0.60	186,000
Low Estimate	176,000	0.20	35,200
			EMV = $333,600

Managing Risk

In today's rapidly changing healthcare marketplace, both conservative and speculative strategies should be considered in determining an organization's optimal service line and in helping the organization manage risk. Speculation is the assumption of considerable financial risk to obtain commensurate gain. A considerable risk is one that is sufficient to affect the acquisition decision. For example, an organization may reject a venture that has a positive risk premium because the added gain is insufficient to make up for the downside risk involved. Commensurate gain means realizing a positive expected profit beyond what could be realized under a low- or no-risk scenario.

Sometimes, adding a seemingly risky asset to a service line actually reduces, or hedges, the overall risk to the organization. For example, if a healthcare organization determines that it is overinvested in skilled nursing care, it might be prudent to hedge this investment by adding seemingly more risky high-tech home health care to its portfolio of services. This hedge works because home health care is a partial substitute for skilled nursing care. If a new payment system to reduce nursing home lengths of stay is introduced, for example, the skilled nursing business will be hurt but the new home health care business will receive a substantial boost. Therefore, the risk of an asset should not be evaluated separately from other owned assets.

Diversification is another method used to manage risk. In designing a service diversification plan, healthcare executives should consider all relevant competitive, entry-barrier, supplier, and purchaser factors. Competitive factors include product differences, brand identity, intermittent overcapacity, and diversity of competitors. In starting a firm, market entry barriers to consider include capital requirements, cost advantages and economies of scale, switching costs, and anticipated retaliation. Factors affecting healthcare provider strength include market concentration, minimum volume needed, impact of substitute inputs (labor for capital) on costs, and quality differentiation. Most critical are purchaser factors, including buyer propensity to substitute services, switching costs, price negotiation leverage, product differences, price sensitivity, and perceived value of service quality.

In evaluating new partnerships, each party must assess risk and return and weigh the chances for mutual benefit. Benefits may include greater access to capital and new markets, and enhanced professional management expertise. In an era of heightened risk for all healthcare players, strategy selection, forecasting, and subjective risk estimation are key skills financial managers must develop. In particular, methods to predict insurance risk should be retooled to prevent adverse selection and reward quality providers, particularly those that serve high-risk populations.

Implementation of DRGs by Medicare starting in 1983 provided the impetus for specialization in the hospital industry. DRG stands for Diagnosis Related Groups, which are the basis of payment for Medicare's new prospective payment system. DRGs represent a system of billing for hospital care, based on a patient's diagnosis rather than on the actual services consumed or the length of stay in the hospital.

DRGs are basically a classification system that distributes all medical diagnoses and procedures into 507 different categories. DRG #45, for instance, is neurological eye disorder, medical; DRG #114 is upper limb and/or toe amputation.

The theory is that all hospital patients assigned to the same DRG represent a homogeneous group—they are similar not only in terms of the broad clinical description of their illness, but also in terms of their length of stay in the hospital, the resources they consume, and the cost of their treatment.

Assuming then that all patients in a DRG will cost the hospital, on average, approximately the same amount to care for, hospitals will now be reimbursed one set fee for each Diagnosis Related Group. The fee is determined prior to the actual treatment—hence, the term "prospective payment."

Another way of looking at this is to say that each DRG represents what a particular hospital should spend, on average, to diagnose and treat a category of illnesses (an SPG, or Strategic Product-line Grouping of like patients).

Rising Specialization

In the 1990s, managed care decreased patient volume, and payers offered tighter hospital reimbursement. Two supply-side responses emerged in the face of bare-bones payment rates and declining patient census. First, a hospital could implement a macro strategy to reap economies of scale through a facility-wide cost containment program or merger. Second, a hospital could implement a micro strategy to specialize, operating fewer but higher-volume departments, and producing departmental economies. Under the specialization strategy each individual department reaps economies through productivity enhancement and trimming variable costs (Yafchak 2000).

Cost analysis of the hospital economy has a long history. Some of the initial economy of scale studies were done on Veterans Administration hospitals with a wide range in the number of beds (from 44 to 1600). This section of the chapter analyzes a national sample of 219 nongovernmental acute care hospitals with 76 to 950 beds (Eastaugh 2001). The primary research question is: Does specialization reduce hospital cost per admission? Previous studies of hospital behavior have used aggregate measures of "services offered" (see **Table 2-2**) from the American Hospital Association's annual survey to assess specialization or diversification. This approach suffers from measurement error: One does not know if the departments have high volume, low volume, or no volume.

With increased competition and discounting, hospitals may react as department stores did in decades past. In the 1950s, for example, every department store tried to operate with 450 product lines—from food to men's formal wear. Since the 1990s, the surviving department stores have specialized in 50 to 90 percent fewer product lines. Consider a second analogy. In 1979, the National Association of Gas Station Owners suggested that every gas station be full-service and have a full-time mechanic on duty. Two decades later, the successful gas stations offer self-service gas and food. Specialization and modest diversification may be optimal strategies for U.S. hospitals that are not the sole provider in their community (Connor 1998). A hospital with poor cardiac surgery or oncology might drop these services and acquire more specialized services like in vitro fertilization. A small, sole-community provider with 25 to 75 beds has a monopoly on the market and lacks the opportunity to specialize and reap economies of scale in high-volume specialty departments.

Table 2-2 Hospital-Related Services

1. Alcoholic/chemical service (outpatient service)
2. Pediatric medical-surgical care
3. Obstetrics unit
4. Medical surgical intensive care
5. Cardiac intensive care
6. Neonatal intensive care
7. Neonatal intermediate care
8. Pediatric intensive care
9. Burn care
10. Physical rehabilitation
11. Psychiatric care
12. Skilled nursing care
13. Intermediate nursing care
14. Adult day care program
15. Home health services
16. Hospice
17. Arthritis treatment center
18. Assisted living
19. Angioplasty
20. Birthing room; LDR room; LDRP room
21. Breast cancer screening
22. Cardiac catheterization laboratory
23. Children wellness program
24. Chiropractic services
25. Dental services
26. Emergency department
27. Trauma center
28. Urgent care center
29. Extra corporeal shock wave lithotripter
30. Freestanding outpatient center
31. Geriatric services
32. Health screenings
33. HIV-AIDS services
34. Hospital-based outpatient care center
35. Meals on wheels
36. Oncology services
37. Occupational health services
38. Open heart surgery
39. Outpatient surgery
40. Pain management program
41. Physical rehabilitation outpatient services
42. Primary care department
43. Psychiatric child-adolescent services
44. Psychiatric emergency services
45. Psychiatric geriatric services
46. Psychiatric outpatient services
47. Psychiatric partial hospitalization program
48. Radiation therapy
49. CT scanner
50. Magnetic resonance imaging (MRI)
51. Position emission tomography (PET)
52. Single photo emission computerized tomography
53. Ultrasound
54. Reproductive health
55. Sports medicine
56. Teen outreach services
57. Transplant services
58. Women's health center/services

Specialization should never be achieved by "dumping" market segments of people—for example, the uninsured—but rather by dropping product lines that are better served by the competition and by recommitting resources to what they do best. This tendency in the 1990s to specialize did not confront hospitals alone: General Motors might be a more successful company if it became Specific Motors. GM did the right thing by dropping Oldsmobile and five other lines. In a decade where automakers and hospitals are now experiencing fiscal troubles, no point of differentiation is likely to prove more powerful than quality. The next section will review previous research on hospital specialization before considering two basic research questions: Are hospitals becoming more specialized? Does specialization seem to reduce cost per admission?

Do Not Trim, Do Not Think

Some people are against trimming costs or trimming product lines. Finkler (1983) offers the traditional argument for avoiding specialization: Hospitals with a broad product scope attract more physicians. As a result, some hospitals offer a broad range of prestige-maximizing high-technology services, often at low volume, and thus at low quality — because you need volume to maintain quality (see chapter 3). Trustees and other interested individuals might accrue intangible benefits, such as pride, from being associated with a hospital that offers so many product lines. However, in the current climate of prospective payment, many outdated hospitals dream of the old days of cost reimbursement when low-volume departments could be maintained. Low-volume departments with high unit costs do not get their inefficiency reimbursed under prospective payment.

The demise of cost reimbursement means that low-volume departments are under scrutiny on the basis of economics (poor profit margins, poor productivity) and quality. Cause and effect on the quality issue is difficult to establish, given two alternative explanations: (1) volume is too low to maintain sufficient quality, but a hospital keeps the product line open so as not to give market share to their competition, or (2) hospitals with poor-quality product line providers are avoided by doctors who send patient referrals, keeping volume sent to these inferior hospitals low. Irrespective of the cause-and-effect dynamics, specialization is associated with maintaining or enhancing the quality of patient care. Specialization allows nurses and physicians to develop more expertise with respect to a specific category of patients.

Some health planners speculate that hospitals refuse to specialize because they would rather engage in a cost-raising "medical arms race." This speculation appears more relevant in a bygone era of cost reimbursement. Farley and Hogan (1990) report that hospitals specialized 9.8 percent in diagnosis-related group-weighted (DRG) terms during the initial years of the Medicare prospective payment system. If the specialization is measured in terms of major diagnostic categories, or major disease categories (MDC), fewer in number than DRGs, they report a higher level of specialization (13.9 percent) during the same two years.

Market Dynamics

For all hospital managers, quality and marketing are becoming increasingly important issues. Developing areas of specialization can bring prestige to a hospital and serve as a magnet for attracting more patients. So-called "centers of excellence" may assist hospitals in gaining access to capital (donors prefer to give to centers for treatment of a particular disease or ailment). In addition to potential quality improvements, the benefits of hospital specialization for society result from eliminating expensive duplication of services and underused technology. Internal corporate planning to cut duplication of departments and equipment in a marketplace can trim costs better than community-based health planning regulations.

The sample hospitals in **Tables 2-3 to 2-6** represent 20 percent of short-term nongovernmental hospitals with more than 75 beds. Only 56 percent of the hospitals were willing and able to provide data for the two study years. There was no statistically significant bias present in the sample based on seven variables: urbanicity, teaching status, size, ownership control, disproportionate share patient volume, Medicare case-mix index, and length-of-stay index.

An unbiased information theory measure of specialization has to be a scalar measure of output that is independent of scale (Barer 1992) so that the analyst can measure any nonlinear impact of economies of scale by including beds and beds-squared in the equation. Utilizing the Farley and Hogan (1990) measure of specialization, let B_c be defined as the baseline (average) proportion of cases in the category $_c$, and F_{cn} is the fraction of cases in the nth hospital observed in category $_c$. The categories for inpatient specialization will be DRGs and MDCs, creating two alternative measures for specialization (DRG-based and MDC-based). The information theory index (I) of specialization for hospital $_n$ collapses information about differences between B_c and F_{cn}, as follows:

$$I_n = \sum_{c=1} F_{cn} \times ln \,(F_{cn} / B_c)$$

This index equals zero when $F_c = B_c$ for all patient categories, and the index increases as case-mix fractions diverge. National case-mix fractions serve as the baseline.

In each year (1991 and 2000), the specialization index was over 14 percent higher in western states and over 12 percent lower in two northeastern states. The sample contains hospitals from every state (219 hospitals). The results in **Table 2-3** suggest that specialization has been highest in competitive West Coast markets and lowest in the rate-regulated states of New York and Massachusetts. (New York and Massachusetts are statistically significant outliers and are reported separately.) Hospitals have less incentive to contain costs by decreasing the array of services offered in stringent rate-setting states, such as New York and Massachusetts, in contrast to flexible rate-setting states, such as Maryland, that allow management to reap all the gains from any resulting cost savings. Because the MDCs are more heterogeneous and fewer in number than the DRGs, their information theory index values are lower than the DRG index (see **Table 2-3**). For example, Major Diagnostic Category 5 (MDC 5), the circulatory system, is a "grab bag" of cardiac surgery, pediatrics, vascular surgery, general surgery, and cardiology.

The DRG-based measure of specialization increased 30.6 percent in the period from 1991 to 2000. The MDC-based measure of specialization increased 39.8 percent in the period from 1991 to 2000. The average hospital in the sample exhibited a slight deviation of service scope, from an average of 43.8 percent of the services listed in **Table 2-3** in 1991 to 39.2 percent of the services in 2000. While managing in turbulent times, it is not incompatible to reduce scope while achieving greater cash flow from a select few specialized departments. Future research should consider what strategy is optimal for various market environments.

A number of factors are hypothesized to affect specialization, including number of beds, rate regulation, and ownership. For-profit hospitals have been found to specialize somewhat more, as have large teaching hospitals (Council of Teaching Hospitals members). All else equal, specialization has been found to be higher in markets with a higher density of health maintenance organizations (HMOs), hospital beds, physicians, and long-term care units.

Table 2–3 Information Theory Index of Case Mix Specialization (I) by Geographic Location, 1991 and 2000 (N=219 hospitals)

	Sample	1991	2000	Percentage Increase 1991–2000
1–4 Index I DRG-based				
1. New York, Massachusetts	N=25	.372	.467	25.6
2. Western United States	N=47	.510	.648	27.1
3. Other 39 States[*]	N=147	.460	.609	32.3
4. All States	N=219	.461	.602	30.6
5–8 Index I MDC-based				
1. New York, Massachusetts	N=25	.144	.186	29.2
2. Western United States	N=47	.198	.254	28.4
3. Other 39 States[*]	N=147	.155	.225	45.1
4. All states	N=219	.161	.225	39.8

[*] Other 39 states not in lines 1 and 2.

The DRG-based specialization index is regressed on the 13 variables outlined to account for cross-sectional variations in case-mix proportions. The results in **Table 2–4** agree with the hypothesized signs from previous studies and support the DRG I-index as a measure of specialization. Specialization is high in moderately sized (100- to 300-bed) hospitals, and specialization declines in hospitals with up to 640 beds. Beyond 640 beds, it appears the scale of financial reserves or institutional slack enables larger hospitals to increase specialization for a wider range of services, which is consistent with other studies (Eastaugh 1992, Eastaugh 2000, Farley and Hogan 1990).

To discover whether specialization can trim unit cost, one has to adjust for case mix in greater detail. Because the sample size of hospitals is not sufficient to introduce one variable for each product in the multiproduct firm, the analyst does the second best thing: builds a hedonic cost function. The hedonic proxy measures for case mix include: our DRG-based specialization index, a length-of-stay weighted case-mix index, and three measures of emergency department and outpatient surgery volume. In building the cost

Table 2-4 Variables Affecting Inpatient Case-Mix Specialization, 1991-2000 (N=219 Hospitals)

Variable Estimate[+]	Hypothesized Sign	Coefficient
A. Capacity (Number of Beds in 100s)		
1. Acute care beds[++]	–	–.0897**
2. Acute care beds squared	+	.0077*
B. Management Focus (ownership, teaching status)		
3. For-profit hospital	+	.0694*
4. Member, COTH teaching hospitals	+	.0952**
5. Affiliated with a medical school	?	.0015
C. Competitive Location and Alternatives		
6. Herfindahl index bed concentration	–	–.1330**
7. In metropolitan SMSA area	+	.0501
8. Number of HMOs in the country	+	.0168**
9. Hospital beds/100 pop. in country	+	.0293
10. Physicians/100 pop. in country	+	.3162**
11. Fraction beds in long-term care units	+	.0441*
D. State Regulatory Pressures		
12. Located in New York or Massachusetts	–	–.0398*
13. Located in western states	+	.0196*
E. Control for Bias in Index Specialization		
14. Inverse of the # of patient records	+	156.1*

+Ordinary least squares regression estimate with DRG-based information theory index of specialization as the dependent variable

++National sample of 219 hospitals with greater than 75 beds

* $p<0.05$, two tailed test

** $p<0.01$, two tailed test

R^2-adjusted = .596

F- Ratio (14df/203df) = 20.21

function in **Table 2-4**, the three measures of factor prices (if labor and debt are more expensive, then cost per admission will be more expensive) and admissions (as a measure for economies of scale rather than bed capacity) must be included (see line 4 of **Table 2-5**). The results in **Table 2-5** indicate that a 30.6 percent rise in specialization yields an 8.2 percent reduction in cost per admission in the period from 1991 to 2000. Reducing costs 1 percent per year over seven years is a small, but not inconsequential, improvement in efficiency. The capacity for generating cost savings is one rationale for the rise in specialization. A second rationale for specialization involves shifts in technology

Table 2-5 Impact of Case-Mix Specialization on Inpatient Hospital Cost per Admission (Based on a Within-Hospital Regression Equation)

Variable Estimate[+]	Hypothesized Sign	Coefficient
A. Hedonic Descriptors for Case Mix		
1. *ln* (DRG-based index)	−	−.1281**
2. *ln* (LOS-weighted case-mix index)	+	.6962**
3. Emergency dept. visits/total visits	+	−.0014
4. Outpatient surgery visits/total visits	+	.0309**
5. Fraction of surgery done outpatient	+	.5951*
B. Competitive Location and Alternatives		
6. Herfindahl index bed concentration	−	−.1098**
7. Percent revenue not from operations	+	.2073*
8. Number of HMOs in the country	−	−.0249**
9. Hospital beds/100 pop. in country	−	−.0876**
10. Physicians/100 pop. in country	−	−.0290*
11. Nonpatient care revenue/total revenue	+	.1774
C. Economies of Scale (Impact of Volume)		
12. *ln* (acute bed admissions)	−	−.1981**
D. Management Focus (Ownership, Teaching Status)		
13. For-profit hospital	−	−.0079*
14. Member, COTH teaching hospitals	+	.1386**
15. Affiliated with a medical school	?	.0018
E. Input Factor Prices (Labor, Debt)		
16. Ratio of long-term debt/total assets	+	.2257**
17. *ln* (total interest expense/long-term)	+	.0235**
18. *ln* (average expense payroll per FTE)	+	.2014**

+ Least squares estimate with *ln* (average cost per admission) as dependent variable and instruments used for *ln* (I) and *ln* (admissions)

* $p<0.05$, two tailed test

** $p<0.01$, two tailed test

R^2-adjusted = .405

F-Ratio = 27.38

and physician preference for certain procedures and product lines. From these regression equations, one cannot ascertain how much of the specialization is provider- or physician-driven, management-driven (selection of product lines), or payment-driven (either the reimbursement rates are too low or the inefficient departments have unusually high average cost).

The coefficients of the within-hospital regression equation explaining shifts in specialization over the period between 1991 and 2000 are presented in **Table 2-6**. The signs are consistent with the cross-sectional results in **Table 2-5**, except that the fifteenth variable (affiliation with a medical school) and the ninth variable (bed density) have different signs. One cannot conclude much from the observation that the HMO density variable is more significant (0.01 level), but the Herfindahl index as a measure of competition is slightly less significant (0.05 level) in **Table 2-6** relative to **Table 2-4**. More competition, as measured by the Herfindahl index, has a modest downward impact on cost (–1.4 percent). Not surprisingly, the western states appear to be associated with more specialization, and the New York and Massachusetts environments tend to retard specialization. To retard specialization also retards profits. In Maryland, hospital operating profit margin declined from 4.1 percent in 1997 to 0.7 percent in the year 2000. The most substantial finding in **Table 2-6** is the large, highly significant coefficient for cost per admission in line 7, suggesting that hospitals facing higher costs per DRG specialize more. One caveat should be introduced: It is difficult to assess reliability when examining cross-sectional data and then comparing it over a period of time.

Specialize Carefully

One of the product lines a nonprofit or for-profit could specialize in is primary care. An urban public hospital could specialize in public health. Not so long ago, there lived a happy paradigm that said hospitals that specialized were too internally focused because they turned away patients and doctors in areas outside their limited product lines. Today the reduction of product lines in a more specialized hospital can reduce the inefficiency (unjustified costs) in individual hospitals. The paradigm for this decade is that specialization breeds quality and cost efficiency. The hospital offering every DRG is too internally focused and provides care at a higher unit cost (with less service quality). The obvious exceptions to this broad generalization are the few very large academic medical centers (AMCs) with departments already large

Table 2-6 Variable Impacting Within-Hospital Variance in Hospital Case-Mix Specialization, 1991-2000 (N= 219 hospitals)

Variable Estimate[+]	Hypothesized Sign	Coefficient
A. Capacity (Number of Beds in 100s)		
1. Acute care beds[++]	–	–.0761**
2. Acute care beds squared	+	.0046*
B. Management Focus (Ownership, Teaching Status)		
3. For-profit hospital	+	.0490
4. Member, COTH teaching hospitals	+	.1023**
5. Affiliated with a medical school	?	–.0037
C. Competitive Location and Alternatives		
6. Herfindahl index bed concentration	–	–.0803**
7. *ln* (average cost per inpatient admit)	+	.2062**
8. Number of HMOs in the country	+	.0091**
9. Hospital beds/100 pop. in country	+	–.0565
10. Physicians/100 pop. in country	+	.3081**
11. Fraction beds in long-term care units	+	.0918*
D. State Regulatory Pressures		
12. Located in New York or Massachusetts	–	–.0719**
13. Located in western states	+	.0407**
E. Control for Bias in Index Specialization		
14. Inverse of the # of patient records	+	238.1**

+Ordinary least squares regression estimate with DRG-based index as dependent variable using an instrument for *ln* (average cost per admission)

++National sample of 219 hospitals with greater than 75 beds

* $p<0.05$, two tailed test

** $p<0.01$, two tailed test

R^2-adjusted = .304

F- Ratio = 22.19

enough to reap any possible economies of scale. About 40 percent of the 122 academic medical centers fall into this last category (16 of the 219 hospitals in this study are AMCs). In the future, the other 900 teaching hospitals may have to specialize or pool their resources and become less full-service (offering under 200 DRGs) and become better positioned to survive in an era of cost competition and quality competition.

Studies of specialization should consider the direction in which the specialization is planned or driven. No current evidence exists to suggest that specialization has harmed access, but in the future specialization may produce less product differentiation, with every hospital moving in the same direction. Under such conditions, all hospitals in a market area might vacate a necessary product line and perhaps harm the health of the population.

One must not forget the role consumers play. Travel time and search time to find the "right hospital" for a given condition will rise if the average hospital offers only 150 DRGs. Future research should consider whether the cost to consumers and physicians in the search process is worth the benefits in terms of rising levels of quality and declining unit cost per admission. With a good public information network, and rising interest in value shopping, specialization may continue to be a bargain for providers and consumers. However, some physicians may not like the fact that they have practice privileges to admit patients at a smaller number of specialized hospitals. On the plus side for hospitals, they may have the economic power to charge a high fee (like a condo fee or rent) to doctors in search of admitting privileges. In hospitals with weak management, the political power of some physicians within a given hospital may lead to underspecialization—the inability of some hospital managers to selectively prune out some product lines. The hospitals with the weak managers will be the first to close.

To maintain an equally high patient census, a hospital that specializes must expand the geographic range of its marketing effort. For example, when the Memorial Medical Center of Long Beach decided to market its specialized advanced cancer treatment program, patients from a wider array of zip codes were admitted. The impact of consumer behavior is more obvious for smaller hospitals. As more hospitals specialize in less than 200 DRGs, patients will have to drive by a number of hospitals to get to the ones that are right for them. More and more patients are choosing the specialized hospitals that create a point of differentiation in their minds, rather than stopping at a full-service hospital offering every DRG.

Future research should consider whether any future improvement in cost efficiency per admission outweighs the cost to patients. If patients have to spend more time (travel time, lost wages) driving to fewer specialized providers, the monetary savings for payers may not be worth the resulting costs to the households. However, Bronstein and Morrisey's (1999) study suggests that patients are willing to travel. They found that 50 percent of rural pregnant women bypassed the nearest rural hospital that provided obstetrics services. These women are willing to drive further for a better provider to meet their needs. If mean travel distance increased by just a few miles, hospital specialization may yield net gains for society that outweigh the costs to consumers—but this generality may not be true in some unstudied rural areas where the opportunity costs for longer distances are more substantial. Equity between types of providers may suggest future alternative methods of reimbursement. Payers may want to move towards prospective payment that pays according to severity-adjusted burden of disease.

Reporting Conventions

Hospitals and nonprofit health maintenance organizations (HMOs) have recently come to adopt the business sector convention of product line and net revenue reporting. If the hospital sector has experienced quantum leaps in financial reporting policies, the progress in managerial cost accounting has been more gradual in the past few years (Eastaugh 2000). Some ambulatory care products are easily process costed, such as diabetes control. However, other items have a wide range of potential customization, including the addition of various options along the way in the treatment process. As a rejoinder to interested medical staff, one might add that to avoid a reductionist "cookbook" standardization of medicine, it is necessary to quantify the cost-behavior ramification of the options. Professional review organizations, or PROs, tend to ignore the subtleties of marginal costing and jump to the larger question of whether much of this care is "necessary." For some diagnosis-related groups (DRGs), variability of costs depends largely on the level of illness severity, which in turn determines the degree of customization (options selected). For example, in major reconstructive vascular surgery, including DRG 111, and to a greater degree for the more prevalent DRG 110, a wide coefficient of variation exists in cost per case, even when the surgeries are done by the same provider team. The range of customized options varies from proximal bypass to distal bypass for limb to salvage to multiple ipsilateral surgery.

The word *customized* denotes a situation that offers a wide range of options within the given DRG and thus a wide range of final product costs (DRGs 25, 82, 108, 169, 213, 254, 296, 324, and 421). The severity system that the HMO or hospital purchases to enhance analytical accuracy can help improve staff scheduling (see chapter 4) and select clinicians (see chapter 3). Without severity system software, the hospital or HMO cannot select equitable staffing patterns or make the correct choice of physicians with which to contract. For example, the daily room charge could be disaggregated into two basic components: fixed per day hotel costs plus nursing costs at Level-1 severity level and variable costs for days in which the patient achieves severity Levels 2, 3, or 4 (sicker and sickest). In effect, hotel costs plus Level-1 severity costs could be process costed, and other severity levels (2, 3, and 4) could be job-order costed. Consider an extreme example: DRG 10 cardiothoracic procedures (except valve and bypass) might have a process-order cost of $11,000 per case, but a severity Level-2 job order costs three times as much. A severity Level-3 job order costs seven times as much, and a severity Level-4 order costs 10 to 14 times as much, depending on the senior attending physicians. Regulators, PPOs, and HMOs might wish to claim that much of this extra care is questionable or could be provided more efficiently. In some cases, however, including DRGs 108, 110, and 111, there appear to be relatively narrow differences in the selection process of customization options among equally board-qualified surgeons when case mix (DRG) is adjusted for severity level.

Standard Costing

From the more limited perspective of cost accounting, as long as the institution can isolate the custom options in serving a patient and standardize unit cost, cost accounting is a simple matter of arithmetic. The two difficult steps in cost accounting are developing standard costs for each service-item option and keeping these standards updated.

Today, methods for handling indirect costs are well established (Suver 1995). Indirect costs are simply allocated from overhead departments to patient care (revenue) departments. Standard costs, on the other hand, are the direct patient-related costs in hospital operation that can be used normatively to assess economic efficiency and productivity. In fact, one cannot perform effective cost accounting without standards (Horngren and Sundem 1997). The three techniques for identification of standards are: (1) nonscientific ("make a guess"), (2) traditional time motion, and (3) the technically sophisticated input-output approach. The most long-standing management sciences approach to standards involves time-motion activity analysis (microcosting) standards. The second meaningful standards-setting approach involves input-output in weighted regression analysis or, alternatively, exponential smoothing regressions that downweight the value of more historic (outdated) observations (McClain and Eastaugh 1993). A third variety of standards is an ad hoc negotiated option or standard, which, for the purposes of the survey instrument, was defined as cost accounting without standards. The following is a summary of the basic categories:

1. Ad hoc estimates of unit cost per service item of informal work sampling without empirical standards (the nonscientific approach)

2. Time-motion work sampling, the management engineering approach to measuring microcosted standards

3. Input-output regression measures of standard costs

All three techniques in practice may involve some degree of negotiation between middle managers and senior managers, but the third technique is by definition a totally negotiated process. For the purposes of our survey, we combined techniques 1 and 2 into a category called "cost accounting with standards." These two techniques are typically used simultaneously or alternatively every few years. The standard-setting technique used varies by cost center, by service item in each cost center, and by year. Consider two examples. First, one might utilize management-engineered microcosting standards, completed in an annual two- to four-week work sample, for 85 percent of the routine service items (tests) in the laboratory department. For the nonroutine 15 percent of lab costs, one might perform input-output regression analysis. Second, one might microcost half of the service items in the diagnostic radiology department every three to five years to keep the standards current but perform input-output regression on the standards in other years. Most costs are distributed in a few years. One-fifth (30 out of 144) of the services in diagnostic radiology captured 95 percent of the expenses in that area of one teaching hospital.

As a last resort, the standards themselves could be externally adopted from other hospitals and adjusted with regression analysis to better fit the institutional application. One might borrow standards from the Maryland Health Services Cost Review Commission, the New York State resource monitoring standards, or some other source. Some hospitals have discovered that the search for analytical precision and theoretical perfection in microcosting is too expensive to do on a regular basis. However, differentiating levels of refinement in cost accounting is key to determining the manner in which variable-cost items are identified and allocated. In other words, a one-time initial investment in microcosting five to nine large departments might pay off in increased accuracy but cost a significant amount of money and slow down implementation.

The basic question is this: Would one like a good product soon or a much better product for management in 12 to 24 months? As an academic, I prefer the second option, the approach that was taken at nine major medical centers in 2002. As a management consultant, one needs to be sure that management will make use of the better — and much more expensive — product. The former head of "Efficiency Review" at a major hospital complained to me that the hospital spent over 15 person/years of salary on a first-rate product that was never utilized. To avoid embedding levels of some other hospital's baseline inefficiency into the standards, these two hospitals "build up" standard costs with local firm-specific data. This route involves management-engineered yardsticks for how many full-time equivalents (FTEs) should really be in a department and offers targets, such as decreasing productive worked hours to 85 percent. The easy method, used in the majority of cases, is to "back in" costs based on the budget and external standards and thus absorb inefficiency into cost standards.

The concept of diminishing returns at increasing expense (administrative cost) is often summarized in the 80–20 Pareto principle: The first 80 percent of cost accounting accuracy can be obtained with 20 percent of available resources, and the last 20 percent hypothetically requires an additional 80 percent effort (too expensive to collect). Are the marginal benefits in microcosting accuracy worth the increased marginal costs ($100 to $180 per patient served), or could the system be validated and updated by sampling on a periodic basis? Is it necessary to microcost at the procedural level, or could one do it every three to five years on a 20 percent sampling basis, along with performing procedure costing for each and every newly initiated procedure? For example, at one teaching hospital seven of 39 service items in hematology capture 90 percent of expenses. Therefore, effort should be concentrated on these seven items. A typical Council of Teaching Hospital facility, which holds 250 to 499 beds, might treat 1,000 separate diseases and perform 9,000 separate procedures (64 new procedures were introduced in 2001 alone). Procedure costing would prove an onerous task. The problem is compounded in the case of academic medical center hospitals with 500 or more beds (n=48 hospitals) that offer 12,800 procedures, with 110 to 150 new procedures (service items) initiated each year.

Level of Analysis

Selective sampling and microcosting at the procedural or DRG level has allowed many innovative chief financial officers to develop software to re-aggregate cost information by 20 to 40 strategic product-line groupings (SPGs, or a clustering of similar DRGs performed by an identical subset of the medical staff). These SPGs are utilized similarly to strategic business units in the administrative sciences literature (Eastaugh 2001). Productivity and variance analysis are obviously more valid and reliable if costs can be combined at the procedural level. In this context, the purist may state that inferior costing of profit and loss by product can do more harm than good if one opens or expands the "wrong" service misidentified as profitable. This statistical Type I error, rejecting the null hypothesis (unprofitable) when it is true (the product line is a poor bet, but the cost accounting system cannot recognize this), is sometimes labeled *failure to maximize specificity.* Moreover, an inaccurate cost accounting system can do harm if it closes or reduces the size of a product line misidentified as unprofitable. This is a statistical Type II error, accepting the null hypothesis (unprofitable) when it is not true. If, in fact, the product line is a good investment, both specificity and sensitivity are high (or over 90 percent). There is no such thing as a 100 percent perfect system. However, misspecified costs yield short-run variance analysis, weak control, and inaccurate long-range financial planning.

Without a measure of actual cost, it is impossible to uniformly price markup relative to actual cost. Therefore, hospitals have never been able to charge uniformly for services in proportion to their costs. Consider the problems with such an inaccurate ratio of cost-to-charge (RCC) costing in the context of an American auto company. The company produces two models, ADRG and BDRG. The company produces car ADRG at $12,000 and sells it for $24,000. The company produces car BDRG at $8,000 and sells it for $12,000. The company sells three times as many model BDRG cars as model ADRG cars.

In this example, the ratio of costs to charges across the company is 0.6, or $[(3 \times 8) + 12] / [(3 \times 12) + 24]$. If the company had been so unsophisticated as to allocate costs by RCC, it would have claimed that car ADRG costs

$14,000 (0.6 x $24,000), and car BDRG costs $7,200 (0.6 x $12,000). Such a primitive RCC methodology overstates the profitability of a BDRG by $800 and underestimates the profitability of an ADRG by $2,400. The principles are the same when we attempt to cost account patient care, with two exceptions: Maintaining technically updated costing standards is more of a problem for medicine and surgery, and health providers typically make a better net profit on the less expensive DRGs such as 86, 96, and angina pectoris (140). Obviously, with economies of scale any DRG can prove profitable with sufficient volume and reasonable levels of provider efficiency. However, certain high-cost DRGs are seldom reported as profitable: craniotomy (DRG 2), hepatobiliary shunt (191), kidney transplants (302), and extensive burns (457).

One should consider two final caveats in the cost accounting process. First, charge items need to be refined into a multitude of service items. For example, one might develop a medical records service item, a discharge and/or admissions service item, and a routine (lowest level of severity or acuity) nursing service item per day. If medical records as a service item have a 70 percent fixed and a 30 percent variable cost, a seemingly homogenous service item may be subdivided into two separate cost accounts (fixed and variable). However, it might be more expensive to discharge a patient to a nursing home than to self-care, but the expense of microcosting this service item into multiple accounts might not justify the administrative expense.

The second caveat concerns reconciliation of standard costs as collected in an extended-charge master file containing data on all service items. Statistical discrepancies in the aggregate across the institution should be very small, amounting to fewer than one percent of expenses at most. However, expecting to reconcile to the last dollar is unrealistic. In reconciling standard costs compared to actual cost information in the general ledger accounts, the difference can be either unfavorable or favorable and attributable to management competence, system error, or exogenous events beyond managerial control. In any case, the variance information can be used to restructure future budgets.

Variance Analysis and Flexible Budgets

As Horngren and Sundem (1997) pointed out, the essential strength of managerial cost accounting is that it links promises made during the budget process back to the responsibility center. For example, if a department chairman claims that the purchase of certain equipment will result in labor savings, but no labor savings are experienced, then this shortfall in performance needs to be either (1) explained away by exogenous circumstances beyond the manager's control or (2) used annually to improve or change the manager in question. This discrepancy between predicted and actual budgeted amounts is called *budget variance* and can be favorable (under budget) or unfavorable (over budget). The traditional business separates total variance into three component parts: (1) price variance (input expense, or what it costs to pay labor or purchase supplies), (2) mix variance, and (3) volume variance. In the hospital context, Finkler (1996) neatly summarized this traditional analysis into a pyramid model that is easy to calculate.

Consider a sample case in which the actual radiology expenses for the month were $91,448, and the budgeted salaries were $90,576. The chief operating officer, unfamiliar with the new flexible budgeting software, claims that the radiology manager does not deserve to go to a national conference because of this $872 unfavorable variance. To defend himself, the radiology manager has to ask how this variance arose. Finkler's pyramid (**Figure 2-1**) provides a good analytical framework. When the most recent rolling budget was made, it was expected that, on average, six relative value units (RVUs) of radiology would be required per diem (Q_i) at an expense of $20.40 per RVU (P), with a patient census of 740 (Q_o). In actuality, there was an average of seven RVUs per day, as the patients were more intensely treated in a shorter duration of stay, and more severely ill patients came from the recently closed public hospital's catchment area. Expenses paid per RVU declined to only $18.40 per RVU thanks to the hard work of the radiology department manager to improve productivity and reduce costs. The number of patients declined to 710 (Q_o) following an 8 percent decline in predicted average length of stay (LOS) and a 4.3 percent increase in admissions.

At the top of the pyramid in **Figure 2-1**, the total variance is described as the difference between the static budget and actual expense, for a net unfavorable $872. For simplicity, the lowercase letter *a* denotes actual costs and *b* denotes budgeted costs. For the pyramid, an actual cost or a budget figure on the left that is smaller than the number on the right implies a favorable variance (radiology price variance); the opposite implies an unfavorable variance (quantity per patient-day variance). From the flexible-budget variance analysis, it might be suggested that the utilization review committee consider the appropriateness of such a substantial increase in radiology services per diem.

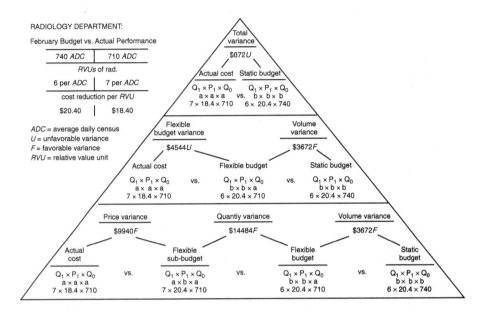

▲ FIGURE 2–1 Variances in a Hospital with Flexible Budgets and Standard Cost Accounting

The medical staff issue is certainly beyond the control of the radiology department. The volume variance in the lower right corner of the pyramid is the same as that in the middle level of the pyramid ($3,672 favorable). The flexible budget variance of $4,544 unfavorable has been subdivided in the bottom of the pyramid into changes in input efficiency (lower cost per RVU) and changes in radiology service mix utilized per case (more RVUs per patients, perhaps without any improvements in efficacy). The department manager is partially responsible for efficiency, in that he could purchase more cost-effectively or schedule better (to reduce overtime hours). The senior management also affects efficiency. The medical staff is largely responsible for patient orders.

Both the subbudget and flexible budget use the $20.40 expense per RVU and the 710 actual patient census. Thus, given the actual workload, the radiologists and other clinicians have produced an unfavorable $14,484 quantity variance. Some fraction of this might result from a more severe case mix. The remaining variance is the price variance, based on the actual cost and the subbudget. Any difference between the actual cost and the subbudget is a result of paying a different amount per RVU produced for the total radiology RVUs needed. This could be even more refined, and the pyramid could be subdivided on a fourth level— the increased (or decreased) RVUs caused by deteriorating (or better) quality control per procedure versus increased RVUs caused by shifts in physician ordering habits. Because quality control was unchanged in our example, the radiology manager is largely responsible for a $9,940 favorable price variance. The radiology manager cannot be assigned any responsibility for the $3,672 favorable volume variance because he or she did not decrease the average duration of patient stay.

Because many managers do not understand flexible budgeting easily, the best software is sufficiently user friendly to present the analysis in simplified language. One pioneer in this area is the New England Medical Center system. The strength of flexible budgets is that they focus on what expenses would have been had the workload output been forecast perfectly. The problem with a static budget is that it simplistically ignores variations that naturally occur as a result of circumstances outside of line-management control and in the control of others, such as medical staff, rate regulators, and other hospital management staff.

Collaborate and Take Action

If competition was the buzzword of the 1990s, collaboration may become the buzzword of this decade. Successful collaboration among hospitals requires improved communication at two levels. The first involves better communication between hospital management and the medical staff, and the second serves to foster better relations between hospitals and includes the sharing of resources. At the first level, improved communication among management and medical staffs can result in lower costs for services and enhanced quality. Management can begin the process by involving the medical staff in the development of preferred practice patterns to enhance productivity. More and more medical staff members are realizing that practice protocols and cost-effective clinical decision making constitute good medicine and good economics. Educational efforts in hospitals should focus on less cooperative physicians who cling to the outdated notion that practice protocols constitute "cookbook medicine." Most physicians now see that the cookbook is a flexible one, partly through the efforts of the Joint Commission on Accreditation of Healthcare Organizations in the development and promotion of clinical protocols. Physicians are starting to forgo tests and procedures when the marginal information gain does not justify the expense.

The second level of communication required for collaboration involves better relations between hospitals. If two hospitals in the same market do not cooperate, the result might be declining cost efficiency and eroding quality of care. For example, assume Hospital M has an excellent cardiac surgery program but a poor oncology program, and Hospital N has an excellent oncology program but a poor cardiac surgery program. Hospital M should close its oncology department and specialize in cardiac surgery; Hospital N should close its cardiac surgery department and specialize in oncology. The two hospitals should then cooperate in referring patients to one another. The SHARP network in Southern California consolidated dozens of hospitals with this strategy; one hospital does oncology while the other does cardiac surgery.

Does quality coexist with cost control? Yes— they are best friends. If your costs are out of control, your statistical quality control is poor in almost all cases. Hospitals that are unable to selectively prune product lines have been characterized as underspecialized. These hospitals are spreading resources so thinly that all departments are suffering.

Specialization and modest diversification might be optimal strategies for U.S. hospitals that are not the sole providers in a community. For a hospital with fewer than 100 beds, the opportunity might not exist to reap economies of scale in high-volume specialty departments. American industry could also benefit from this same recommendation to specialize through cooperation. The point of differentiation likely to prove most powerful is quality. As hospitals analyze their future roles, new areas of specialization and collaboration will emerge to ensure competitive increases in the quality of services offered.

Financial Accounting

Improvements in standard costing have helped reduce management uncertainty and fuel the trends toward hospital specialization and HMO carve-out contracts. Financial accounting has been more stable over time thanks to the landmark work of Ohio State Professor William Cleverley (1997). Since 1980, he has recommended that hospitals record their income in the same way that any other business concern does. In the spirit of true cost and revenue accounting, the hospital industry began to report revenue at expected payment levels. In the past, hospitals had recorded revenue as gross revenue, as if every patient paid list price (charges), with deductions for debt, charity care, and contractual or courtesy allowances, such as those for members of the clergy. The pressure for this change in reporting conventions emanated from the need for the hospitals' books to make sense for trustees with knowledge of the business world and from external relationships with five other key actors: lawmakers, state regulators, discount payers (Medicaid, HMOs, PPOs, and so on), bankers, and bond rating agencies.

The Enron scandal of 2002 taught us about the impact of bad accounting. Since the 1990s, most hospitals have been reporting gross patient revenue as the actual amount that the payers provide—that is, as true revenue. The industry should have adopted this policy independent of any external reporting concerns. Such information is important for meeting the internal fiduciary responsibility to stay viable and up to date as an institution. For example, internal decision making requires one to know how much preferred provider organization payer A is paying in relation to Blue Cross plan B. A hospital may not have any leverage negotiating better process with Medicare, but the leverage to trade-off discounts for improved patient volume does exist on a local level. Having a more accurate estimate of the benefits and costs of alternative arrangements is better than hoping it all works out okay.

Financial ratio analysis can be used for normative one-year peer comparisons or for time trend analysis. **Table 2-7** offers financial ratio medians for four sectors of the mid-Atlantic census divisions. These medians are derived from information taken from financial statements filed with the Securities and Exchange Commission. The financial averages for these four sectors are therefore representative of medium and large for-profit firms. These industry ratio medians do not represent nonprofit firms. Local peer hospitals could analyze their data relative to column one of **Table 2-7** and ask the following: (1) Is our liquidity (ability to meet short-term obligations) better (higher) or worse? (2) Is our capital structure more or less dependent on debt than the competition? and (3) Is profitability better or worse? Irrespective of these normative questions, time trend questions such as these can be addressed: Is liquidity getting better? Is profitability getting better? Is asset turnover improving?

In 2002, more than 70 percent of the 16,000 nursing homes in the United States were for-profit. Ten percent of nursing homes' finances were covered by Medicare, nearly 52 percent were covered by Medicaid, and about 38 percent were covered by out-of-pocket cash. Private insurance represented only 2.7 percent of nursing home revenues. If we compare the columns in **Table 2-7**, nursing homes have half the profitability of hospitals.

Rather than being profitable, nursing homes always rank at the bottom among 171 major industry groups in terms of profitability. Whereas nursing homes are joining chains more and more frequently, hospitals seem to be entering merger agreements more and more frequently. For example, over the past decade the number of Massachusetts hospitals has declined from 121 to 51 due to mergers and closures. Local planners in the state suggest the number of hospitals will decline to fewer than 30 by 2007.

Table 2-7 Financial Ratio Medians for Mid-Atlantic Providers, 2003

Financial Ratio	Hospital (SIC* code 806x)	Hospital and Medical Service Plans (SIC Code 6324)	Patient Offices (SIC Code 8011)	Skilled and Intermediate Care Facilities (SIC Code 805x)
Liquidity				
Current	1.42	1.19	2.17	1.45
Days in receivables	54.2	20.9	59.9	61.4
Days' cash-on-hand	8.2	87.3	14.1	17.7
Capital Structure				
Equity financing percent	34.8	48.5	50.4	38.1
Long-term debt to equity percent	51.6	13.0	31.3	51.5
Cash flow to total debt percent	18.4	15.7	21.6	12.3
Times interest earned	30.2	13.3	4.2	2.1
Activity				
Total asset turnover	0.9	1.6	0.8	0.9
Fixed asset turnover	1.6	15.8	4.8	2.0
Current asset turnover	4.1	3.0	2.1	4.0
Profitability				
Total margin percent	4.3	2.9	4.2	2.1
Return on equity percent	11.4	10.7	9.2	5.5

*SIC = Standard industry code assigned by the Department of Commerce. Source: Data from Department of Commerce, 2002.

Mergers and Diversification

The rate of hospital mergers might increase in the next decade. Mergers are like human relationships; they can range from love and marriage, to courtship followed by friendship, to fast pillage and one-night stands. Employees in merging companies often experience turmoil and confusion often undermining the most careful financial and strategic plans. Financial managers do a good job by avoiding the "Noah's Ark" syndrome and cutting administrative fat rather than keeping two of every job position following a merger. In terms of employee morale, one quick, big cut in jobs is better than the indecision of multiple small cuts over many months. The latter strategy introduces too much uncertainty into employees' lives.

Mergers or aggressive diversification into new lines of business, when successful, can:

1. Allow accumulation of equity capital to offset anticipated lower capital and operating payment rates

2. Provide a storehouse of liquid assets for feeding the mothership hospital

3. Generate wealth sheltered from the malpractice attorneys and rate regulators (which can also be channeled back to the mothership to cover unexpected contingencies)

Diversification also can generate operational efficiencies for the hospital. For example, if the hospital controls the capacity of its home health agency or nursing home, it can facilitate better inpatient discharge planning. One can only speculate whether all this diversification and corporate restructuring will increase profitability and reduce business risk for the core mothership. The logic is obvious: Spin off into some nonregulated or less-regulated sources of revenue to underwrite the overregulated hospital. Future research should consider three basic factors: (1) effect on revenue stability (revenue risk), (2) effect on debt dependency and capital structure (financial risk), and (3) effect on the variability of the cost structure (expense risk).

If the new market does not reach the achieved crucial mass and exceed the break-even point in a reasonable time, the first entrant will usually label the venture a failure. In the health context, the message might be to not try significant investment in a capital-intensive new technology, such as plasma aphaeresis, until a first entrant succeeds somewhere in the nation. If the initial investment at risk is not substantial, hospitals need not be so risk-averse. However, if the investment at risk is substantial, a second entrant in the market often can experience the safety of diversification into a proven market soon to reach appreciable size (market demand). On the other hand, the first entrant might still reap some intangible benefits, such as better knowledge of the market and consumer tastes (preferences), and remarket elsewhere.

Any facility should *ex ante* (up front) calculate the expected break-even point and estimate a reasonable time to expect results (achieve the break-even point). Such calculations will open to ex-post-judgment (whether a second injection of capital is needed to get the new service off the ground). A good marketing survey of the external environment is probably the most critical determinant of successful diversification ventures. When a hospital seems to jump off a cliff, either through excessive diversification or total inaction, if a researcher inquires as to why, 99 percent of the time everything the individual managers did made perfect sense as a response to internal politics. In other words, the fatal mistake was to let internal pressures block out external reality concerning risk and payoff.

In long-term care, continuing care retirement centers (CCRC) offer good examples of testing the market. CCRCs should take advantage of what marketing professionals call *double-loop learning* and realize after a second look at the issue that the assumptions underpinning the projections are overoptimistic. For example, if one is building a CCRC in a community with too much spending power and too many rich elderly homeowners, then they have the financial capability to purchase full-service private care in their own homes. On a second loop in the learning process, the CCRC may wish to downsize the facility.

Diversification: The Upside

Diversification can produce a more adaptable, flexible healthcare system that offers the institution new avenues to equity markets and offers patients greater continuity of care. Internal, strategic, and competitive benefits can be gained through new ventures. What is viewed at one facility as a burden that saps management talent can be viewed by a more adaptable institution as an invigorating challenge for management and staff. A diversification effort, when carried out appropriately, can be a powerful mode of altering the institution's competitive position, especially as management gains sufficient experience with assessing business risk. Optimally, diversification is not a risk strategy, but a syndication-of-risk strategy. New-venture strategies should be analyzed using the portfolio theory of business management, where multiple business concerns can dampen the extremes of variability in cash flow in any single business.

Some types of diversification appear to be simple examples of imitative entry or bandwagoning, such as the explosion of podiatric services or speech pathology services. Posture variables considered by administrators and trustees include whether the new proposed hospital-based service offers a favorable degree of product differentiation relative to the service offered by incumbents (physicians currently providing the service in private offices). For example, does the hospital offer better quality or better convenience to its intermediate consumers (physicians) to practice medicine more productively, better provision of consumer education to foster increased utilization of health services, or better access to the ultimate consumers (patients)? The hospital, as a centralized service distribution innovator, has the potential to reduce the time cost to physicians and the travel time cost to patients in the provision of many services. **Figure 2-2** offers some of the popular services for diversification (not including long-term care).

Diversification is a delicate undertaking that involves many nonfinancial concerns. A rational portfolio framework must consider how to select new ventures, determine which internal and external partners are appropriate, and decide how much capital investment will be required. One should not oversimplify the situation and jump from a quick-and-dirty competitor analysis to a decision. To paraphrase H. L. Mencken, for each complex alternative there is a simple explanation, and it is very often incorrect. The diversification plan can be accomplished through acquisitions, internal joint-venture spinoffs, partial-ownership joint ventures, contractual minority investments, or joint cooperative agreements.

Divestment is the strategy of choice for services with a weak competitive position, poor profitability, and a sufficient supply of other providers offering the service for society. On the other hand, certain services may be divested too quickly because management does not have the persistence to give the product line a chance to gain market share and begin to produce profits following a redesigned marketing program, changes in the basic product, and recapitalization (if needed). The phase-out pricing option listed in chapter 8 will help timid managers slay the sacred cows—unnecessary product lines

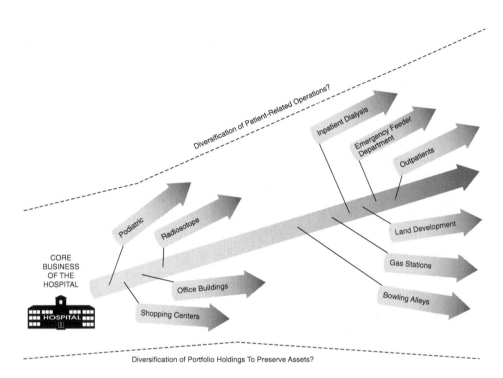

▲ FIGURE 2–2 Two Roads for Diversification: The High Road? The Low Road? or Both Roads?

that will never survive these competitive times. The forward-looking diversified institution should be better able to adapt to unforeseen, and many times unforeseeable, changes in the payment climate. Good cost accounting and prudent specialization are keys for success.

The GME Quandry: Who Should Pay and How Much?

The graduate medical education (GME) component of medical care costs is frequently given adequate earmarked support via funds from Departments of Education in Canada and Europe. The American tradition is to subsidize such costs indirectly through the "back door" of patient hospital bills. For example, the 2002 survey of the Association of American Medical Colleges (AAMC) reported 80 percent of residents' stipends and fringe benefits were derived from hospital patient revenues (AAMC 2003). The Commonwealth Task Force on Academic Health Centers report suggests collection of a tax on all hospital admissions to reimburse hospitals for sponsoring GME

(Commonwealth Fund 2002). This is a rather attractive payment solution for teaching hospitals because it involves minimum disruption of business as usual. Such a proposed tax on hospital admissions, a sort of "sick tax" for education, has the administrative advantage of distributing the costs of teaching hospitals across all inpatients without disaggregating how much of this cash flow underwrites (1) appropriate treatment of a more severely ill case mix, (2) charity care for the poor, or (3) inappropriate expensive care.

Teaching costs are not easy to assess. It is very difficult to partition joint activities such as teaching, research, and patient care. *Joint activity* is a term used to describe the simultaneous production of multiple outputs during a given activity. Joint activity is most obvious when multiple individuals are involved in multiple tasks at the patient's beside. However, joint activity also occurs in instances in which a single individual is involved in multiple tasks or activities. Here a joint product may be indicated by comparative amounts of time taken to perform a task. If an attending physician acting alone, for example, performs a patient-care task in an average of 12 minutes and a second-year resident takes an average of 18 minutes, then the resident's time may be attributed in part to patient care and in part to education. The attending physician's average time in this example is presumed to have no educational content. Thus, if the task is performed in that given period of time, whether by attending physicians or second-year residents, it is taken entirely as an input to patient care. But if the time taken is greater, then a portion becomes an input to education, on the normative premise that the individuals performing the tasks are not yet as skilled, on average, as the attending physicians and therefore must still be learning.

The most basic question to consider is the reason joint-production institutions exist. Joint production most often derives from economies of simultaneous production. Joint production also might arise from joint factor supply, especially in a profession such as medicine. For example, if a factor required to produce instructional outputs, such as faculty members, is to be made available only if allowed to produce research, joint factor supply exists. One should see the folly in buying a minimum of research time if the only objective is to hire a teaching faculty. Fortunately, deans in the real world are concerned with the quality and quantity of patient care, research, and education. Deans must consider issues such as how much additional faculty practice-plan effort on patient care must be requested to restrain tuition rate increase, secure adequate faculty resources, optimize the prestige of the research program, and still produce the level of educational output to which the residency program is committed.

The federal government has effectively resisted pressure to bail out teaching hospitals and medical schools despite the fact that they are precious national resources. The basic dilemma hospitals and schools face is whether they can acquire renewed federal support and maintain their current degree of autonomy from government bureaucrats. Congress's problem is how to allocate resources effectively among many competing high-priority national needs in the face of limited discretionary funds. Ironically, Congress created the specialist oversupply problem through generous Medicare payments to hospital specialist training grounds, and now it is attempting to reduce the number of specialists.

Payers and politicians complain about the oversupply of specialists, but 100 percent of federal GME dollars (up to $108,000 per resident) goes to hospitals. Hospitals train specialists, and if public policy also pays to train more specialists, a glut results. Payment comes in two forms. First are the $2.3 billion annual Medicare funds for direct GME (DGME) payments to hospitals for salaries, fringe benefits, supervisory teaching physician costs, and miscellaneous overhead. Second are the indirect medical education (IME) payments, which are based on the teaching hospital's ratio of interns and residents to beds. The IME payment is tacked onto each patient discharge bill, for which Medicare pays $4.8 billion annually (Office of National Cost Estimates 2002).

▶ **Summary Points:**

- Market economic forces apply to both for-profit and not-for-profit healthcare facilities.

- One of these forces is specialization.

- Cost effectiveness and quality go "hand-in-hand."

> ### *Research and Discussion Questions:*
>
> * What are "public goods?" What are "private goods?"
>
> * What does "marginal economics" mean?
>
> * What does "quality of care" mean?
>
> * Does cost efficiency mean least costly? Why?

References

Association of American Medical Colleges. 2003. Annual Report, Washington, DC: AAMC Press.

Baldridge, M. 1990. Awards, July 10. Washington, DC: National Institute of Standards of Technology.

Barer, M. 1992. Case-mix adjustment in hospital cost analysis: Information theory revisited. *Journal of Health Economics* (1): 53–60.

Berwick, D., Goodfrey, A., and Roessner, J. 1990. *Curing health care: New strategies for quality improvement.* San Francisco: Jossey-Bass.

Bronstein, J., and Morrisey, M. 1999. Determinants of rural travel distance for obstetrics care. *Medical Care* 28(9): 853–866.

Carter, G., Bell, R., and Dubois, R. 2000. Clinically detailed risk information system for cost. *Health Care Finance Review* 21(1): 65–85.

Cleverley, W. 1997. *Essentials of healthcare finance.* Gaithersburg, MD: Aspen.

Commonwealth Fund 2002. Report on the Task Force on Academic Health Centers, New York: Commonwealth Fund.

Connor, R., Feldman, R., and Dowd, B. 1998. Hospital costs and prices. *International Journal of the Economics of Business* 5(2): 159–180.

Dalton, K., Norton, E., and Kilpatrick, K. 2001. Longitudinal study on the effects of GME on hospital operating costs. *Health Services Research* 36(1): 1267–1291.

Drucker, P. 1996. *Managing the nonprofit organization.* New York: HarperCollins.

Eastaugh, S. 1992. Hospital specialization and cost efficiency: Benefits of trimming product-lines. *Hospital and Health Services Administration* 37(2): 223–236.

Eastaugh, S. 1993. *Health economics: Efficiency, quality and equity.* Westport, CT: Greenwood Press.

Eastaugh, S. 1994. Diversification and financial management. *Medical Care* 22(8): 704–723.

Eastaugh, S. 2000. New ventures require accurate risk analysis. *Healthcare Financial Management* 50(1): 54–57.

Eastaugh, S. 2001. Managing risk in a risky world. *Journal of Healthcare Finance* 25(3): 10–17.

Eastaugh, S. 2001. Cost effective potential. *Managed Care Quarterly* 9(1): 23–33.

Farley, D., and Hogan, C. 1990. Case-mix specialization in the market for hospital services. *Health Services Research* 26(5): 757–783.

Feldstein, M. 1989. *Hospital costs and health insurance.* Cambridge, MA: Harvard.

Finkler, S. 1983. The hospital as a sales maximizing entity. *Health Services Research* 18(2): 130–139.

Finkler, S. 1996. *Budgeting concepts for nurse managers.* Orlando, FL: Grune and Stratton.

Horngren, C., and Sundem, G. 1997. *Introduction to management accounting.* Englewood Cliffs, NJ: Prentice-Hall.

McClain, J., and Eastaugh, S. 1993. How to forecast to contain your variable costs: Exponential smoothing techniques. *Hospital Topics* 61(6): 4–7.

Office of National Cost Estimates. 2002. *Trends in health care spending.* Washington, DC: U.S. Government Printing Office.

Suver, J. 1995. *Management accounting for health care organizations.* Oak Brook, IL: Healthcare Finance Management Association.

Yafchak, R. 2000. Longitudinal study of economies of scale in the hospital industry. *Journal of Healthcare Finance* 27(1): 67–89.

Zwanziger, J., Melnick, G., and Bamezai, A. 2000. Effect of selective contracting on hospital costs and revenues. *Health Services Research* 35(4): 849–867.

Chapter 3

The Physician Marketplace

In analyzing physicians, a useful mnemonic is TUMS: tantalized by technology, uncomfortable with uncertainty, motivated by money, scared by suit.

– Richard Riegelman, MD

He who pays the piper can call the tune.

– Old English proverb

The state medical society is essentially a trade union. They have a very narrow outlook, viewing utilization profiles or quality reports as information that should be kept from the public.

– Benjamin Barnes, MD

Concerning the coming surplus of 60,000 physician specialists, I use "surplus" with caution because I do not believe the United States will ever see a surplus such as exists in some Western European countries, where trained physicians have taken jobs as taxicab drivers and have applied for welfare.

– Alvin Tarlov, MD

▶ Critical points in this chapter:

- Physician competition
- Allocative efficiency
- Supply and demand
- Bundling, unbundling, upcoding, and code creep

To the general public, physicians are like cops: The aggregate supply appears to be adequate, but there is never one around when you need one. The growing supply of physicians is important because physicians add to the medical cost-inflation problem. Depending on whether expenditures per physician grow at the historical 30-year rate or at the projected rate of the consumer price index, the rising supply of physicians could add between $16 billion and $24 billion to national health expenditures by 2008. The traditional labor economist view of this issue suggests we reduce the rise in the number of physicians and nonphysician practitioners to help hold down healthcare costs (Brown 2001). Some medical schools have followed this traditional analysis and reduced class size. Is this viewpoint fair to nonphysician practitioners? Is it fair to U.S. consumers desiring more and more doctors and concierge-style personalized practice plans that offer 90 minutes per visit?

Demand for physician services over the past 70 years has grown 50 percent faster than gross domestic product (GDP). Conservative economists take a *laissez-faire* approach: If citizens want more physician services, new doctors should come forth to meet the demand. One recent study from the Medical College of Wisconsin suggests that the United States will have a shortage of 200,000 physicians by 2020 (Cooper et al. 2002). Does this suggest that we should expand class size and build more medical schools? Allocation efficiency is the central issue for policymakers. Rather than focus on total supply numbers, we must focus on practice location and type of physician (primary care or specialist). Do we want to live in a nation where 40 million Americans get 90-minute talks with their "concierge doctor," and 40 million uninsured individuals get no basic primary care?

Physicians: Director of the Ship

It is often stated that physicians control 75 percent of resource decisions in our $1.4 trillion health economy. Physician supply is a critical human resource issue because physicians have some control over the volume of patient demand and, as Christensen (1998) points out, can partially offset the impact of fee freezes (price controls) by expanding volume. Christensen studied 1,000 internists and general practitioners in Colorado and reported a volume offset of approximately 50 percent. Volume increased most rapidly for radiological procedures and diagnostic surgery. In addition to the quantity and adaptability of the physician community, the composition of physicians by specialty distribution is a major issue for public policy because specialists are more expensive than generalists (Physician Payment Review Commission 2002).

Since the publication of the Tarlov Graduate Medical Education National Advisory Committee American Study, the concept of a physician glut (oversupply) has become part of the conventional wisdom. In the context of the 1990s the term glut might be a misnomer, like the term physician shortage in the 1960s. In his classic book *The Doctor Shortage*, Fein (1967) pointed to the two real problems: maldistribution of physician supply by geographic location and specialty choice (too many specialists). As the reports in 2002 by the Council of Graduate Medical Education (COGME), which was set up by Congress in the 1980s to advise it and the Department of Health and Human Services (HHS) on trends in physician supply, pointed out, these maldistribution problems have diminished as the supply of physicians per capita has increased. To the novice, reducing the supply of specialists entering the marketplace would seem to be a simple matter of (1) reducing the number of medical school graduates and (2) changing the emphasis in graduate medical education from specialization to general care. However, finance can shift only some career decisions. The medical school faculty culture will be slow to change. The near-universality of the perception that academically capable students are not encouraged toward primary care is another indicator of the low regard for generalists among many faculty members.

Since 1944, the number of active physicians per capita has doubled from 138 to 274 per 100,000. Yet the nation does not have enough primary care physicians. What do we do when the supply of specialists exceeds 154 per 100,000 population by the year 2010, as is currently projected? The estimated need for specialists at that time is expected to be only 85 per 100,000 at best, assuming only a modest growth in managed care. Some "old timers" are fighting back and saying every nation should have more specialists.

In the United States in 2001, there was one cardiologist for every 12,000 people, compared to one for every 1,000,000 in the United Kingdom (American Medical Association [AMA] 2002). However, the public wants more specialists to talk to patients and confer a generalist's style of care. Conservative physicians will dislike the competition they have been promoting. Many physicians who have had experience with competition and are now facing declining patient volume dream of returning to a less competitive era. Nobody likes competition in what he or she produces, but we all like competition and choice in what we buy. An oversupply of specialists has led to an overutilization of services. For example, the U.S. rate for percutaneous transluminal coronary angioplasty and coronary bypass surgery is seven times the rate of the United Kingdom, although both countries have comparable rates of coronary artery disease.

Recent Trends in Physician Supply

Our past solutions often create our current problems. To offer incentives for inner-city hospitals to serve the poor, teaching hospitals began to receive additional payments for interns and residents in 1983. Currently, teaching hospitals are paid an average of $80,000 per year per resident for as many residents as the hospitals choose to hire (Office of National Cost Estimates 2002). Teaching hospitals have responded to this open-ended entitlement by increasing the number of residency positions by 26 percent since 1988. Medicare has become the $6 billion annual engine for the production of specialists, and no equivalent bonus payment goes to primary care training, which is one reason there are too many specialists and too many residents. In 2002, there were 94,300 residents undergoing training in the United States, 79 percent of whom were U.S. citizens graduating from U.S. medical schools. Only 20 percent of foreign-born residents return home after completing their training. And while the number of U.S. medical school graduates entering subspecialty training is decreasing (for example, the number of U.S., Canadian, and osteopathic graduates in internal medicine subspecialty training dropped from 5,371 in 1993 to 3,817 in 2001), the difference is more than made up by the increasing enrollment of foreign medical school graduates in subspecialty programs (AMA 2002).

As the marketplace sends signals that certain specialties are in oversupply, and annual incomes decline, residents avoid graduate medical education in certain areas. Without federal intervention, the number of young residents training to become anesthesiologists, for example, has declined from 1,491 in 1994 to 406 in 2002.

We must better balance the supply of specialists and generalists. According to the Bureau of Health Professions' data, there were almost equal numbers of specialists and general physicians (defined as family practitioners, general internists, and general pediatricians) in 1967. Supplies per 100,000 persons were 56.8 specialists and 57 generalists. But just three years later, in 1970, there were 65 specialists per 100,000 persons while the generalist ratio had declined to 49.8 per 100,000 persons. After that, the number of generalist physicians rose gradually to peak at 72 per 100,000 persons in 2002. Demand-expanding and demand-constraining forces flow like a tide over a medical community hardly conscious of economic forces. Technological change could increase patient demand beyond all projections, whereas corporate and federal attempts to ration services could decrease the demand for physician services. Whether society has an undersupply or an oversupply of physicians depends on two factors: demand (highly unpredictable) and supply. With federal incentives, we may reach a 50–50 mix of generalist to specialist physicians by 2015. Most medical school deans endorsed this goal in the Pew Commission Report (2001).

The federal government has designated medically underserved areas in rural and inner-city locations. One program in North Carolina and a second 22-year-old program in Pennsylvania have been very successful in increasing the rural physician workforce. Jefferson Medical College has set up a special program in this field for 25 years (Rabinowitz 2000). Jefferson Program graduates are more likely to practice in a rural area (34 percent vs. 11 percent), more likely to practice in underserved areas (30 percent vs. 9 percent), and more likely to practice family medicine (52 percent vs. 10 percent), than graduates of other programs.

Congress took action to restrict the flow of foreign medical graduates (FMG) since the mid-1980s. Public hospitals and small marginal teaching hospitals are still highly dependent on an FMG work force to deliver patient care. But in 1999, COGME, the Council on Graduate Medical Education, proposed decreasing the number of residency slots to discourage further importation of FMGs. The Council has recommended that the number of entry residency positions be held to 110 percent of the number of U.S. medical school graduates. The current level of entry residency positions is 126 percent of the number of students graduating from U.S. medical schools each year. In addition, the elder senior medical staff might continue to lengthen the apprenticeship to enhance quality of care and might also keep their competition in the educational pipeline for as long as possible. Some of the younger physicians in training wish that their elders would listen to Hippocrates and reflect that "life is so short and the craft so long to learn." Lucky Hippocrates never faced an $80,000 debt service from his medical education.

A career in medicine is being viewed as increasingly regulated and less profitable than in prior decades. According to the AMA survey of socioeconomic characteristics of medical practice (2002), physician incomes after inflation increased only 1.1 percent from 1988 to 2002. However, the cost of a medical education markedly outpaced inflation. Average tuition at medical schools outpaced inflation by 208 percent over the last decade. Those without substantial wealth have to incur a substantial debt before graduation day. Nearly one in every three graduates was more than $80,000 in debt by graduation. The rise in bureaucratic paperwork and increasing competition within the profession are steering young people away from a career in medicine.

Clearly, nonfinancial factors such as loss of autonomy or prestige contribute to the flat trend in applications to medical schools. In four of the last five years, medical school applications have declined (Tienan 2002). Medicine is not a poverty profession. As an index of physicians' economic status within a society, one can consider the ratio of physicians' net income to gross domestic product per capita in a nation. By that yardstick, in 2002, West German physicians outpaced the general public in Germany by a ratio of 6.8 to 1, closely followed by U.S. and Japanese physicians in their countries (6.4 to 1). However, these pretax medical practice figures understate the economic advantage among Japanese physicians, who have such high status that by law they pay no income taxes. In contrast, physicians' income in most of Western Europe outpaces the general public's by 3.8 to 4.3. Because of the high tax rates in these countries with national health insurance, it is futile to negotiate higher salaries, so the clinicians negotiate about working hours and working conditions (Eastaugh 1995).

While American physicians fear the idea of government-negotiated salaries, the cost-escalation problem is driving Congress to consider broad systemic reforms in the payment of physicians. Unconstrained, physician expenses will rise to $1,600 per capita, or 2.6 percent of gross national product (GNP), by the year 2005.

Principal Methods for Paying the Doctor

The three basic methods of compensating clinicians are salary, capitation, and fee-for-service. Each method has relative strengths and weaknesses. The primary advantages of a salaried system are cost control and a controlled workweek (many young physicians like the lifestyle advantage of working a salaried shift and going home). If a physician is salaried (paid per unit of time), the organizational risk involves poor productivity and the potential underprovision of care. The salaried individual can try to come in late, leave early, and do a minimum amount of work per hour. Because of this obvious moral hazard to underprovide service, salaried contracts increasingly come with an incentive compensation provision to pay more for enhanced productivity. Clever salaried contracts try to promote the carrot (additional pay for additional work above the average), rather than to emphasize the stick (sanctions if one fails to meet a quota for workload per month).

The second method for paying physicians involves capitation. Pure capitation pays the physician a fixed payment per person joining his or her panel of potential patients. The incentives are to keep the patients happy and healthy (happy so they do not disenroll and healthy so they do not overutilize expensive healthcare resources). Capitation offers no incentives to overprovide expensive care, and it offers the long-run incentive to provide preventive care (thus saving money in the future). In our mobile U.S. society, this last incentive is probably overstated because subscribers change jobs and health plans often. Thus the capitated system providing the preventive care accrues only a small fraction of any resulting financial benefits. Capitated managed care systems use a gatekeeper with the dual responsibility to do no harm to the patient while acting as an explicit guardian of the health plan's financial welfare. Capitated systems run the risk of undercare, so quality must be closely monitored. Capitated systems also run the risk of overreferral in that gatekeepers may minimize their workload by shunting too many patients to specialists elsewhere in the health plan. This can be controlled through the process of utilization review and reinforced through financial incentives by providing less holdout pay at year's end. A number of managed care systems have demonstrated that physicians can practice excellent and cost-effective medicine under a capitated contract. Unnecessary admissions and routine tests (chest roentgenograms) can be reduced without detriment to the patient. Consequently, capitated payment has grown most rapidly as a method of paying physicians.

Under fee-for-service payment per unit work, the clinician's income is directly related to work ethic and business acumen. However, just as capitation runs the potential risk of conflict of interest for financial reasons, fee-for-service offers the conflict of interest to steer patients to tests or facilities from which the physician reaps financial returns (the physician owns the equipment that does the test or receives kickback incentive pay for referrals). For example, it looks greedy to the public if the clinician is a business partner with the laboratory and the radiology imaging center. Congress is increasingly wary of the argument that the physician is unconcerned with cash flow and owns such facilities only to ensure the quality of patient care. Fee-for-service physicians get paid more if they provide more services, but they also get paid more (1) if they are paid as owners of the equipment that does the test or procedure and are paid again to interpret the results and (2) if they are paid for upcoding (upgrading) the current procedural terminology (CPT) code on the reimbursement requests to insurance companies for work done in order to receive higher payment rates. The fee-for-service system has been very inflationary because all the incentives stimulate overprovision of inappropriate or unnecessary care. For example, a total hysterectomy (58150) might be coded as exploration of the abdomen (49000), removal of ovaries and tubes (58720), appendectomy (44955), and lysis of adhesions (58740). According to the CPT manual, this coding is incorrect because all of these procedures are bundled together as total hysterectomy (58150), and the moral hazard exists to select the code that maximizes payment. In contrast, salaried or capitated physicians have no incentive to own healthcare facilities or upcode the patient record in CPT coding.

Wanted: Some Effective Controls on Quantity and Quality

Capitation systems are growing in popularity because governments and insurance companies want to negotiate with bundling of services, fewer sellers, and risk-contracting care organizations (a few hundred plans willing to take an annual per-person check as payment in full). Both in terms of cost control and administrative simplicity, dealing with capitated plans is superior to dealing separately with 790,000 physicians and all ancillary service providers and their unbundled piles of bills. However, organized medicine fears declining professional autonomy and loss of the prerogative to exceed the employers' norms for standard care if clinicians are only salaried or capitated employees of some faceless corporation. A change in physician attitudes might emerge over the next decade as guidelines and models are developed for plans that have excellent quality as well as excellent cost-efficiency. Billions of dollars could be saved each year if physicians practiced in the same style as those at

Stanford, the Mayo Clinic, or Case Western Reserve. These competitive medical organizations (CMO) act as islands for 5 percent to 20 percent of the physicians in an area, enhance quality, take responsibility for patient needs, and make prudent decisions concerning discretionary care (Eastaugh 1995).

Naïve policymakers question the concept of discretionary care, saying that the world is black or white, that care is either unnecessary or necessary, and that there is no middle category. One could take the CMO concept one step further and suggest that such organizations represent pathway guidelines for better community medical practice at a reasonable cost. Pathway guidelines serve as yardsticks for cost-effective clinical decision-making and as a standard to demonstrate that good medicine and good economics can coexist. Too much attention has been focused on a second type of guideline: boundary guidelines for payers to define the range of medical practice beyond which a clinician incurs the wrath of payers. If the practitioner exceeds the boundary, the computer suggests an administrative sanction, and after a number of due-process hearings, a monetary penalty might result. This second type of guideline gives the topic a bad reputation and has led to the denotation "cookbook medicine." Physicians are not ignorant or venal, but many clinicians need help with positive, proactive pathway guidelines. If physicians wish to preserve their autonomy, they should participate actively in the development of these guidelines. The guidelines are suggestions, and the computer is more of an educational tool than an enemy to be consorted with as part of a standard operating procedure. In summary, boundary guidelines clamp down on "bad" physicians, whereas pathway guidelines assist the profession.

What constitutes appropriate care and an optimal pathway can be established in three basic ways: the implicit ad hoc method, the risk-benefit method, and the cost-benefit method. Decision trees in academic settings focus on the cost-benefit method (an action is appropriate if the marginal benefit exceeds the marginal cost, with the intangible benefits shadow priced). The risk-benefit approach suffers because the method includes only traditional medical risks and excludes monetary costs. The implicit approach used in hospital utilization review is hard to export to other settings and has questionable validity, given that we know little of what the reviewer had in mind during the ad hoc process of making judgments.

Controlling the Volume of Services

The great equation in medical economics involves the control of expenditures (E), which are equal to price (P) times quantity (Q). All payers desire to control their expenditures by trimming P and constraining Q (the volume of services). The healthcare system is a very adaptable balloon, where squeezing down on only one factor (P) can cause a bulge in another area (increased volume). Price controls without volume controls yield little in the way of cost control. Service volume per capita is clearly out of control. Physicians can expand volume by a stepped-up quantity of procedures, operations, and provider-initiated follow-up visits. Moreover, with 8,200 codes available to label physician services, including 10 subjective codes for the basic office visit, code creep (upcoding) becomes prevalent. The fine detail of the codes allows the smart physician to unbundle the patient experience or upcode individual items (the minimal visit is upcoded as brief, and the extended visit is upcoded as a comprehensive office visit). Hospitals played the same game with diagnosis-related group creeping of patient classifications to the better-paying and higher code groups.

Some of the added volume and intensity might represent real health benefits to patients, but the Centers for Medicare and Medicaid Services (CMS, formerly HCFA) has labeled some of the increase unnecessary. The number-one physician reimbursement issue seems to involve controlling the growth in per capita service volume. The most effective single solution is capitation. Capitation decentralizes decisions about which patient receives what and how much, while heightening the need for quality assurance and minimizing the chance of underprovision of care. Capitation will not be the voluntary choice of all Americans, as evidenced by the fact that capitated Medicare currently covers only six million Americans (Office of National Cost Estimates 2002).

The number-two physician reimbursement issue involves selecting a fair workload scale for equitable payment among physician specialties. Current Medicare fees are based on the work of Harvard Professor Bill Hsiao. Hsiao (1989) worked for five years to develop a resource-based relative-value scale (RBRVS) as an alternative to the current charge-based system. Resource inputs by physicians include (1) total work input performed by the physician for each service, (2) practice costs (including office overhead and malpractice premiums), and (3) the cost of specialty training (the opportunity for spending 13 years going to medical school and training to become a cardiac surgeon). The Hsiao study, with the help of the AMA and a number of specialty societies, presented fairly valid and reliable estimates of physicians' work according to four dimensions: time, psychological stress, mental effort and judgment, and technical skill plus physical effort.

The Hsiao study has been subject to two criticisms, one minor and one major. The minor point concerns the heavy emphasis on time measurement: Other professionals' (lawyers, for example) charges are not so perfectly correlated to their work time expended. This point is easily dismissed for three reasons: (1) in the name of scientific accuracy, using resource-based relative-value units (RBRVU) is better than perpetuating tradition; (2) orientation to time might stimulate physicians to enhance productivity; and (3) other professions make less use of government funds or insurance dollars (if we had government paying half the legal fees, then RBRVUs would be necessary for that profession). On a more important point, the RBRVS study methodology could be improved if a refined estimate for improvement of patient health status could become a major measure of workload. If improvement of health status replaced activity as the purists' measure for effective workload, the providers who offered better care and produced higher quality patient outcomes would get paid more for their efforts and skill. In the business world, this mechanism would be called *pay for performance* (see chapter 4). Obviously, not all activity proves to be beneficial, given that the real output in an ideal study would be improvement in health status. If a refined health-status measure were developed, the clinicians who produced higher quality patient outcomes would get paid more for their effort and skill.

Improving the System

The Hsiao study answers the basic research question of how much to pay for cognitive services relative to procedures. The payment system is biased toward paying for procedures done to the patient, rather than for talking to or thinking about the patient. The specialist who spends 25 minutes inserting a Swan-Ganz catheter into a patient in heart failure receives $295, but the physician who spends 60 minutes doing a history and physical on the same patient to arrive at the diagnosis is paid only $70. Under the Hsiao system, physicians would be paid more equitably per unit of work (there would not be a ten fold variation in the last column of **Table 3–1**). If gains and losses among physicians had been redistributed in a zero-sum fashion among the various specialties, $140,000 of yearly income would have been carved out of the average thoracic surgeon's $350,000 income and given to primary care.

Hsiao and the Physician Payment Review Commission (PPRC 2002) utilized the human-capital concept that resources devoted to increasing an individual's skills or knowledge, such as education, can be thought of as investment in future income. Income includes monetary compensation and the psychic benefits from any undertaking. For example, most people derive monetary income from their jobs and psychic income from their leisure activities. Most theoretical discussions of human capital include all forms of income as the result of the stock of human capital with which individuals are endowed at birth plus any subsequent investment in human capital (medical school education, varying lengths of time in residency, and fellowship programs). An individual's pool of skills and knowledge is the input he or she can use to create a product, whether it is a food, a service, or a leisure activity, that will generate monetary or psychic income.

Table 3-1 Physicians' Charges and Workload in an RBRVS			
Service Workload	Charge ($)	Work Units	Charge per Work Unit ($)
Follow-up visit of family physician to nursing home patient, with extended service	$37	159	$0.23
Diagnostic proctosigmoidoscopy examination of colon	53	118	0.45
Simple repair of superficial wound, 2.5 cm to 7.5 cm	66	75	0.88
Delivery of child (vaginal)	481	407	1.18
Repair of inguinal hernia (in the groin)	732	476	1.54
Triple coronary artery bypass	4,663	2,871	1.62
Insertion of permanent pacemaker (ventricular)	1,440	620	2.32

Economic studies with regard to human capital have led to many estimates of the implicit return in earnings from investments in different levels of education. These analyses are weak in that they cannot include the psychic income that people derive from their work and leisure activities. Conservative physicians will continue to protest "comparable-worth" attempts to set fair payment levels, given different levels of education. Determining fair payments also requires a determination of the rate of return that nonphysician practitioners should realize on their investment in education.

The federal government recognizes 12 classes of patient visits: new and established patient office visits, initial and subsequent hospital visits, initial and follow-up consultations, initial and subsequent nursing facility visits, initial and subsequent rest home visits, and new and established patient home visits. This classification allows variation in payment per level of service, reflecting differences in effort (work per unit time) and practice costs for different types of visits and for visits in different sites.

A number of studies (Dunn and Latimer 1997, Pope and Burge 1996) have validated the Hsiao Harvard approach and improved the allocation of practice expenses approach based on the simple notion that at the service level, work and practice expense relative values should mirror their respective revenue shares. Like the current charge-based practice expense relative values and the Hsiao Harvard approach, service-level revenue shares are calculated as the volume-weighted average of shares for the specialists providing services. These shares are used with the existing physician work relative value to calculate the total practice expense relative value of each service. If, for example, the work value for a service is one RVU and the practice expense share of that service is 50 percent, then the approach would yield a practice expense relative value of one RVU. If work value is one RVU and the practice expense share is 67 percent, then the practice expense relative values equal the ratio of the net income to practice expense revenue shares.

Pope and Burge (1996) allocated total practice expense relative values based on physician work. Practice expense resources required by a given service do not necessarily correlate with the physician work needed to provide the service, however. Thus, this approach does not necessarily yield resource-based values at the service level. The aggregate practice expense relative values for an entire specialty should be relatively correct (**Table 3-2**).

Table 3–2 Variation in Expenses as a Percentage of Practice Revenue of Six Types of Physicians

Service	Practice Costs as Percentage of Revenues	Salaries and Fringes	Administration	Malpractice
Family practice	52	42	3	12
General surgery	45	38	3	29
Internal medicine	48	43	3	10
Ophthalmology	48	41	3	8
Orthopedics	51	45	3	20
Urology	44	41	5	17

Source: Reprinted from 2002 Annual Report to Congress, Physician Payment Review Commission.

Join Together or Suffer Alone

As the formation of the AMA was an event to combat cults in the nineteenth century, aggressive specialty unions might form in the future to defend specialists' declining incomes and strike for improved patient care. Unionization, once a dirty word in the medical world, is spreading. The California-based Union of American Physicians and Dentists has 29 state chapters. Politically conservative physicians might have to face two economic truths. First, they must realize that unions are not always bad. Currently, 306 hospitals have physicians affiliated with the AFL-CIO. Second, they must realize that clinicians in overdoctored locations increasingly face the probability of going broke. Running excess providers out of business is a major cost-containment agenda for those who pay for medical services. Payers hope that economic failure of excess physicians and hospitals will eject the fixed cost pathology from the system and drive costs down. To survive in the marketplace, physicians require better productivity and a voice to negotiate on their behalf. If the profession does not act as a group and continues to pursue only individual business interests, medicine will be no more protected or respected than used-car dealerships. Likewise, those who disrespect business skills, productivity, marketing to the public, and patients' shifting tastes will also face an early retirement (Valentine and Jacobs 2001).

A New Era of Federal Price Setting

HCFA administrator Gail R. Wilensky characterized the RBRVS payment system initiated for Medicare in 1992 as the dawn of government-administered pricing in medicine. If our goal is to contain the growth in expenditures, a product of price times volume, a simple system of price controls might be ineffective because of expansion in volume. Global-based budgets (GBB) that contain expenditures, with so-called behavioral offsets (for volume expansion), have proved successful in countries including Germany, Sweden, and South Korea. Annual social arbitration over spending caps could set incomes for all sectors of the health economy: physicians, hospitals, home health care, and long-term care. If the volume growth outpaces the global budget by 4.5 percent, prices are subsequently deflated by 4.5 percent. In the decentralized German system, fee negotiations between hospitals and sickness funds require final approval from state governments, but the overall management of policy is typified by compromise and consensus building. Local governments, sickness funds, labor unions, hospitals, and physician groups (geographic-based councils known as the *Arztekammern*, with an average membership of 7,000 physicians) annually agree on fees and annual expenses in each sector of the health economy (Eastaugh 1993). If physician fees exceed their targets in one time period, they are subsequently reduced in future periods to penalize providers for cost overruns due to unplanned volume shifts. In the jargon of accounting, this political process is described as variance analysis under a limited budget (the global pie of dollars for local health care). If the budget variance is unfavorable (overbudget), the fees are deflated in proportion to the "unnecessary part of the increase in volume." The hope is that this process will yield a more efficient, effective, and equitable healthcare system.

One final caveat should be considered. Building consensus for GBB is more difficult in the U.S. context of separation of powers. GBBs are more easily created in parliamentary systems with inherent consensus between legislative and executive branches. However, just because a GBB is more difficult to initiate does not mean that it would be any less effective at cost control once created. All nations with GBBs spend one-third less of their economy on health care than the United States does.

Moreover, creation of a GBB might catalyze breakdown of the gridlock against national healthcare reform for the 41 million uninsured Americans and those otherwise squeezed by the current situation. Implementation of a GBB will not cause the United States to spend 4 percent of GNP less on health care (Eastaugh 1993), but it will free up the resources necessary to make healthcare coverage more affordable. GBBs can reduce the need for explicit rationing (the Oregon Medicaid program, Eastaugh 1995). Also, the distributional impact of GBB may yield more funding for long-term care.

The Medicare fee schedule differentials between specialties must be more substantial to affect new physicians, unless we go to an all-payer global budgeting system for setting prices and expense targets for all patients and providers. Will the Hsiao, Braun, Yntema, and Becker (1992) methodology lead to a better (more equitable) distribution of incomes and services? Germany tried this broad approach with a major revision of physicians' fees in 1987. The impact was minimal in that (1) no substantial substitution effect occurred between technical procedures and patient-centered primary care and (2) income rankings of specialists did not change by more than two points. However, average income at the lowest end of the physician scale, gynecology and pediatrics, did increase substantially.

Physicians' Supply Curves

Whether a physician works more or less as a result of an increase or decrease in physician wages is an important subject for public policy. Depending on the physicians' labor supply curve, physicians could decide to work harder and substitute more patient care for leisure (the substitution effect). Alternatively, physicians could decide that their income is sufficiently high to afford increased leisure time in preference to a higher workload. They would consequently work less (the income effect). An important point to remember is that even if the supply curve for a given individual physician is backward-bending (SB in **Figure 3-1**), the physicians' aggregate labor supply curve may instead be uniformly upward-sloping (SF in **Figure 3-1**), as is usually the case in most labor markets.

The research issues are clear. Brown and Lapan (1989) corroborated the backward-bending labor supply hypothesis. Although they utilized aggregate time-series data, they operated under the hypothesis that physicians are price-taking utility maximizers rather than price setters. Their findings supported the view that physicians are on the backward-bending portion of the labor supply curve. A second interesting finding of this study was that nonphysician inputs (physician extenders, aides, and so on) substitute for declines in physician labor, so that the supply curve of physician-office services is always positively sloped (curve SF in **Figure 3-1**). These findings use aggregate data to corroborate Reinhardt's results (1985), using data for individual physician practices. To protect their market share, specialists might fight back with controversial hospitalist programs that keep office-based physicians in the office and open access programs that allow patients to bypass primary care physicians and go directly to specialists. Hospitalist programs to integrate care and manage costs are very popular with payers.

Some of consumer demand for physician services is being met by other providers. We currently have 274 active physicians per 100,000 citizens. Physician extenders currently provide the output equivalent of 30 physicians per 100,000 persons. We currently have 104,000 physician assistants, nurse-midwives, and nurse practitioners; 56,000 acupuncturists and chiropractors; and 37,000 other PEs specializing in optometry, anesthesia, or mental health.

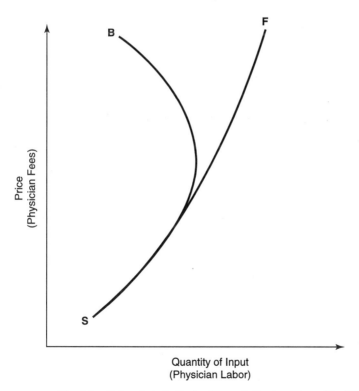

▲ FIGURE 3–1 Physician Labor Supply Curve: Upward-Sloping Normality (*SF*) or Backward-Bending Response (*SB*)

Hospital Practice Privileges

Fewer than 1,000 physicians had their licenses suspended or revoked for inappropriate or unnecessary practice behavior in 2001. The federal professional review organizations (PRO) sanctioned fewer than 300 physicians during 2001 (AMA 2002). However, as hospitals win court cases related to staff privilege decisions based on quality or efficiency concerns, hospital managers and medical staff are getting more selective about the physicians to whom they award admitting privileges. Self-serving members of the medical staff might want to close the doors on their hospital's medical staff in a crowded marketplace and force the institution to cease taking new applications from potential competitors. In negotiating compensation agreements with hospital-based physicians, management clearly likes the leverage to negotiate from a large pool of potential replacement clinicians. All types of physicians have potential anticompetitive reasons for closing their segment of the medical staff (raising antitrust legal concerns), but hospital managers and trustees are more interested in the composition of their medical staff and their cost behavior relative to levels of payment (Reeves 2001).

Institutions might no longer allow privileges to physicians who erode the financial standing of the institution through imprudent, wasteful use of hospital resources to admit patients. Hospitals that allow inefficient physicians to admit patients might go so heavily into debt that their survival is in question. In 2002, one-third of all hospital clinical departments were closed to new medical staff appointments; most of these were internally reviewing whether certain clinicians should have their privileges renewed (American Hospital Association 2002). Legally, it is easier not to renew privileges than to actually revoke privileges. The percentage of physicians with admitting privileges at any hospital has been declining each year since 1982, according to AMA survey statistics. Almost half of the physicians with privileges at only one hospital will have a tough time establishing relations with other local hospitals. Inefficient ordering and treatment habits are liabilities for the individual physician in a market in which fees increasingly are paid prospectively (inefficiency is not reimbursed by a pass-through of costs for the hospital) and in which hospital privileges are in short supply. The practice-profile cost per case experience of a physician should be appropriately adjusted for diagnosis-related group (DRG) mix and case severity to make any data-based credentialing process fair (for medical staff membership).

Increasingly, physician managers have adopted the concept of strategic product-line groupings (SPG). **Table 3-3** provides the medical staff with sensitivity estimates of how much to trim in the other three areas if performance in one area declines. For example, the clinicians running SPG7 decide that they cannot improve length of stay (see Options 8 or 9 in **Table 3-3**) or adjust behavior in radiology (Options 1–3 and 5). Such estimates depended greatly on the blend of variable and fixed costs for the specific hospital under study. Therefore, the analysis must be done at each facility every one to three months. For example, there is enormous variability in the fixed-variable cost ratios of tests done in chemistry labs, ranging from less than 24 percent variable cost for some to more than 90 percent variable cost for others. Information on the distribution of tests in the "highly fixed" cost category, compared to those in the "highly variable" cost category, should be useful in the design of physician educational programs for cost containment.

Retail Managed Care

Managed care systems have changed providers' viewpoint on marketing. Much of this change came about in the last 10 years.

The hospital industry had been rather slow in recognizing the need for differential advantages marketing. In the minds of the AMA authors of the advertising code, the public had no right to know whether a competitor has less modern facilities, a less well trained staff, or inferior quality of care. Today, health marketing campaigns are more consumer oriented and less physician oriented. If one assumes that the retailer controls the production channel, as in the case of an HMO, the plan can achieve maximum profits by hiring physician services at below-market prices. A second alternative is to assume that the physicians and hospitals of HMO plans pursue profit maximization while allowing a "necessary" profit margin to the other party. Such a compromise may result in an inefficient equilibrium at a price between Q' and Q" in **Figure 3-2**. To maximize profits, physicians set marginal physician revenue equal to their marginal costs, implying a transaction with the hospital involving Q' units of care at price P'. To maximize hospital revenues in excess of costs, hospitals would prefer a transaction with the physician involving fewer units of service (Q') at a higher level of reimbursement (P").

Prepaid group health plans are one of the few markets in which health facility managers and physicians are on a relatively equivalent bargaining basis.

Table 3-3 Options for Achieving a Break-Even Cost-Behavior Profile for SPG 7

Option	LOS (Length of Stay)[a]	Inhalation Therapy,[b] IVs, and Miscellaneous Therapy	Lab[c]	Radiology
1	−15 percent	0	0	0
2	−10 percent	−27 percent	0	0
3	−10 percent	−10 percent	−23 percent	0
4	−10 percent[d]	−10 percent	−10 percent	−18 percent
5	−5 percent	−20 percent	−24 percent	0
6	−5 percent	-20 percent	−10 percent	−19 percent
7	−5 percent	−16.8 percent	−16.8 percent	−16.8 percent
8	0	−27 percent	−22 percent	−39.7 percent
9	0	−29.8 percent	−29.8 percent	−29.8 percent

Note: SPG 7 consists of 16 DRGs produced by 13 attending physicians.

[a] The semivariable and variable cost savings from reduction in length of stay (LOS) are distributed as follows: 45 percent in forgone hotel costs; 27.1 percent in forgone nursing services; 13.3 percent in forgone therapy (inhalation therapy, IVs, medications, recovery room, operating room, anesthesia, etc.); 8.5 percent in forgone lab tests; and 6.1 percent in forgone radiologic services.

[b] For this hospital and this SPG 7, the example is only atypical to the extent that overutilization of inhalation therapy was a major problem identified in peer review audits. Requiring a 27 percent aggregate reduction in inhalation therapy could easily be accomplished with a 75 percent reduction in use by four of the 13 physicians offering this SPG, with no change in behavior required of the other nine physicians (who were already using 24 percent to 32 percent less inhalation therapy than the group average).

[c] Use per diem.

[d] The cost savings from a 5 percent drop in LOS equals a 27 percent drop in therapy per diem (for the reduced number of per diems remaining after the LOS reduction), which is equivalent to a 43 percent drop in lab tests per diem and a 59 percent drop in radiology usage per diem.

The management of a new HMO must frequently report to the private risk bearers who supplied the venture capital, and HMO sponsors are always putting on the pressure and searching the market for better managers.

Respect for the patient/consumer/customer was a marketing revolution, although a bloodless one in which physicians Marcus Welby and Ben Casey lost. Paternalism is dying; patients are beginning to aggressively seek new alternatives and better information. During the two decades of cost reimbursement, with little pressure to market, the cost crisis was a byproduct of the system and the incentive structure was not of cost per se. One could ignore consumers, run up a big bill, and get paid dollar for dollar. What a great deal!

However, competition, with emphasis on purchasing on an economic basis, had to rear its head. We all like competition in what we buy, not in what we sell, and healthcare providers were no different. With the rise of competition came increasing interest in consumer satisfaction, marketing, discovering what the patients wanted, cutting excess costs, and offering the service at a favorable price. Innovation occurred on five major fronts:

1. Competitive pricing and contracting (HMOs, PPOs, and managed care)
2. Staffing in proportion to workload (dumping underproductive staff)
3. Financial disincentives against overhospitalizing and testing
4. Incentives to invest in aftercare and long-term care
5. Sufficient supply of both physicians and empty hospital beds

This new world might stimulate continued growth in salaried physicians. The prototype for physician groups in the next century might be the airline pilot unions. Airline pilots have experienced a drop in earnings, but the work

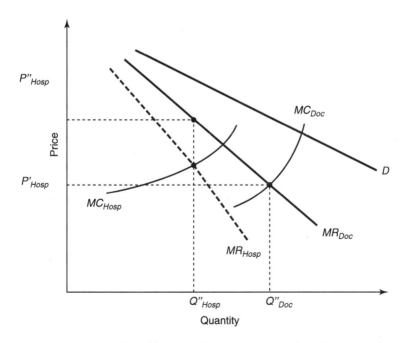

▲ **Figure 3–2** Potential Equilibrium in the Doctor–Hospital Producer–Retailer Production Channel for Hospital Services

week is shorter, less hectic, and allows more time for family life. The pilot unions have a done an admirable job in the areas of quality assurance, statistical quality control, and customer safety. Quality improvements lead to increased volume, potential economies of scale, and competitive advantage. In health care, costs might decline because physicians will earn less individually and as a group. Enhanced quality will diminish both internal (rework of faulty documents, wasted materials, and loss of morale) and external quality-maintenance costs that affect customers and include losses through malpractice judgment and negative word-of-mouth advertising. Quality gains reduce pressures for tighter oversight for the Joint Commission on Accreditation of Healthcare Organization (JCAHO or the Joint Commission) and from the public. The increase in the quality-maintenance budget might prove that inferior care is the most costly care, and that doing the job right the first time is cheaper than cleaning up mistakes.

The challenge for physicians and managers is not to break even on every product line. There will always be some cross-subsidization in the hospital sector. The real challenge is to have all parties working toward common goals: quality care, institutional financial health, and enough retained earnings to keep the hospital-physician workshop state-of-the-art. This last goal must be balanced with the broader social goal of not having too much wasteful excess capacity or excess patient admissions. Preferred practice patterns will help reduce wasteful habits.

Supplier-induced demand offers the obvious possibility of a conflict of interest: The physician provides extra service to generate income. The evidence is usually indirect by nature. For example, Broward County, Florida has 23 physician-owned magnetic resonance imaging (MRI) machines on which 48 MRI procedures per 1,000 persons are performed per year. Baltimore County, Maryland has three physician-owned MRIs and two medical schools, but only 18 MRI procedures were performed per 1,000 persons. Are the physicians at Johns Hopkins and the University of Maryland underserving their patients, or is it more likely that the Florida physicians are generating unnecessary patient volume to cost-justify (break even) or profit from their MRI business ventures? Is the number for MRIs per 1,000 citizens too low in Baltimore or too high in Florida? Classic economic theory would predict that competition would keep the price of an MRI scan down in Florida. However, the charge in Broward County is nearly double the Baltimore price, and all the extra utilization is performed on nonpoor, insured patients.

Maryland is one of the best states for effective regulation of the healthcare marketplace (Eastaugh 1995).

In the next chapter, we will turn our focus to technical efficiency, called productivity. Our concern is how best to set staffing patterns for optimal patient service delivery.

▶ **Summary Points:**

- Our past solutions often create our current problems.

- Physicians react to market forces and remuneration strategies much like most of us react.

- Pathway guidelines, clinical decision-making "cookbook medicine," and decision trees are aspects of evidence-based medicine (EBM). One aspect of EBM is the reduction in variability in medical practice.

Research and Discussion Questions:

- Suggest some economic incentives to increase the supply of primary care (family practice) physicians, and to increase the supply of physicians in inner-city and rural areas.

- Physician Assistants and Nurse Practitioners (PAs and NPs) are partial substitutes for physicians. What does this mean?

- Why is the reduction in medical practice variation critical for cost containment?

References

American Hospital Association. 2002. *The emerging roles of physicians*. Chicago: American Hospital Association.

American Medical Association. 2002. *Physician characteristics and distribution in the United States*. Chicago: American Medical Association.

Ash, A., and Ellis, R. 1999. *Diagnostic cost groups DCG methodology*. University Working Paper. Boston: Boston University.

Association of American Medical Colleges. 2002. *Supplying physicians for future needs*. Washington, DC: Association of American Medical Colleges.

Brown, D., and Lapan, H. 1989. Supply of physician services. *Economic Inquiry* 17(2): 262–279.

Brown, M. 2001. Physician manpower. *Journal of Healthcare Finance* 27(4): 55–64.

Christensen, S. 1998. Estimate of behavioral responses. In *Physician payment reform under Medicare* (Appendix B). Washington, DC: Congressional Budget Office.

Cooper, R., Getzen, T., McKee, H., and Lavd, P. 2002. Economic and demographic trends signal an impending physician shortage. *Health Affairs* 21(1): 140–154.

Dunn, D., and Latimer, E. 1997. *Derivation of relative values for practice expense using extant data*. Report to the Health Care Financing Administration (Contract No. 500-92-0023). Cambridge, MA: Harvard School of Public Health.

Eastaugh, S. 1993. *Health economics: Efficiency, quality, and equity*. Westport, CT: Greenwood.

Eastaugh, S. 1995. CQI and planning expansion of primary care. *Academic Medicine* 70(6): 465–469.

Fein, R. 1967. *The doctor shortage*. Washington, DC: Brookings.

Hsiao, W. 1989. Potential effects of an RBRVS-based payment system on health care costs and hospitals. *Frontiers of Health Services Management* 6(1): 40–43.

Hsiao, W., Braun, P., Yntema, D., and Becker, E. 1988. Estimating physicians' work for a resource-based relative-value scale. *New England Journal of Medicine* 319(13): 834–841.

Institute of Medicine. 2002. *The nation's physician workforce: Options for balancing supply and requirements*. Washington, DC: National Academy of Sciences.

Mundinger, M. 2000. Primary care outcomes in patients treated by nurse practitioners or physicians: A randomized trial. *Journal of the American Medical Association* 283(1): 59–68.

Mullan, F. 2000. The case for more U.S. medical students. *New England Journal of Medicine* 343(3): 213–217.

Office of National Cost Estimates. 2002. *Trends in health care spending.* Washington, DC: U.S. Government Printing Office.

Pew Commission. 2001. Health workforce. *Journal of Allied Health* 30(3): 160–167.

Pope, G., and Burge, R. 1996. *Derivation of relative values for practice expense using extant data.* Report to the Health care Financing Administration (Contract No. 500-92-0020). Washington, DC: U.S. Government Printing Office.

Physician Payment Review Commission. 2002. *Annual report to Congress.* Washington, DC: Government Printing Office.

Rabinowitz, H., Diamond, J., Markham, F., and Hazelwood, C. 2000. Program to increase the number of family physicians in rural and underserved areas. *JAMA* 281(3):255–260.

Reeves, C. 2001. *Compliance for medical practices.* Vienna: Management Concepts.

Reinhardt, U. 1985. *Physician productivity.* Cambridge, MA: Ballinger.

Sunshine, J. 2000. Employment among recent residency program graduates. *JAMA* 281(7): 611–616.

Tarlov, A. 1990. How many physicians is enough? *JAMA* 263(13): 571–573.

Tienan, J. 2002. Med school downer: Applications decline for 4th year in a row; experts cite anti-affirmative action initiatives. *Modern Healthcare* 1(6): 18–19.

Tufts New England Medical Center. 2002. *The mechanics of physician selection and patient enrollment.* Boston: Tufts.

Valentine, S., and Jacobs, L. 2001. *Medical group management.* Vienna: Management Concepts.

Chapter 4

Productivity Enhancement and Incentive Compensation

Thinking that the facility cannot improve productivity substantially is the principal affliction of the health care industry. Productivity is the first test of management's competence. One should get the greatest output for the least input effort, better balancing all factors of service delivery to achieve the most with the smallest resource effort.

– Peter F. Drucker

Do not confuse bad management with destiny. You can improve your position with the right management and incentives.

– Alfred Sloan

▶ **Critical points in this chapter:**

- Technical efficiency
- Prospective payment
- Acuity-driven workload staffing
- Statistical quality control

This chapter explores a number of ideas concerning productivity improvement—for example, "cutting staff harms service quality," "more staff buys more quality," "reducing staff translates into reduced employee morale," and "performance gains accrue only to those who work harder." Alternative mechanisms by which the organization may work smarter rather than harder are also advanced. Implementing efficient scheduling systems and work-unit reorganizations, especially when reinforced by an incentive-pay plan, can reduce costs significantly. Productive managers must be change agents, not overcommitted to the existing ways of doing things. In the future, productivity will not be just a minor part of the management job or simply an area for added emphasis; it will be the whole job for managers.

Productivity, in its simplest form, equals output divided by resource inputs. Productivity can be improved by expanding output, by contracting inputs, or by having the rate of change in output volume outperform the rate of change in input resources. For example, the ratio of output to input improves (that is, we do more with fewer resources) if volume increases 8 percent and staff hours increase by less than 8 percent. Alternatively, if staff hours decline by 8 percent and volume decreases by less than 10 percent, productivity is increased. Thus productivity can be improved by reducing costs, increasing output, or both.

However, hospital services are special kinds of output. Producing more services than are medically necessary, even if they are produced at a lower unit cost, has little to do with a real increase in productivity. A hospital's production of unnecessary services is inefficient, and the institution will not be compensated for them under evolving managed care systems. The third-party payers will be cooperating with peer review organizations to curtail the production of unnecessary services. Cost reduction, not output expansion, is the key to future productivity improvement in most hospital markets. One measure of hospital output, patient days, has been declining at a rather fast rate. The "recession" in patient days might represent a permanent shift in provider behavior rather than a cyclical recurring problem. With fewer patients in bed, obviously fewer staff members are needed, although some of these "extra" employees can be trained to work in ambulatory care or other settings.

Aren't Our Present Productivity Measures Good Enough?

It was curious to hear a manager recently exclaim: "So what if patient census dropped 6 percent last year? All departments are reporting more units of activity, so productivity is up and staff should be increased, not decreased!" On the contrary, the efficiency of activity production is essentially irrelevant. Another service industry, police protection, affords an interesting comparison. The important variable for the public is crimes prevented and solved, not staff hours of internal office activity generated, tabulated, or filed. It is easy to get lost in a mass of numbers, producing measures of insignificant activity that turn out to have no meaning. The reporting and analysis process saps endless hours of management time throughout various departments, and such productivity information systems do not engender read cost reductions.

In the world of prospective payment, the basic unit of productivity is the diagnosis-related group (DRG) case treated, not the activity units accumulated. There has long been a need for a final-product perspective in health care, and we now have resource usage groupings (RUG) in nursing homes and ambulatory cost groups in ambulatory care. Counting relative value units (RVU) misses the target completely. It is largely irrelevant to measure "the product" with nurse relative intensity measure points or laboratory standardized unit value College of American Pathologists points accumulated. Although counts of RVUs are improvements over simple procedure counts and tallies, the appearance of high levels of activity can result from inefficient allocation of responsibilities rather than from the group being overstaffed or "overproductive." When productivity experts talk in terms of RVUs, they lapse into jargon that is an industrial engineer's version of the secret lodge handshake. Even the most technically savvy senior managers are likely to doze off when they are bombarded with indecipherable RVU trends dear only to the hearts of management engineers. Who cares if RVU workload is improving because overreporting is on the increase? What matters to the chief executive officers is that patient census has declined 6 percent, cash flow is down 6 percent, and the facility will be running at a big deficit. We in academia lecture on pristine systems development, but the analyses of RVUs and other activity measures are largely unproductive contributions to the management process. The compilation of activity measures is of little use in setting staffing levels and even less useful for cost accounting.

Productivity is not easy to measure in all departments. Overemphasis of small activity measures is the principal weakness of traditional productivity analysis, and the normative staffing study is not very useful in achieving cost-saving results. But if these traditional means of dealing with the issue of productivity are not going to work in health care, what can we do to ensure that services are provided at the lowest cost?

What Must Be Done to Improve Productivity?

The basic requirement of a successful productivity program is that the senior managers and trustees must really want cost reduction. They cannot follow the path of least resistance. Peter Drucker often has said that productivity is the first test of management's competence, and that we should reward managers who do more with less, who reduce staff and costs to the public.

Move Rapidly

The best productivity programs are rapid, large in scale, cost-beneficial, and provide benchmarks for assessing future performance. Productivity improvement studies do not need to be multiyear and very costly. The first stage of operational assessment can be rapid (three to five months) and quite cost-beneficial. Substantial cost reductions can be obtained in the short run, whereas second and third stages of more refined improvements (scheduling systems, for example) and incentives are put in place for permanent, long-run cost containment. Timing depends on the size and scope of the facility and the areas under study, but rapid plan development and implementation is essential for both financial and nonfinancial reasons. Allowing the assessment to go beyond a few months would create undue uncertainties among anxious employees.

Start Big

The department under study should be large if the gains are to be large. For example, a 5 percent improvement in nurse productivity would dwarf a 30 percent improvement in labor productivity of central supply, pharmacy, housekeeping, laundry, plant, and maintenance. That management frequently complains of "having the best laundry costs and the worst hospital cost increases" illustrates a major point. Significant cuts in the big cost areas in a hospital or clinic cannot be avoided in the vain hope that cost containment either can be easy or confined to cosmetic reductions in staff. Merely conducting an overhead variance analysis and cutting the number of housekeepers, administrative residents, and summer interns will not get to the heart of facility problems in managing productivity improvements.

Ask the Right Questions

Trustees and senior management should ask critical questions such as these: What staffing ratio do we really need? How did other peers achieve expanded output with much lower growth in staff? What new equipment and organizational changes can be used to reduce staff and make the work force more effective? Examples from other institutions convince management that new methods of organizing and scheduling can be made to work. Normative comparisons of "best actors" among peers (those exhibiting the best levels of productivity) also can be useful in making ballpark "guesstimates" of the potential for staff reductions.

Programs that focus on the activities of individual workers ignore the two greatest keys to productivity improvement: organization and work-team scheduling. Much can be achieved by examining what is being done and how employees are being organized into work teams (Stage I) and how middle-level managers can schedule more efficiently (Stage II).

Stage I: Operational Assessment

The conceptual approach argues that it is possible to determine precisely the number and types of employees a given facility needs to supply quality patient care and meet its other objectives (teaching and research). Exceeding this number does not increase quality; it simply creates unnecessary costs. Stage I, the initial operational assessment, involves finding answers to two basic questions: How many people should work here? and What is the best mix of staff and other resources? Four basic actions make up the formal operational assessment:

1. Review historical, current, and budgeted staffing levels.
2. Evaluate facility layout, equipment, intraunit functional relationships, and interdepartamental coordination.
3. Identify operational deficiencies and recommend improvements.

4. Analyze all current forms and management reports for the appropriateness and timeliness of the information.

Management's ability to focus on those actions and ideas that highlight unnecessary costs determines the real usefulness of the assessment. Hammer and Champy (1998) defined this basic reengineering phase as fundamentally rethinking and radically redesigning processes to achieve dramatic improvements in critical measures of performance, such as cost, quality, and service.

Focus on Basic Problems

The study should be based on these principles:

1. Don't organize for what is done less than 2 percent of the time.
2. Streamline overlapping functions and excessive layers of supervision.
3. Reduce those departments that exhibit excess capacity.

The efficiency of standing orders and standard operating procedures (SOP), such as letting nurses restart IVs, needs to be assessed. Nurse activities that need increased delegation to other staff, such as patient transport, running errands, or making beds, should be evaluated. Situations worsened by rigid specialization (a small water spill that takes less time for a nurse to clean up alone than to make three calls to housekeeping) also should be identified.

Reorganize and Retrain for Improved Productivity

Nursing and ancillary departments should reorganize and retrain for improved productivity. Flexibility in staffing is the key to adjusting to the flux in demands during peak periods while keeping staffing levels down. For example, operating room (OR) workers, from nurses to housekeeping, can be pulled together into one team so that housekeeping can assist in pulling supplies for the next case, thus enhancing productivity. If the ancillary department is having an easy level of volume on the night shift, have it work on the setups for the next day. The key to better productivity is to smooth out the work flows and minimize idle time associated with the work. Japanese hospitals use the "utility infielder" approach: They cross-train all staff in two areas so that other departments can be cross-covered in the same day or within the same month. Staffing can be reduced 15 percent by using this approach; at the same time, workers with two roles to play experience improved job satisfaction and morale (Eastaugh 1992).

Define Necessary Staff Qualifications

A good operational assessment of any work unit should include study of each task to determine the level of staff qualifications required. Aggregate numbers of recommended full-time equivalents (FTE) are not the principal output of Stage I analysis. Let us return to nursing as an example. Equally important as the ratio of nurses to patients is an optimal mix of nurses employed for the given tasks assigned. Staffing an excess number of registered nurses (RN) in the name of quality enhancement was the biggest problem in nursing cost containment in the early 1990s. The organization of the work to be done and the skill mix of the employees are the crucial issues in staffing. Although the emergency department needs critical care nurses, for example, delegation of more tasks to aides and clerks can help to control payroll expenses (Schmidt 2002).

Use an Adequate Reporting System

Functional procedural flowchart analysis and task evaluation are two key tools in operational assessment. Nursing productivity studies, in particular, are often hampered by poor information systems and support systems. Although some facilities allocate float nurses' work effort back to the home department, rather than to the understaffed units or subspecialty areas (such as the OR), other facilities draw all float-pool personnel from an outside registry and define float time as a cost center with no information concerning where the work effort should actually have been allocated. Useful operational assessment depends on accurate, comparable information. The essential elements in Stage I of a productivity improvement program are summarized in the top half of **Figure 4-1**. Chapter 5 offers a nurse productivity study. Nurses are critical because they make up two-thirds of healthcare employees. Nurses exhibit the highest level of job frustration of any profession. We must better treat our overworked generation of nurses and attract a new generation of nurses.

Stage II: Who Can Be Scheduling Better?

Stage II, operational assessment, yields better work assignments, identifies lost resources and unnecessary activities, and suggests ways to foster efficient interdepartmental coordination. Major productivity improvement, however, depends on one basic element: scheduling. Three critical actors—the patient, the employee, and the physician—must be scheduled for improved productivity. Better scheduling of all three groups can reduce unnecessary activity flow, reduce unit costs, improve patient satisfaction, and reduce waiting time for both providers and patients (Eastaugh 1999, Shorr 2002).

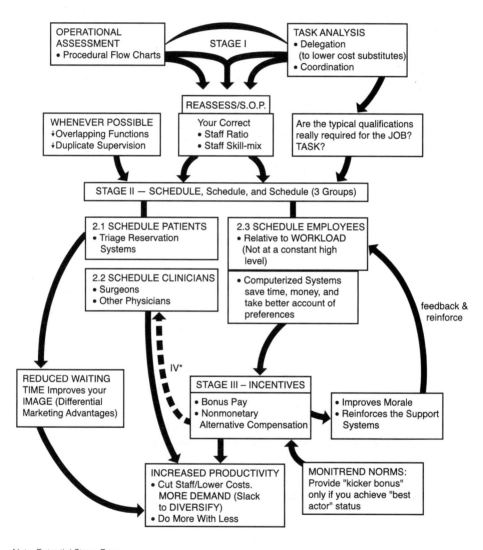

Note: Potential Stage Four,
*IV – Either form of incentive compensation can be paid to physicians with appropriate attention to IRS restrictions (link it to a productivity index, and *not* "profits," "gross," or "net income" if your institution is tax-exempt).

▲ **Figure 4–1** Three-Stage Approach to Productivity Improvement

Forecast Actual Workloads

Staffing-level assessment in Stage I refers to the number of personnel; scheduling refers to when the personnel are working and when patients are expected to arrive. Obviously, the staffing ratios should be set in proportion to forecast workloads. In scheduling nurses, for example, if the workload on day shifts is three times as high as that on night shifts, it would be illogical to provide the same number of nurses over all three shifts. Similarly, even when workload is unscheduled, as in the emergency room, patterns of utilization are predictable. A sample survey over a few months demonstrates the days and shifts that have the highest workload, and staffing should be proportionate to this predicted demand. Additional adjustment for seasonal changes and case-mix severity can be made (McClain and Eastaugh 1993). The result will be that the emergency department will not be staffed so that the day shift experiences 12 visits per nurse and the night shift experiences only four visits per nurse.

Preserve Employee Morale

A basic requirement of a scheduling system is that it preserve morale and meet the personal needs of employees for days off, vacations, birthdays, and holidays. In addition, employees must believe that the scheduling process is fair and impartial.

Use an Automated Scheduling System

Unfortunately, many hospitals use manual scheduling systems that are unresponsive to subtle shifts in workload and that are perceived as being unfair. It is amazing that personnel are still manually scheduled in an industry that spends more than five billion dollars each week. For example, if 12 nurses are scheduled over a month so that each nurse works 22 days, disregarding all other constraints, there would be 1.5 million possible schedules. It is hard to imagine that human ingenuity, even under no other constraints, could develop the best schedule. A computerized scheduling system can select the best schedule without hours of paperwork, hassles, and appeals. The computer can provide convincing documentation of fairness, demonstrating that weekend assignments and shift changes (AM to PM to nights) have been equalized. Frequently one finds capable employees being promoted to "scheduler" without ever having been taught the importance of, or techniques for, efficient scheduling. Computer-generated schedules are guided by efficiency and equality, and not by interpersonal relationships.

Nurses should be allocated to account for acuity of the level of care a patient needs. The goal is acuity-driven workload staffing, not merely census-driven staffing. However, even the most refined industrial engineering methodology can be undercut if management eschews flexibility in favor of a fixed decision rule, for example, that each nurse is allowed every other weekend off. Such a rule results in overstaffing on the weekend or on one or two of the weekdays. Nursing costs and morale can be improved by forecasting nontraditional staffing arrangements. Flexible use of part-time staff and combinations of two 12-hour shifts and two 8-hour shifts for some full-time nurses can ensure a better match between workload and FTEs. The worst of all possible worlds exists when facilities are forced to overstaff nurses on weekends and some weekdays, yet run short of staff on the busy weekdays (Eastaugh 2001).

Schedule Physicians Better

Scheduling systems for physicians also can reduce costs through reducing downtime (wasted time). When an OR mishandles case scheduling, cost overruns result from either underutilization or overtime wages. Henry Ford Hospital has instituted a highly successful scheduling system in the ORs and in a number of other settings. A triage reservation system for ambulatory clinics can be implemented by scheduling 25 percent more patients per hour (five per hour, instead of every 15 minutes), at staggered times (easy cases at 10 and 10:05, two cases at 10:20 and 10:25, and the hardest case served from 10:40 to 11:00), with varying duration of necessary visiting time with the physician. The organization works smarter, but no individual experiences a perceptible shift toward working harder. Slack periods or downtime simply declines in frequency and duration (Eastaugh 1986).

The University of Michigan Medical Center has been a pioneer in OR scheduling. Operating room scheduling efficiency is improved by scheduling on the basis of patient DRG, severity level, and surgeon (speed based on past experience). Scheduling policies were made uniform across all departments, and a service-specific scheduler was assigned in each area (one person for cardiac surgery, one for ophthalmology, one for general surgery). The specialist in scheduling knows how to collect information, stagger schedule time blocks, minimize misscheduled cases, call surgeons if necessary, and collectively make optimal use of the 33 OR suites (they experienced only 10 percent downtime in 2002).

Juran's (2002) statistical quality control making use of process-flow diagrams or flowcharts are especially useful in service industries to identify all the unseen steps in a work process. Trend charts offer graphs of the clinical outcomes, productivity shifts, or fiscal changes as a result of the work process plotted over time. The most advanced of the Deming method techniques are control charts that plot the range of variation in a system between the 10 percent and the 90 percent confidence intervals. When used for internal management purposes, they are run charts with statistically determined lower and upper limits for performance. As long as the process variable under study falls within these limits, the system is labeled "in control," and variation therein stems from common causes (seasonality, typical shifts in work force on July 1, and so on). To attempt to correct individual shifts in the system leads to overcorrection (tampering), thus causing more variation in performance (not less). The goal of the method is to narrow the range between the upper and lower limits by seeking to eliminate the common causes of inefficiency that occur day-in and day-out.

Incidentally, there is nothing sacred about the 10 percent/90 percent confidence intervals. Studies have been done for patient-transport departments with 5 percent/95 percent confidence limits and for labs with 20 percent/80 percent confidence limits. How much variation can and should be accepted is a management decision. When a point falls outside the confidence interval, it is a special case that the department team should investigate. Common causes of variation may include a flu epidemic or the need to train new recruits to the department; a special cause would be equipment breakdown or information-system breakdown.

In summary, the Juran approach emphasizes identifying problem areas, team building, implementing successful remedies, and holding and extending performance gains. The job of quality control never ends because improvements are often reversible. Procedural changes, such as distributing new criteria, require effort to maintain the new high levels of performance and productivity. By avoiding mistakes and useless units of activity, gains in productivity occur as quality improves.

Develop an Accurate System of Productivity Measurement and Workload-Driven Staff-Scheduling Systems

Responsive daily adjustment of the scheduling system is necessary. For example, department managers should report labor hours and scheduled workload to the chief executive officer (CEO) by 8:15 AM and distribute data to vice-presidents by 9:15 AM, while vice-presidents have until 11 AM to investigate and correct variances (such as whether the facility is overstaffing or understaffing at this time). Overstaffing should lead to adjustment in future schedules, and if possible, personnel can be asked to take time off.

Understaffing should not be solved simply by paying more overtime (although paying a little overtime is preferred to full-time overstaffing). Instead, understaffing should be treated by reallocation of labor and cross-utilization of staff. To help cross-utilization and avoid balkanized job descriptions and employees with poor attitudes ("that's not my job"), employees should be cross-trained in multiple jobs. This Japanese utility infielder approach to cross-training requires the facility to pay for education programs and certification tests in multiple disciplines. The organization benefits from (1) a more engaged and challenged work force, (2) lower employee turnover, (3) better daily staffing flexibility to move idle workers to overworked departments, and (4) monthly flexibility to plan vacation slots and cross-utilize staff. Technicians can learn electrocardiograms (ECG), nurses and NEs can be cross-trained in ancillary skills, and RNs can be cross-trained in several nursing specialties.

Trim Bureaucracy

Many cost-conscious hospitals recently worked to reduce management layers of supervision and limit the number of vice-presidents to a select few (rather than three per 100 beds, the median peak level in the "good old days" of 1996). One hospital's nursing department had seven layers of supervisory staff trimmed to two (department director and vice-president for patient care); eight vice-presidents were eliminated in 1998 and 36 managerial support staff were fired. Hospitals should also try to minimize the number of departments with fewer than eight or nine FTEs by consolidating departments with similar skill requirements and functions. Hospitals, like health maintenance organizations, need to reduce bureaucracy as a semifixed cost of business. Hospitals should not utilize census-driven staffing. A staffing and scheduling system based on monitoring case-mix complexity, such as the one at Riverside Hospital, is a better alternative. Being output-driven (workload-based) in setting staff levels is superior to simply linking staffing to census.

Stage III: When Can Incentives Be Provided?

It is relatively easy to cut costs by cutting services or service quality. A two-stage strategy was outlined that manages the difficult task of cost reduction without service reduction or quality reduction. Little attention, however, has been paid to the use of motivational tools. Incentives can improve employee attitudes concerning the innovations implemented under the first two stages. Monetary incentives involving the provision of incentives will reinforce the new scheduling systems and new modes of work units. Adherence to reorganization into efficient work units (Stage I) and compliance with scheduling systems (Stage II) has been very successfully reinforced through the payment of incentive compensation.

Put Incentives in Context

There are many jobs in the hospital industry in which employees have considerable discretion over how they manage their work. Employees and medical staff have control over their personal commitment and their productivity. They can withhold it, or they can give it in exchange for something they value, such as cash, vacation time, or nonmonetary rewards. Management needs to present carefully a philosophical and financial context for the announcement of incentive programs. Employee perception is critical. A system of perceived bribes will not change behavior, but incentive pay as a substitute for even more belt-tightening does improve productivity and morale.

Communicate the Benefits of Cost Reduction

Many administrators believe that reducing staff results in employees working harder and translates into lower employee morale. Indeed, it is true that if the staff cuts appear abrupt and arbitrary and offer no incentive "carrot" to maintain performance, morale might decline and the most outstanding workers might look elsewhere for job security. Staff cuts can improve morale, however, if employees share in the benefits of cost reduction and understand the new incentives and why things must change. For example, the institution and the employees both can be in a better financial position following a 10 percent reduction in employees and an average of a 9 percent increase in compensation per employee.

Help Employees "Work Smarter"

Management should explain to employees the reasons fiscal realities make net cost and employee reductions imperative rather than elective. If the remaining employees receive significant incentive bonuses, they are less likely to unionize or strike. Incentive pay offers substantial benefits beyond the reductions in rates of absenteeism (Reynolds 2002). The keys are to provide bonus incentive pay by work subunits, thus reinforcing friendly acceptance of the efficient work and scheduling system, and to work smarter, not harder, thanks to these systems. If your department achieves the best productivity of peers in your region, offer a "kicker bonus" for being number one so you can avoid the trap of "chasing your own tail" in trying to forever reduce staff to earn a bonus.

Use Incentives to Improve Quality Care

Incentives are quite effective at stimulating the best employees to push the existing SOPs to the limits of efficiency without harming service quality. Who are the best employees? They are those innovative employees who exhibit episodic rule breaking under the SOP, not merely to add variety to their work life, but to demonstrate that SOPs or Joint Commission standards do little to foster efficiency or quality. Implementation of incentives, following a conceptual study on task requirements, common skills, job training, flexible staffing, and scheduling, causes the total organization to focus on making a given line of work most productive. With the help of incentives, a hospital can establish and maintain a dedication to high level of productivity, craft excellence, and quality service.

The Dos and Don'ts of Structuring an Incentive Plan

One of the great unanticipated benefits of a well-designed incentive compensation program is the potential for enhanced physician and employee loyalty. Employees are important, implicit components of the marketing program because word-of-mouth advertising is important in any service industry. If employees are jealous of an incentive plan that excludes them, they may act in a more abrupt or uncaring manner. Likewise, if employees believe that pay has no relationship to performance, they will bad-mouth the institution. But if employees are offered incentives, morale typically improves and all concerned get serious about doing the things that really need doing. This includes minimizing unnecessary activity, working smarter, and, in the process, cooperating to reduce staffing levels to more closely approximate case-mix-adjusted workload. Physicians are usually important elements of marketing — enhancing physician loyalty through incentive plans translates into more patients. As a general rule, for every physician who believes that incentive plans are a mistake and threatens to admit patients elsewhere, many other physicians will take the initiative and refer more patients to the facility with the better incentive plan.

As mentioned earlier, the incentive plan should be groupwide and not individual-specific. An individual-specific plan, especially if it is short-run and patient-specific, can rapidly erode medical staff support for the incentive plan. All of the problem areas are interrelated: Poor morale can yield decreased scheduling efficiency, longer patient waiting time, increased consumer dissatisfaction, decreased efficiency, consequent high costs, and reduced business from cost-conscious payers. In summary, an incentive plan open to the majority of employees seems the best compromise to support harmony and efficiency while trading off the administrative costs of offering the plan to everyone.

Conveying a sense of ownership might evolve increasingly into offering employees an equity share in the organization. Managers, employees, and physicians might come to own stock in their core business (the hospital itself), or some co-op subchapter T corporation of the hospital, or a for-profit subsidiary of the hospital. Defenders of the status quo in nonprofit hospital administration will resist this trend, just as they resisted pay increases for hospital employees in the 1970s and resisted calling administrators "managers" in the 1980s and "executives" in the 1990s. This archaic thinking is often wrong and thus demonstrates a remarkable degree of consistency. Times change, and economic efficiency must improve, but this need not result in any erosion of the mission.

The challenge for senior management and trustees is to find a means whereby all parties are motivated to work toward a common goal. Counterproductive workers might be weeded out so that creative entrepreneurs can do much more. Reductions in salary expenses by firing nonproductive employees would provide the resources for offering incentive compensation and, more important, the resources for institutional survival and better care in an era of total revenue controls. The incentive plan has four crucial features:

1. Departments requesting more financial support will have to face some of the economic consequences of their extravagance (inefficiency is no longer a reimbursement expense).

2. The plan should involve no downside risk of reduced salary.

3. The plan should offer a "kicker bonus" for those who achieve the target level of performance in order to maintain the incentive to economize.

4. The plan should be group-specific until the department divides the compensation pool among individuals.

The department-level director in charge of the compensation pool can also reward excellent noneconomic performance, such as for research and teaching. This builds a spirit of harmony in the teaching hospital context (Eastaugh, Sahney, and Steinhauer 1993) and helps to underwrite improvements in graduate medical education and to encourage biomedical research. The incentive compensation system should be viewed as a means of realizing central control and encouraging local department initiative and autonomy. Management must be vigilant, however, to prevent departmental "turf war" behavior— that is, shifting work to others to appear more efficient on paper.

Fairness and Efficiency

If some clinical areas are viewed as intrinsically lucrative, one could consider pooling 10 percent to 20 percent of the net institutional bonus compensation pool and distributing it equally to all employees. This would add to an institutional feeling of cohesion and teamwork and make the program de facto 10 percent to 20 percent "gainsharing" and 80 percent to 90 percent department sharing. Innovation in cost control may be quantum, that is, in leaps and spurts. For example, if an individual department does not perform well in 2003 but earned a great bonus payment in 2002, at least it shares in some small bonus in 2003 under a limited gainsharing program.

Table 4-1 Seven Alternative Incentive Compensation or Reward Systems

Sharing Reward Plan	Formula Basis	Goals (Type of Situation)	Level (Timing)	Split of Benefits	Reserves
Gainsharing Incentive Compensation Plans					
1. Scanlon	Labor costs: sales	A. Reduction in labor expenses B. Suggestion committee C. Common-fate atmosphere (crisis situation)	Firmwide (quarterly)	75 percent to labor	10 percent set aside
2. Desirable compensation ration (Henry Ford Hospital)	Total labor costs: net revenue (kicker) bonus—if this desirable compensation ratio equals the best and lowest, among peers	A. Reduction of labor expense or expansion of revenue B. Merit-based pay for performance (ongoing situation)	Work group (annual)	60–80 percent to labor & MDs	10 percent distributed hospitalwide the following year
3. Improshare (J.F.K. Hospital, Edison, NJ)	Nonfinancial base productive hours factor	A. Improvement in productivity B. Reduction in nonproductive hours (ongoing situation)	Work group (weekly)	50 percent to labor	10–25 percent rolling average

(continues)

Sharing Reward Plan	Formula Basis	Goals (Type of Situation)	Level (Timing)	Split of Benefits	Reserves
4. Rucker	Labor costs: sales, allowances, materials, supplies	A. Quick reduction of costs B. Suggestion committee C. "Open books" spirit of trust (short-run crisis)	Firmwide (monthly)	100 percent to labor	25 percent
5. Profit sharing (Humana)	Bottom-line profits	A. Control cost of behavior B. Expansion of operating profits (ongoing situation)	Work group (quarterly)	10–40 percent to labor	50 percent to 50 percent deferred income available
Innovative Reward Systems (Independent of the Compensation System)					
6. Team suggestion (Raritan Bay Med. Center, NJ)	5–20 percent split of the savings among team members	A. Suggestion system B. Earning points to purchase merchandise (ongoing situation)	Work group (payout as earned)	15–20 percent to labor	Possible
7. Performance management system (NME)	Percent of share of the value of improvements (sales, cost)	A. High customization for a big firm/chain B. Driven by senior management objectives	Strategic business units	10–30 percent to labor	Possible

Incentive Compensation Plans

There are four basic gainsharing incentive plans: Scanlon, Improshare, Rucker, and profit sharing. These gainsharing plans engender bottom-to-top employee involvement and are considered a component part of a total compensation plan (**Table 4-1**, lines 1-5). However, an alternative innovative reward system can be run independently of the compensation program (**Table 4-1**, lines 6-7). Performance management systems offer equal payout to work-unit members for achievement of various financial or physical corporate objectives. Performance management system programs typically result in a modest 4 percent to 6 percent improvement across the board in manager incomes. Second, team suggestion programs (**Table 4-1**, line 7) pay out a fixed percentage (20 percent to 25 percent) of work units' successfully implemented cost savings or business-expansion ideas. The team suggestion payout is typically made with merchandise, not cash, as the employee earns "recognition credits" redeemable for items in the "Green Stamp" award book. While human resources personnel point to the "cute reaction" of employees who bring their gifts to the workplace to "show them off," such merchandise incentive plans have a number of drawbacks. Operating the gift plan has significant administrative costs, and employees come to resent the limited lists of available items. Despite this, one New Jersey hospital reported good long-run financial and employee performance from a merchandise incentive suggestion program.

Cash is a much less paternalistic form of incentive. However, one of the disadvantages of cash as a motivator is that the bonus checks are perceived to be too modest in size if they are delivered weekly (Improshare) or monthly. The traditional profit-sharing plans avoid this problem by offering annual payouts and quarterly accounting reports of bonus earnings. A number of other plans overemphasize timing — that is, the need to have the payout within weeks of the performance improvement (Scanlon, Rucker, and Improshare). The concerned individual can keep a tally of how much bonus pay he or she has earned and realize the direct connection between actions and benefits without having the cash in pocket.

One of the central strengths of the Improshare gainsharing plan is that the incentive payout is work-unit-specific (those who earn it receive it), whereas the Scanlon and Rucker plans suffer from being hospital-wide in focus. Improshare managers report another benefit. Their employees are doing departmental functions that they "never had time to do." However, it is important to be aware that in the documentation of more RVUs of activity, these employees can generate more useless activity that does not improve actual productivity. The incentive plan must offer incentive pay to streamline and eliminate useless departmental functions and free up more productive hours of nonadministrative activity.

Final Points

One should infer from this chapter that a well-designed plan should have five E-Q-U-I-P attributes:

1. *E*stablish a merit-based performance climate with pay for performance rewards for superior workers and idea makers (entrepreneurs).

2. *Q*uality should be emphasized by making the incentive bonus pay significant in size (and linked to a quality-enhancing customer orientation) to overcome the antiproductive orientation that if you try, if you come to work, you should all get the same pay.

3. *U*nproductive workers should face sanctions and no pay increases, so hopefully they will leave the facility (and go to the competition).

4. *I*ncentives should be offered in the spirit of a "cut of the action" or, in less entrepreneurial rhetoric, a common-fate atmosphere that requires change and continuous improvement if the institution is to survive.

5. *P*romote a spirit of job security and trust built upon the preexisting compensation system and performance-appraisal framework.

Further research is needed to analyze the ways these incentive reward programs affect the total institution. Organizational theorists have developed a number of competing hypotheses to explain explicit and implicit contractual relationships among senior managers, middle managers, employees, and independent contractors. Response to incentives can be analyzed under two alternative hypotheses: 1) productivity depends on efforts that are difficult to observe, or 2) ability is unknown and is revealed (learned) over time. If the preexisting productivity measurement system is crude or continues to remain highly imperfect (due to the nature of the job), past performance might remain irrelevant in predicting current or future performance. Under the second hypothesis, incentive compensation could merely unlock the door of innate managerial ability, which is initially unknown but revealed over time.

A number of noted members of the economics profession have written extensively on the relationship between progress and the law of comparative advantage. If each good or service is supplied by the most productive producer, all of society will be richer. To be against productivity is to be against medical progress. Productivity gains will help underwrite our future improvements in service delivery and technology. These programs will provide the linchpin to ensure that we continue to deliver a quality service at an affordable cost for all concerned.

▶ **Summary Points:**

- Functional procedural flowchart analysis and task evaluation are two key tools in operational assessment.

- A computerized scheduling system can select the best schedule.

- Incentive plans must be viewed as fair and removed from politics or personal relationships.

Research and Discussion Questions:

- What do you see as the pros and cons of the different types of gainsharing incentive plans?

- Other than money, what rewards can be given to above-average employees?

References

Charns, A., Cooper, W., and Rhodes, R. 1989. Evaluating program and management efficiency: DEA analysis. *Management Sciences* 27(6): 668–697.

Clemmer, I. 2002. *Firing on all cylinders*. Homewood, IL: Business One Irwin.

Currid, C. 2002. *Reengineering toolkit: 15 tools and technologies for reengineering your organization*. Rocklin, CA: Prima Publishing.

Decker, P. 1998. JCAHO tool for your workforce. *Health Care Supervisor* 16(3): 54–62.

Dekay, M., and Asch, D. 1998. The balancing act, the evil twin, and the pure play. *Medical Decision Making* 18(1): 35–37.

Deming, W. 1993. *The new economics*. Cambridge, MA: MIT Press.

Dolan, K. 1998. Are you paying enough? *Medical Economics* 75(1): 99–112.

Dolan, P. 1998. The measurement of individual utility and social welfare. *Journal of Health Economics* 17(1): 39–51.

Drucker, P. 1996. *Managing the nonprofit organization*. New York: HarperCollins.

Eastaugh, S. 1985. Improving hospital productivity under PPS: Managing cost reductions without harming service quality on access. *Hospital and Health Services Administration* 30(4): 97–111.

Eastaugh, S. 1985. Organization, scheduling are main keys to improving productivity in hospitals. *FAH Review* 18(6): 61–63.

Eastaugh, S. 1986. Work smarter, not harder. *Health Executive* 1(2): 56.

Eastaugh, S. 1990. Hospital nursing technical efficiency: Nursing extenders and enhanced productivity. *Hospital and Health Services Administration* 35(4): 561–573.

Eastaugh, S. 1992. Healthy management alternatives for better productivity. *Harvard Business Review* 70(1): 161–162.

Eastaugh, S., and Regan, M. 1990. Nurse extenders offer a way to trim staff expenses. *Healthcare Financial Management* 44(4): 58–62.

Eastaugh, S., Sahney, V., and Steinhauer, B. 1993. Alternative compensation incentives for stimulating improved productivity. *Journal of Health Administration Education* 1(2): 117–137.

Fare, R., and Gosskopf, S. 1997. Productivity growth in health care delivery. *Medical Care* 35(4): 354–363.

Gilbert, J. 1996. *Productivity management: A step-by-step guide for health care professionals*. Chicago: American Hospital Association.

Ginsberg, P., and Pickreign, J. 1997. Tracking health care costs. *Health Affairs* 16(4): 151–155.

Gordon, S. 1998. Three nurses on the front lines. *Health Affairs* 17(1): 261–263.

Hammer, M., and Champy, J. 1998. *Reengineering the corporation: A manifesto for business revolution*. New York: HarperCollins.

Jadad, A. 1998. Evidence-based decision making. *Medical Decision Making* 18(1): 2–9.

Juran, J. 2002. Quality control. New York: McGraw-Hill.

Kerr, S. 1998. *Ultimate rewards: What motivates*. Boston: Harvard Business School.

Kettlitz, G. 1998. Employee tenure among nurses. *Health Care Supervisor* 16(3): 54–62.

Kruger, R. 1998. *Focus groups: A practical guide for applied research*. Newbury Park, CA: Sage.

Laverty, S. 1998. Incentive compensation. *Healthcare Financial Management* 52(1): 56–60.

Lenert, L. 1998. Utility elicitations. *Medical Decision Making* 18(1): 76–83.

McClain, J., and Eastaugh, S. 1993. How to forecast to contain your variable costs. *Hospital Topics* 61(6): 4–9.

McConnell, C. 1998a. Employee involvement motivation. *Health Care Supervisor* 16(3): 69–85.

McConnell, C. 1998b. *The effective health care supervisor*. Gaithersburg, MD: Aspen.

Moran, D. 1997. Federal regulation of managed care: An impulse in search of a theory? *Health Affairs* 16(6): 7–20.

Pauker, S., and Pauker, S. 1998. Torts, tradeoffs, and thresholds. *Medical Decision Making* 18(1): 29–32.

Perry, K. 1998. Wider choices, happier staff. *Medical Economics* 75(2): 117–127.

Reynolds, M. 2002. Gainsharing. *Healthcare Financial Management* 55(1): 60–66.

Schmidt, K. 2002. Electronic medical records. *Healthcare Financial Management* 55(1): 52–58.

Scott, K. 1998. Physician retention. *Health Care Financial Management* 52(1): 75–77.

Sherer, J. 1997. Human side of change: Downsizing and reengineering. *Health Care Executive* 12(4): 8–14.

Shorr, A. 2002. *The optimizer: Productivity evaluation methodology for scheduling*. Tarzana, CA: Shorr.

Sloan, A. 1940. *My years at General Motors*. New York: Doubleday.

Smither, J. 2002. *Performance appraisal*. San Francisco: Jossey–Bass.

Theodossiou, I. 1998. The effects of low pay and unemployment on psychological well-being: A logistic regression approach. *Journal of Health Economics* 17(1): 85–104.

Ulrich, D. 1998. New mandate for human resources. *Harvard Business Review* 76(1): 124–134.

Umiker, W. 1998a. *Management skills for the new healthcare supervisor.* Gaithersburg, MD: Aspen.

Umiker, W. 1998b. Practical reward strategies. *Health Care Supervisor* 16(3): 63–68.

Weir, R. 1997. Efficacy and effectiveness of process consultation in improving staff morale and absenteeism. *Medical Care* 35(4): 334–352.

Chapter 5

Production Functions

Big change is here, like it or not. Major change is in view. Change breeds doubt. Doubt kindles choice. Choice is opportunity, opportunity to do better.

– James Suver

When you are through improving, you are through.

– B. Schembechler

▶ **Critical points in this chapter:**

- Complements and substitutes

- Wage inflation and deflation

- Production function

Introduction

Two powerful trends suggest that productivity varies widely among hospitals as a function of staffing patterns, methods of organization, and the degree of reliance on nurse extender technicians. Nurse extenders can enhance the marginal value product of the most educated nurses as the RNs concentrate their workday around patient care activities. The results suggest that nurse extenders free RNs from the burden of non-nursing tasks.

As previously stated, productivity is the first test of management's competence. A hospital manager should get the greatest output for the least input effort, balancing all factors of care delivery to achieve the most with an optimal level of quality. A number of exogenous factors can affect productivity. For example, nurse staff flexibility is enhanced during tight low-wage inflation periods. When nurse wage inflation is under control, nurses are less likely to protest productivity improvement programs. Hospital nurse productivity did not improve in the 1980s. During that time, nurse wages inflated 2.3 percent annually, while those of comparable professions, such as teachers, increased by only 2.0 percent. In the 1990s, nurse wages deflated 0.4 percent annually, whereas those of comparable professions increased by 1.1 percent annually. Recent bare-bones reimbursement policy changes, such as the Balanced Budget Act of 1997, have had a major impact on the wages of the profession.

The hospital nursing profession is undergoing a major transformation. Task delegation and the allocation of nurses within the hospital has become a major medical economics issue. Nursing department employees represent 62 percent of hospital employees and 36 percent of hospital expenses. Hospitals have increased their employment of full-time registered nurses (RN) per 100 patient days by 49 percent in the period from 1993 to 1999. The report of the Secretary's Commission on Nursing indicates that the hospitals reporting the most severe RN shortages have been the leaders in replacing licensed practical nurses (LPN) with more expensive RNs. Alternative labor input, in the form of the technician nurse extender (NE) is an increasingly popular approach to alleviating the problem of inadequate nurse staffing levels. While a careful empirical study has not yet been done to assess the degree to which employment of NEs and efficient task delegation to clerks can enhance department productivity and free nurses to perform their unique clinical activities, in theory, NEs can intensify the marginal value product of the most educated nurses as RNs are able to concentrate their workday around the most severely ill patients.

Background

Nurses have struggled for the past century to find a socially valued place and a distinct identity. Hospital nursing has undergone a number of major organizational shifts, from functional nursing in the 1940s, to team nursing in the 1960s, to primary nursing in the 1980s. The innovation of team nursing in the 1960s set the experienced RN as team leader, working with nursing aides and LPNs. The team leader delegated much of the patient care to the team members and planned the care for each patient during that specific shift. Team nursing had the financial benefits of cost effectiveness and the positive and negative aspects of any task-oriented system. Hospital administrators liked team nursing's focus on centralization of control, while nurse educators desired a new system that would focus on autonomy of the BSN-trained RN (and maximize reliance on RNs, while decreasing employment of LPNs).

Primary nursing became popular in the 1980s as nursing focused on the need for autonomy and the evolution of a knowledge-based professional practice. Primary nursing involves decentralization of the nursing unit and the establishment of a responsibility relationship between a nurse and the patient. The primary nurse writes a 24-hour care plan for each patient, and the associate nurse implements the plan when the primary nurse is not working. Primary nursing has the advantage of improved continuity of care but carries the cost of a smaller number of patients per RN.

The nurse extender concept, as a substitute or complement to primary care nursing, has become increasingly popular. The NE technologist label is an attempt to rid the profession of any sexist bent and to recruit men (NEs are typically two-thirds male and earn 20 to 40 percent less per hour than RNs). Nurse extender technicians became popular because the hospital sector experienced difficulty in finding a sufficient supply of RNs for primary nursing staffs. Some nursing groups were not receptive to the NE concept because of fears that it represented a return to team nursing and would merely confer a new job title on under-trained LPNs. However, task delegation to NEs by itself does not undermine the standardization of nurse education. In fact, the realization that the nation needs more caregivers and that NEs will still be under the control of the nursing department prompted the nursing literature to become less militant. Now an NE is referred to in the literature as a "technical assistant to an experienced RN as a primary partnership," or an "executive administrative assistant assisting the executive nurse." Such glowing titles may seem unimportant to economists, but in the workplace it is important for job retention that NEs not be labeled reborn LPNs who do "scutwork" or "menial tasks." One profession's menial task is another profession's vital activity, so NEs spend most of their workday performing a "noninterpretive" collection of vital signs, EKGs, and lab slips.

Data and Methods

Production-function studies of technical efficiency (productivity) have been done by economists since the 1930s. Production functions are useful in understanding how resources are combined by the department or firm (hospital) to produce some particular level of output and ascertain how these resources complement or substitute for one another in the service production process. A number of recent studies have analyzed production functions in business and in the hospital sector.

The first major study of U.S. hospital production functions involved a sample of 60 nonteaching hospitals in Ohio. Hellinger utilized a translog (transcendental logarithmic) production function, which attenuates or eliminates restrictions on the functional form, thereby leaving much generality and flexibility in the service production estimation process (in contrast to the traditional Cobb-Douglas model). The translog form used in this study involves two basic assumptions. First, managers monitor nursing costs when deciding the appropriate staff mix and range or level of hospital output and nurse workload. This assumption does not mean that nurse managers are perfect cost-minimizers operating at the production possibility frontier of 100 percent technical efficiency. The second assumption is that nursing departments exhibit constant returns to scale in producing their output. Consequently, there is no reason to presuppose that nurses are any more productive in a 900-bed hospital than in a 90-bed hospital. (Previous hospital cost studies, not focused on the nursing department, report very shallow economies of scale of only 8 percent.)

In comparing isoquants—curves producing the same output for different quantities of inputs—two extreme situations can exist. Under perfect complementary production between inputs, no substitution at all is possible between inputs A and B, and inputs A and B must always be used in fixed proportions (isoquants are straight, downward-sloping lines). Under the opposite extreme, perfect substitutability between inputs defines the isoquants as perfect right angles. In the first step in the data analysis, a translog production function will be estimated from data at 37 hospitals. The second step measures the curvature of the nursing isoquants and thereby the substitution among inputs (the elasticity of substitution).

Since nursing is a complex production process, we will be assessing a production process with five-dimensional isoquants. Between each pair of inputs, partial elasticities of substitution will be measured (RN x NE substitution). The five basic inputs studied include (1) NEs; (2) RNs; (3) H=housestaff residents and interns performing some nursing activities while understaffed; (4) A=clerks, LPNs, and nurse aids; and (5) E=capital.

Collection of data on labor inputs is straightforward and has been done in a number of previous studies. Nursing output is specified by a point-scoring system sold by the largest proprietary vendor of nurse workload and nurse scheduling systems (Atlas MediQual). This same system tracks work hours to measure the contribution of nonphysician labor inputs (input factors 1, 2, and 4). Housestaff resident and intern input was not measured on an annual basis, only on a one-shot, sampling basis in one year (1997). Filled residency slots have been largely time-invariant for the 16 sample teaching hospitals, and physician labor in nursing activities ranges only from 0.1 to 1.1 percent of nursing activities. To not include this measured work input in the analysis would slightly overstate the productivity of nursing departments in certain hospitals.

One last caveat must be presented concerning measurement error in this study: measurement of capital inputs must avoid the pitfall of using depreciation charges to more accurately reflect differences in the age and productivity of the capital stock. I have used the same index employed in a previous study to adjust the capital expenses for differences across the 37 sample hospitals in the average age of their capital stock. For each hospital, the ratio of accumulated depreciation to total assets is taken as a measure of age. Age-adjusted capital input was calculated as follows:

$$E = UA \times Exp\ (M-R) \tag{1}$$

Where   *UA = unadjusted capital expenses*

R = ratio of accumulated depreciation to total assets

M = mean value of R for the sample

Exp = inverse natural logarithm

The sample is a convenience sample of hospitals with nursing activity research programs. Obviously, the sample is not generalizable to all U.S. hospitals. The more progressive hospitals, with active support for health services research, may have production technologies (scheduling and staff education) that are more advanced than the average U.S. hospital. Each of the sample hospitals subscribed to the same nurse workload system, and the hospitals ranged in size from 114 beds to 950 beds. The hypothetical frontier production can be expressed as:

$$y_{ij} = \prod_{k} (X_{ijk})^{\beta k} e^{u_{ij}} \qquad (2)$$

Where y_{ij} = the nurse output of the jth hospital in the ith period
for periods 1-4 (1997–2000)

X_{ijk} = kth input applied by the jth hospital in the ith period

If the hospital realized its full technical efficiency at 100 percent, then u_j takes the value zero, and if not u_j takes a value less than zero depending on the extent of its lost productivity. The $e^{u_{ij}}$ term provides a measure of hospital-specific productivity, and improvement in $e^{u_{ij}}$ will be reflected in higher mean productivity over time. Inefficiency is:

$$U_{ij} = \ln y_{ij} - \left(\sum \beta_k \ln X_{ijk} + v_{ij} \right) \qquad (3)$$

Estimation of u_j and e^{u_j} is possible once density functions for u and v are assumed. Let u follow a half-normal distribution and let v follow the full normal distribution. (The validity of the half-normal distribution was verified at the end of the analysis by plotting the combined residual [$u+v$], the hospital's technical efficiency and the output levels.) Equation 2 can be rewritten:

$$Y_{ij} = \prod_{k} (X_{ijk})^{\beta k} e^{E_{ij}} \qquad (4)$$

Where $E_{ij} = u_j + v_{ij}$

The estimation of the maximum possible stochastic output, had the hospital realized its full technical efficiency, is carried out by applying maximum likelihood methods to equation 4. With this model one can estimate individual hospital technical efficiencies together with the mean technical efficiency using four years of panel data (dummy variable D [0,1] for the three years after the base year 1997). One can hopefully also target some factors causing variation in technical efficiencies in nursing among the 37 sample hospitals.

Empirical Results

Maximum likelihood methods of estimation were applied to equation 4 and the parameter estimates of the translog model are presented in **Table 5-1**. The ratio of hospital-specific variability in productivity was significant at the 0.1 level, indicating that productivity dominates in explaining the total variability of nurse output produced. Judging by the significance of the dummy variables, we can reject the hypothesis that productivity was time-invariant over the four years. Most of the parameters not involving the two weakest variables (H and E) are significant at the .05 level.

A second alternative, partial elasticity, can also be derived. The Allen elasticity of substitution holds constant the quantities of all other inputs, in addition to the level of nurse output. The Allen elasticities are related

Table 5-1 Translog Production Function for Medical/Surgical Nursing Services Delivery, 1997–2000			
Variable	Parameter Estimate* (Maximum Likelihood)	Variable	Parameter Estimate* (Maximum Likelihood)
D_1, 1998	0.009	βRN, E	0.133
	(10.7)		(25.1)
D_2, 1999	0.023	βRN, NE	–0.116
	(31.2)		(30.6)
D_3, 2000	0.029	βA, NE	0.129
	(44.5)		(14.2)
βNE, E	0.106	βA, H	0.018
	(9.8)		(2.9)
βH, E	0.103	βA, RN	–0.025
	(21.4)		(7.0)
βH, NE	0.126	βA, E	0.092
	(38.0)		(11.3)
βRN, H	–0.492	Constant α	0.057
	(8.9)		(9.1)
t-values in parentheses; log likelihood = –39.649			

Note: NE = nurse extenders, RNs; H = housestaff residents and interns doing some nursing activities while understaffed; A = clerks and LPNs and nurse aides; E = capital.

econometrically to the cross-price elasticity of demand for factors — for example, the demand for input 1 (NEs) to change the price of input 2 (RNs). The sign of a cross-price elasticity of demand (column 3 of **Table 5-2**) by itself is an indicator of gross substitution — a negative sign indicating complementary factors, a positive sign indicating substitution. As line 11 of **Table 5-2** reveals, a negative sign on the elasticity of demand for NE labor with respect to the price of RN labor indicates that as RN labor becomes more costly, the labor of NEs is used more extensively in place of RNs. The NEs and RNs are complementary team members, not in competition with each other. On the other hand, this suggests that rapidly inflating costs of all RN nursing staff trades efficiency by avoiding the opportunity for NE-induced productivity gains. Moreover, using nonemployee RNs, temporary agency nurses, can cost many urban hospitals up to $65 to $95 per hour/per nurse.

Table 5-2 Partial Elasticities of Substitution for the Input Factors of Medical/Surgical Nursing Productivity

	Input Pairs	Partial Elasticity	Relationship
1.	NE/NE	−0.196*	Complements
2.	RN/RN	−0.180	Complements
3.	H/H	−0.157	Complements
4.	A/A	−0.092	Complements
5.	E/E	−0.315	Complements
6.	NE/E	0.413	Substitutes
7.	H/E	0.809	Substitutes
8.	H/NE	0.741	Substitutes
9.	RN/H	−0.262	Complements
10.	RN/E	0.478	Substitutes
11.	RN/NE	−0.436	Complements
12.	A/NE	0.502	Substitutes
13.	A/H	−0.040	Complements
14.	A/RN	−0.275	Complements
15.	A/E	0.417	Substitutes

The own-price elasticities have the expected negative sign.

Note: NE = nurse extenders, RNs; H = housestaff residents and interns doing some nursing activities while understaffed; A = clerks and LPNs and nurse aides; E = capital.

The NEs substitute fairly well and fluidly for clerks and LPNs (line 12) while complementing RNs. A positive sign in line 8 (**Table 5-2**) on the elasticity of demand for NE labor with respect to the price of household (resident) labor indicates that, as housestaff labor (H) becomes more costly per hour, the labor of NEs is used more extensively in place of residents. As some state regulators and hospital managers have moved to restrict the housestaff work week — yielding fewer hours at the same fixed annual wage — the hourly wage of the housestaff and the employment level of NEs have risen. However, the negative sign in line 9 of **Table 5-2** reveals that no increase in RN employment can be expected as some states implement a maximum hourly work week for residents and interns.

Lines 6, 7, 10, and 15 in **Table 5-2** have the expected positive signs, indicating that labor can substitute for capital (.01 level of significance). Line 7 has the highest observed elasticity, suggesting that the highly skilled MD component of housestaff — their technical diagnostic skill as doctors — partially substitutes for more equipment and physical capital. This generalization may be increasingly true in the future as more residents benefit from economic grand rounds, "think before ordering tests" educational programs, and the cost-effective clinical decision making ethic of younger doctors trained in health economics.

From observing the three dummy variables at the top of **Table 5-1**, more productivity for this sample of 37 hospitals was not time-invariant over the four-year period. Mean nurse productivity for each cross-section equation improved from 0.73 to 0.81 from 1997 to 2000. In the most recent year, nursing departments were realizing only 81 percent of their technical efficiency (productivity). While averages are interesting, distributions are more policy relevant. **Table 5-3** lists the average productivity level across the 37 nursing departments and the factor input (NEs) with the two highest t-values (from **Table 5-1**). Individual nurse productivity ratings range from .60 to .93. **Table 5-3** suggests discrete differences in production technologies as well as differences in input mix. This wide range could in theory reflect differences in organizational efficiency or differences in the availability and use of factor inputs (a shortage of nurses). However, the eight hospitals with the worst nursing productivity at the top of **Table 5-3** employed no NE technicians, operated a 100-percent RN primary care nursing organization, and exhibited productivity 11 to 21 percent below average. The nine hospitals in **Table 5-3** with the highest levels of nurse productivity made heavy use of

NEs: three used the team nursing organizational concept, but six employed primary care nursing with a 61 to 66 percent BSN-trained RN staff.

Table 5-3 Frequency Distribution of Nursing Departments Productivity and Nurse Extender Staffing-Mix

Productivity Level (range)*	Number of Hospitals	Ratio of NEs to RNs
0.60–0.65	4	0.0
0.66–0.70	4	0.0
0.71–0.75	3	0.23
0.76–0.80	8	0.48
0.81–0.85	9	0.59
0.86–0.90	5	0.82
0.91–0.93	4	0.81
Total	**37**	**mean = 0.48**

0.81 = average productivity

Discussion and Conclusions

In summary, the results suggest that: (1) primary care nursing can be either highly productive or highly inefficient; (2) the all-RN nursing staff, used in only eight of the 37 hospitals, reports the worst productivity performance; (3) a shortage of nurses did not drag down productivity levels in **Table 5-3** as the four cities with the tightest nursing markets contained the five hospitals with the highest levels of productivity; and (4) employment of nurse extenders reduces wasted labor and enhances productivity.

The last of these four conclusions indicates a number of avenues for future research. For example, the results at the end of the last column in **Table 5-3** weakly indicate that NEs, as with any labor input, may approach a level of diminishing returns. Does having eight to 10 NEs per 10 RNs constitute a zone of diminishing returns? Does a primary care nursing staff with greater than 70 percent BSN-trained RNs constitute an inefficient staff-mix of diminishing returns? Does deploying five to eight NEs per 10 RNs harm patient care quality? Judging by the deployment of NEs at prestigious teaching hospitals, task delegation can enhance the quality of patient care.

Lastly, what additional tasks can be delegated to NEs beyond obtaining vital signs and EKG results, patient transport, procuring supplies and equipment, procedural assistance, and paperwork (such as lab slips)? Some of the 28 hospitals utilizing NEs have begun to utilize specialist technicians to dress wounds and do other nursing functions. Other activities performed by nurse extenders are outlined in **Table 5-4**. Progressive nurse managers will participate in careful studies to set standards, study task delegation feasibility, and circumscribe the job descriptions for NE technicians.

We must improve nurse productivity and attract more young people to the profession. Quality of care is jeopardized by the convergence of three trends: a rapid increase in the number of elderly Americans requiring

---

Table 5-4 Selective Examples of Nonnursing Menial Tasks versus Important Nursing Tasks

Nonnursing Tasks*	Important Nursing Tasks
Taking vital signs	Interpreting vital signs
Transporting patients	Assessing and monitoring physical conditions
Housekeeping and bedmaking	Monitoring technological equipment such as infusion pumps and swan-ganz catheters
Preparing meal trays	Administering tube and IV feedings
Assisting with physician procedures (pelvic exams)	Administering IV therapy: nitroglycerine, insulin, TPA drips
Venipuncture (drawing blood)	Completing evaluation/outcome documentation
Getting supplies and equipment	Planning for discharges
Performing secretarial duties (lab slips)	Placing of special tubes such as NGs, foleys, and oxygen therapy
Obtaining EKGs	Counting narcotics

Nonnursing tasks, often called "scutwork," are activities easily delegated to NEs in a high-productivity unit.

medical care, the retirement or dropout of an already aging and overworked generation of nurses, and the steep decline in the number of people entering the nursing profession. We must not focus just on technology and high-tech skill sets. Technology cannot change beds, dispense medicine, or bathe and dress people. There simply will not be enough people to provide the touch, the smile, and the skill to care for our sick.

Linear programming scheduling systems, incentives, and workload technologies can attack the problems of burnout and frustration. In 2003, the JCAHO and the two national nursing associations are working at 59 "magnet hospitals," where nurses are given larger supervisory roles. These magnet hospitals retain nurses an average of more than eight years, twice as long a others without such programs.

At a time when hospital care is becoming more complex and patients are becoming sicker, productivity enhancement is critical. With future funding limitations, "bare-bones" reimbursement dictates that the recent tradition of 100-percent RN primary care nursing must be abandoned. Development of an efficient staff-mix criterion in nursing should enhance nursing's rising sense of professionalism. Maximizing RN hospital employment levels is hardly a desirable or economical goal unless the United States has a gross oversupply of nurses. Since no such oversupply exists, increased reliance on NEs is good economics and good medicine.

▶ Summary Points:

- While some processes exhibit "economies of scale," not all do (many nursing functions do not).

- "Human" factors are important determinants of economic functions (titles and risk acceptance).

- Specialization, both at the RN level and at multiple skill levels, increases productivity performance.

> ### Research and Discussion Questions:
>
> * How important are non-economic incentives, such as titles, to production performance?
>
> * How could you measure this importance in economic terms? (Note: Reconsider your answers after reading Chapter 7.)

References

Ashby, J., Guterman, S., and Greene, T. 2000. An analysis of hospital productivity and product change. *Health Affairs* 19(5): 197–205.

Cardinal Health Information. 2001. Dublin, Ohio.

Drucker, P. 1990. *Managing the nonprofit organization*. New York: Harper Collins.

Eastaugh, S. 1989. Impact of the nurse training act on the supply of nurses. *Inquiry* 22(4): 404–417.

Eastaugh, S. 1999. *Health care finance*. Gaithersburg, MD: Aspen.

Eastaugh, S.1990. Hospital nursing technical efficiency. *Hospital and Health Services Administration* 35(4): 561–572.

Eastaugh, S., and Regan, M. 1990. Nurse extenders offer a way to trim staff expenses. *Healthcare Financial Management* 44(4): 58–62.

Eastaugh, S. 1995. *Health economics: Efficiency, quality, and equity*. Westport, CT: Auburn.

Eastaugh, S. 2001. GWU Working Paper. "Hospital costs and specialization."

Eastaugh, S., and Young, A. 1991. Econometric study of the financing of graduate medical education, Volume 3 Report. DHHS 100–89–0155. Washington, DC: U.S. Department of Health and Human Services.

Feldstein, M. 1989. *Hospital costs and health insurance*. Cambridge, MA: Harvard University Press.

Johnston, J. 1989. *Econometric methods*, 3rd ed. London: McGraw-Hill.

Hellinger, F. 1975. Specification of a hospital production function. *Applied Economics* 7(2): 149–60.

Hollingsworth, B., Maniadakis, N., and Thanassoulis, E. 1999. Efficiency: Measured response, DEA at 75 hospitals. *Health Services Journal U.K.* 109(5682): 20–29.

Hollingsworth, B., Dawson, P., and Maniadako, N. 1998. Efficiency measurement of health care: A review of non-parametric methods and applications. *Health Care Management Science* 2(3): 161–172.

Lenehan, G. 1988. The AMA's registered care technologist proposal: Old wine in new bottles. *Journal of Emergency Nursing* 14, 5268–5271.

McCarthy, S. 1989. The future of nursing practice and implications for nurse education. *Journal of Professional Nursing* 5(3) 121–168.

MediQual. 2001. Marborough, MA: Atlas.

Secretary's Commission on Nursing. Final Report, Volume 3. 1990. Washington, DC: U.S. Department of Health and Human Services.

Shukla, R. 1983. All RN model of nursing care delivery: A cost-benefit evaluation. *Inquiry* 20(3): 173–184.

Shukla, R. 1983. Technical and structural support systems and nurse utilization. *Inquiry* 20(4): 381–389.

Walker, D. 2000. Compensation: Rewarding productivity of the knowledge worker. *Journal of Ambulatory Care Management* 23(4): 48–59.

Zegeye, A., and Rosenblum, L. 2000. Measuring productivity in an importer world. *Applied Economics* 32(1): 91–105.

Chapter 6

Technology Assessment and Cost-Effectiveness

Technology is most effective when it prevents problems. It is better to put a fence at the top of the cliff than an ambulance at the bottom.

– James Mason

If humans are distinguished from other primates by their need to take drugs, then physicians must be distinguished by their need to order tests.

– William Osler, M.D.

Medline Research Service does not list the word "health" in its index. In a teaching hospital there is no such thing as a healthy patient. A healthy patient is one that has not been sufficiently worked up at a high cost. Come to a teaching hospital as a Medicare patient with the complaint of "stiff hands in the morning" and we will send you to rheumatology for a workup to discover Lupus in one case per 1,000 screened.

– John G. Freymann, M.D.

▶ **Critical points in this chapter:**

- Discounting and NPV
- Cost-effectiveness analysis (CEA)
- Quality of life (QOL)
- Quality adjusted life year (QALY))
- Marginal information gain (MIG)

Cost-effectiveness and cost-benefit analysis have been applied in many preventive, diagnostic, and treatment contexts. Over the past decade, methods have improved for prospectively collecting better data sets and incorporating intangible life valuations into the calculus for weighing benefits against costs. Further cooperation among clinicians, economists, and epidemiologists is a healthy trend. Political scientists are prone to argue over valuation in dollars, reflecting a basic misunderstanding of the trade-off concept and the need to combine and compare benefits and costs in comparable units.

Economic evaluation of new or expensive technologies has become a central issue in the public debate about rising healthcare costs. Historically, the growth in technology has stimulated a concomitant increase in the numbers and salaries of healthcare employees. Physicians and economists frequently express their hope that these expensive technologies are partially justified by their quality-enhancing properties. Sometimes expensive new technologies can be cost saving (as in the case of a kidney transplant), while in other cases they are not.

The objective of cost-benefit analysis is to maximize net benefits (benefits minus costs, appropriately discounted over time). Cost-effectiveness analysis is used for ranking preferred alternatives for achieving a single goal or a specified basket of benefits. Cost-effectiveness analysis is not any easier to perform than cost-benefit analysis if multiple varieties of benefit are specified (person-years, work-loss days, reduced angina), except that in doing cost-benefit analysis the intangible benefits must be valued in commensurate dollar terms. Operationally, ethical questions can be raised if the benefits and costs accrue to different social groups. For example, a clinic scheduling system that minimizes wasted time for the physician through multiple overlapping appointments might generate a net benefit of a few hundred dollars per physician at the expense of many more dollars of patient time.

Quality-Adjusted Life Years (QALY)

QALYs are the gold standard for most cost-effectiveness studies published since 1980. Singer and Younossi (2001) used QALYs as their benefit outcome measure for a cost-effectiveness study of screening for Hepatitis C. The analysis does not support the widespread screening for Hepatitis C among asymptomatic average-risk adults. The cost-effectiveness results were most sensitive to patient awareness of quality of life concerns. Screening was preferred when more than half the patients who tested positive for Hepatitis C actually initiated treatment, or if the annual progression to cirrhosis was greater than 2.5 percent.

Different patient populations will have varying levels of cost effectiveness. Vijan's (2001) analysis of colon cancer screening tests revealed an incremental cost effectiveness from $20,000 to $300,000 per QALY saved. Cost of colonoscopy and proportion of cancer arising from polyps affect cost effectiveness. In all screening studies, recommendations should be tailored to varying compliance levels in different practice settings. The example concerning hypertension at the end of this chapter is a classic example of this point.

Blute (2000) analyzed the cost effectiveness of microwave thermotherapy in patients with benign prostatic hyperplasia and concluded it exhibited the highest five-year utility value (4.4 QALYs) compared to medical treatment. The incremental cost per QALY gained was $39,000 for thermotherapy compared with medical therapy. Many nations cannot afford this level of fiscal support. The World Bank considers three types of evaluations for comparing alternatives: cost minimization, incremental net benefit, and incremental cost effectiveness (Eastaugh 2000).

Many services that are effective are not insured. Why are proven preventive services underinsured? Even in the event that preventive services are cost-saving, the gains may be so far in the future or the elasticity of supply in the industry may be so high that insurance companies are unable to reap any benefits. One of the problems with preventive screening examinations is that the cost of treating false-positive results, along with the adverse psychological effects, might outweigh the benefit of detecting a disease in its early stages (Ferrucci 2001).

It is not necessary to conduct economic analysis and randomized clinical trials on every new technology, and certainly not on most existing ones. However, the uncontrollable economic pressures for efficiency are apt to result in more careful economic analysis. Some of these studies will severely disrupt the conventional wisdom. For example, Russell (1995) studied a number of preventive programs and concluded that society's total healthcare costs increased (most prevention was a cost add-on, not a cost-saving investment). Investments that cost very little on a per-person basis become very costly when applied on a national basis. Russell cited the example of a blood pressure check, which is very inexpensive on an individual basis, but becomes very costly when applied to 20 million to 30 million people. A well-targeted work-site blood pressure control program can result in $1.72 to $2.72 in reduced healthcare claims per dollar spent operating the program (Foote and Erfurt 1991).

To make the research relevant to clinicians, one must define a basket of benefits (major complications). Magid, Douglas, and Schwartz (1996) did this in comparing treatment strategies for women with uncomplicated cervical chlymadial infections: (1) initial therapy with doxycycline, 100 mg orally twice daily for 7 days (estimated cost, $5.51); and (2) initial therapy with azithromycin, 1 g orally administered in a single dose (estimated cost, $18.75). In univariate sensitivity analyses, the azithromycin strategy prevented more major complications but was more expensive than the doxycycline strategy when doxycycline effectiveness was greater than 0.93. In a multivariate sensitivity analysis combining 11 parameter estimates selected so that the cost-effectiveness of the doxycycline strategy would be maximized relative to that of the azithromycin strategy, the azithromycin strategy resulted in fewer complications but was more costly. The incremental cost-effectiveness was $521 per additional major complication prevented.

Methods of Analysis

Public and political disenchantment has been high with model builders who provide narrow definitions of direct benefits and ignore the limitations of their very crude databases. A good economic analysis must: (1) make the evaluation as complex as necessary, (2) assign values to resources that reflect their opportunity costs, (3) avoid zero counting of resources, and (4) avoid double counting of resources. The typical accounting costs of billed charges or incurred expenses define cost too narrowly for the economic analyst. Confusion frequently exists when members of the medical profession attempt to do a cost analysis. For example, the cost to society of not having airbags must not exclude accident victims who are dead on arrival. In the arena of cost-effectiveness analysis between medical treatment versus surgery, surgeons frequently omit from the analysis those who die during surgery to make surgery look better relative to medical treatment. The tendency is to go far afield in counting benefits and to neglect some costs, such as the pain of surgery or the overhead costs of the operating room. The cost of cash expenditures is defined too narrowly. True cost to society can only be measured in opportunity cost terms, or in terms of the value of the benefit sacrificed to obtain it.

Estimating the economic burden of a disease involves the measurement of prevalence, the assessment of effect on health status and on others' well-being, and the eventual quantification of direct and indirect costs associated with these effects. For example, the cost of alcohol abuse was an estimated $98 billion in 2000. Half of the alcohol abuse burden on the economy resulted from lost economic production ($160 billion), $26 billion was generated in direct healthcare service costs, and $25 billion resulted from motor vehicle accidents, fires, crime, and other less tangible effects (Eastaugh 2000).

A number of sources of uncertainty exist for making economic decisions. The first source of analytical uncertainty results from incomplete mastery of available knowledge in medicine coupled with the fact that medicine is in a constant state of flux and revision. A second source results from limitations in current medical knowledge. Human immunodeficiency virus-1 (HIV-1), HIV-2, Lyme disease, Legionnaires' disease, and eosinophilia-myalgia syndrome were characterized only recently, and new disease entities are discovered every year. The third source of uncertainty, derived from the first two, is the difficulty in distinguishing between ignorance and the limitations of current medical knowledge; that is, the fear of the untaught versus the fear of the unknown.

The critical point to convey to the reader is that cost-effectiveness analysis and cost-benefit analysis are taking their appropriate positions more and more frequently in the evaluation (prediffusion) stage prior to the marketing decision. The rationale of this emerging public policy is that the costs (in lives and in dollars) of forgoing economic and efficacy evaluation often might be much greater than the costs of a well-designed evaluation. One "consumerist" benefit of increasing reliance on economic evaluation is that it must force those in power to be explicit about (1) valuation-of-life biases (across social class) in cost-benefit calculations and (2) the resource cutoff level utilized in cost-effectiveness analysis.

As the public grows to understand the degree to which medicine involves decision making under uncertainty, the physician-god model must give way to a more realistic paradigm. Consumers might better think of their physician as a "senior partner" (SP) in health care. This abrupt relabeling of the professional title, from MD to SP, highlights the rising popularity of health promotion and education and the declining perception of infallibility in medicine. Moreover, outcome measures of quality and patient satisfaction and compliance are inseparable. Patient compliance is critical to improving health status.

SPs enhance patient compliance and provide a better level of informed consent; omniscient practitioners claim that their "hands are touched by the gods." Gods give out proclamations; SPs give probability estimates and explain them. For some patients, the explanation of odds and conditional probabilities might be complex enough that they are best referred to as overinformed consent. The sensitive SP knows when to stop with the detail, whereas a god would never become schooled in such detail or provide it to a patient. The SP will wait for the junior partner (patient) to say either "Enough detail; go to XYZ" or "What shall we do, Doctor?"

Net Present Value Analysis: Discounting

What noneconomists most frequently misunderstand is that inflation is only one part of the rationale for discounting. Even if all benefits were adjusted for the projected rate of inflation, discounting would still be necessary to account for the social rate of time preference. Discounting future years of life implies no utilitarian value judgment. It only presumes that benefits and costs are juxtaposed and measured in commensurable dollar units at a single given discount rate. Choice of a discount rate is of no consequence for a short-lived program with benefits and costs concentrated within one to two years.

Selection of the rate of discount is a crucial parameter in most net-present-value calculations. A prediction that technology will become more cost-increasing in the future argues for selection of a lower discount rate in order to make lifesaving more valuable in future years. The viewpoint is supported by the suggestion that technology is reaching a state of diminishing returns where even an optimistic 50 percent reduction in the three leading causes of death (cardiovascular disease, cancer, and motor vehicle accidents) would add less than one year of life for people aged 15 to 65. There are three basic varieties of discount rates: (1) the corporate discount rate if the private sector borrowed the funds, (2) the government borrowing rate on bond issues in the marketplace, and (3) the social discount rate to enable programs and procedures with benefits far in the future to prove more acceptable.

The social discount rate (Pigou 1920) is probably used most often because of the strength of its intergenerational equity argument. For example, a $25 million one-shot project in 2001 with a payoff of $75 million in the year 2021 has a positive net present value only if the discount rate is 6 percent or less. The typical social discount rate is on the order of 4 percent to 6 percent.

However, a bias against the value of future generations might still remain apparent to some futurists if they realized that at a 5 percent discount rate, 30 deaths in 2071 are exactly equivalent to one death in 2001. To those political scientists and welfare economists concerned with the ethical issues, any discount rate will have some slight bias in favor of present generations. (A counterargument might be Keynes's rejoinder that "in the long run we are all dead.")

Opportunity cost principles argue for a high discount rate. The true cost of a healthcare investment is the return that could have been achieved if the resources had gone elsewhere in the private sector. The relevant comparison is not the expected rate of return but the expected rate of return net of the subjective costs of risk-bearing. The first option, the corporate discount rate, is obviously overinflated because it includes both a risk premium and a markup for corporate taxes. The second choice, government borrowing rates, serves as the middle estimate in most analyses. Given the implicit assumption that the discount rate is not changing over time, the most prudent course of action is to perform a sensitivity analysis of the net present value under a range of discount rates. If a sensitivity analysis can demonstrate that selection of a discount rate does not affect the recommendations, then the tenuousness of the assumption will not be a source for concern.

Applications of Cost-Effectiveness Analysis

The purpose of cost-effectiveness analysis in the therapeutic arena is to identify the preferred alternatives. Physician preoccupation with survival probabilities must not preclude measurement of quality-of-life factors in performing a cost-effectiveness analysis. Cost-effectiveness analysis still requires that intangible factors be measured; however, they do not have to be valued. Typically, the search for preferred alternatives involves comparisons of less invasive treatment. Further research is needed as to the timing and content of the best means of promoting cost-effective clinical decisions. Ethical and social issues raised by cost-benefit and cost-effectiveness applications are also discussed. The need for more cost-effective clinical decision making is clear: When we have 5 percent to 10 percent overuse and excess care, we waste $55 billion to $110 billion.

The medical staff should promote efficient, sequential scheduling of tests: Order only sodium and potassium electrolytes, and not the full panel of electrolytes, if these two tests are sufficient. If there is no suggestive evidence from the peripheral smear, do not order unnecessary tests such as iron studies or multiple vitamin levels for anemic patients. Do not spend $9 million for routine liver-function tests of patients on disulfiram to detect only one case of Hepatitis. Other cost reduction ideas include reducing the flow of anesthesia from five to two liters per minute, thus saving $8 per hour and not eroding the quality of care. Nearly half of the basic preoperative tests (electrolytes, complete blood count [CBC], PT/PTT) need not be done if previous testing was normal within the past year, and no clinical indication for retesting exists. Fax machines have improved the information flow between the hospital and physicians' offices, thus decreasing the amount of repeat testing.

Consumerism should also play a part in the cost-effective medical staff. Make the consumer king. That is, teach diabetics to use pocket insulin-dosage computers to enhance independence and self-esteem, and save money by reducing the rate of hospital admissions among brittle diabetics. Often what is less costly is better for the patient: Use a $19 pulse oximeter to get the same basic information as arterial blood gases, thus saving $75 and reducing the discomfort for the patient (as long as acidosis or CO_2 retention is not suspected). The style of medical practice is moving toward cost-effective clinical decision making. Most nephrologists do not order a metabolic workup for the first kidney stone. Pulmonary specialists order spirometry rather than expensive but more complete pulmonary function testing for the preoperative chronic emphysema patient. Emergency medicine physicians have come up with five rules to cut costs: not X-raying everyone with low back strain; not ordering Chem-7s and CBCs on young healthy patients with a day or two of gastroenteritis; getting a chest X-ray rather than rib films on young patients with rib fractures; not getting an EDIVP on every young healthy patient with clinical evidence of kidney stone; and dipping urine as a screening test rather than using microscopy on every urine sample.

Technology assessment proceeds in sequential stages. Physicians dominate the first stage of analysis, examining short-term safety and descriptive analysis (does the new technique or procedure yield improvements?). Statisticians dominate the second stage of technology assessment with a middle-term study of efficacy utilizing randomized controlled clinical trials. Diagnostic efficacy studies report sensitivity and specificity. Economists and policy makers dominate the third stage of technology assessment: clinical cost-effectiveness (is it less costly than the alternative options at achieving a prescribed package of "effects," such as X percent less pain or Y percent less morbidity?) and long-run cost-benefit (does the ratio of benefit to cost exceed one, counting all costs and benefits to society?). Since cost-benefit analysis should include intangible benefits, such as pain reduction, to be comprehensive, it is necessary to shadow-price patients' willingness-to-pay preferences regarding a given medical technology.

Because some might not have conceptualized excess utilization in graphic terms, **Figure 6–1** illustrates three possible scenarios for medical treatment production functions. Curve *AB* represents a cost-beneficial treatment mode such as heart pacemakers. If the technology were inappropriately utilized or prophylactically prescribed for an indiscriminately large fraction of the population, the assessed technology could move along the curve into the region *BC* where benefits do not justify costs. Hypothetical curve *DE* might represent the benefit-cost range when surgeons perform only 210,000 coronary artery bypass operations annually, but the treatment may appear unjustified (region *EF*) if the operative incidence increases.

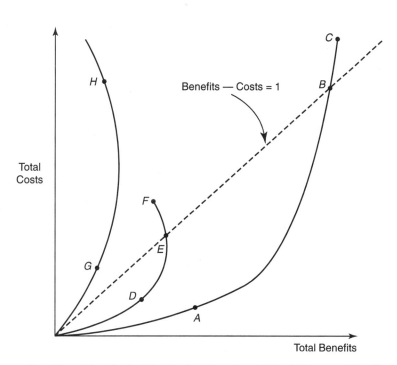

▲ FIGURE 6–1 Three Hypothetical Production Functions of Total Treatment Benefits as a Function of Total Costs

The less tangible quality-of-life benefits comprise a growing proportion of medical care benefits. For example, elective surgical expenditures are properly intended to achieve goals less tangible than mortality or morbidity rate reduction, such as relief of disability, pain, and disfigurement. Such quality-of-life factors are to be identified and quantified in terms of their equivalent social costs by shadow pricing, and finally to be balanced against commensurate shadow prices of quantity of life. Advocates of the willingness-to-pay approach suggest the maximization of lives saved as the social objective function.

The Tunnel of Technology and Costly Marginal Information Gains

Cost-effectiveness analysis is a popular topic in the medical journals. We live in an information age. Physicians are not unlike other professionals in wanting the most marginal information gain as an agent for their clients. Unfortunately, benefits are often mainly to physicians' curiosity ("an interesting question answered" or "a rare zebra case found and ready for publication") rather than to the healthcare benefit from overtreating or overtesting their patients. One study described a treatment style that runs independent of patient needs after reporting a disappointingly low predictive value of magnetic resonance imaging (MRI) scanning for nodal involvement in cancer staging. This diagnostic strategy may be questionable if the marginal information gain (MIG) to the physician is outweighed by the more specific information (but discomfort to the patient) to be gained by surgical biopsy. If providers did not operate clinics and hospitals like tunnels of technology, maximizing costs, we would have less need for cost-benefit and cost-effectiveness analyses in health care. One health maintenance organization (HMO) chain president said in 2001: Teaching hospitals can learn to do cost analysis and cut costs, or they can all close.

One promising trend is the recent evolution of economic theory into cost-effective protocols. Using a protocol, Phoebe Putney Memorial Hospital, in Albany, Georgia, reduced patient time on ventilators by 60 percent, reduced intensive care unit (ICU) length of stay by 65 percent, and reduced overall hospital length of stay for ICU patients by 50 percent. Quality of care actually improved; mortality was reduced by 47 percent and readmissions to the ICU were cut in half. One of the key factors was the use of protocol-standardizing patient care. Physicians and nurses agree that standardizing does in fact reduce costs and result in better clinical outcomes. Phoebe Putney managers hired a full-time intensivist—a physician whose only job is to oversee the process and make sure the ICU protocol is followed. In too many hospitals, intensive care is fraught with idiosyncratic treatment approaches and outmoded, expensive services, and saddled with high costs (Dunn 1997). Some programs have obvious cost savings potential, like smoking cessation for mothers. Lightwood (2000) reports that an annual drop of one percentage point in smoking prevalence would prevent 1,300 low birth weight live births and save $21 million in direct medical costs in the first year of the program; it would prevent 57,200 low birth weight infants and save $572 million in direct medical costs in seven years. However, most of modern medicine is not so clear-cut in the quick return on the healthcare intervention.

The growth in third-party financing of medical care has frequently been criticized for funding excessive or inappropriate therapies. One postulated negative effect of health insurance is the increased financing of useless technologies like gastric freezing for ulcers. Another postulated negative byproduct of the growth in health insurance is the utilization of treatments to an excess (see points *C*, *F*, and *H* in **Figure 6–1**). The growth in health insurance coverage provided healthcare institutions with the wherewithal to expand service capability and produce service at the point where the cost exceeds the benefit. As health insurance becomes more comprehensive and the consumer's out-of-pocket cost falls to zero, health-service institutions continue to provide care beyond the point where marginal cost is equal to marginal benefit (Q_2) up to point Q_3 (see **Figure 6-2**). The situation is somewhat analogous to that of the consumer who visits an automobile showroom and asks the dealer to select a car for him, price being no object. Because the dealer's profit margin is higher if he provides a Mercedes rather than a Mustang, the customer will never see the Mustang.

The present U.S. economy cannot afford a Mercedes for every consumer (point Q_3). The defense of production at point Q_3 is the argument by the U.S. medical establishment that it must do the utmost for each patient irrespective of cost. Many economists argue that society can barely afford the Mustang unless it decreases utilization rates by increasing the coinsurance paid by patients. Future physicians should realize that relaxing the degree of clinical discrimination and increasing the quantity of care provided per illness episode (intensity) will be curtailed by the managed care revolution. The public voted with their feet for Mustang medicine by signing up for low-cost HMOs. We realize the limits of Mercedes medicine in that doing the utmost for everybody will save a few lives, but at an ever-diminishing rate. Production of $Q_3 - Q_1$ additional units of medical service ignores the opportunity cost of spending that money on housing or pollution control. Some analysts would hope that every dollar wasted in the medical economy is a dollar not used on big corporations (Kissling 2001). However, the broader health economy prevention and public health are being squeezed by the growth in the medical economy.

Economic evaluations must take into consideration the difference between efficacy and effectiveness. Efficacy is the maximum possible benefit, often achieved with controlled trials, and effectiveness is the actual decrease in disease achieved when the intervention is applied over a large, non-homogeneous population (Meltzer 2001).

The goal of physician education programs is to apprise physicians of the appropriate use of tests, procedures, and treatment options. Educational efforts come in a number of formats, offered in combination, including didactic lectures, restructuring of order forms, cost feedback, concurrent or retrospective protocol review, and other retrospective medical record audits. The

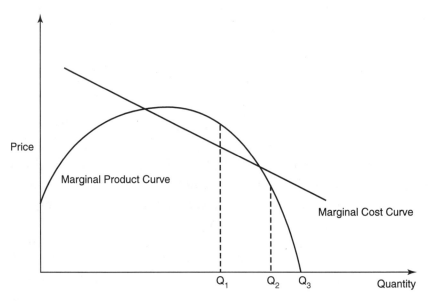

▲ Figure 6–2 Hypothetical Marginal Benefit and Marginal Cost Curves

didactic course approach typically makes four basic points: (1) work cost-effectively (home health care or ambulatory surgery); (2) perform a cost-benefit assessment of the case management alternatives; (3) avoid unnecessary, outmoded, or duplicative procedures; and (4) encourage preventive and health promotion activities. On this last point, health promotion can do more than reduce future illness; it can also reduce duration of stay, patient anxiety, and complications.

Measures of Health Status

Historically, a country's health status was measured by life expectancy. The long-standing measure, however, is giving way to newer gauges of health status:

QALY: Quality-adjusted life years calculate life expectancy adjusted for quality of life, where quality of life is measured on a scale from 1 (full health) to 0 (dead).

QALY = utility x probability x increased life expectancy

DALY: Disability-adjusted life years lost combines years of life lost (YLL) through premature death (before 82.5 years for a woman and before 80 years for a man) plus years lived with the disability (YLD).

DALE: Disability-adjusted life expectancy separates life expectancy into good-health years and years lived with the disability. While DALE is estimated to exceed 60 years in half the countries in the WHO, it is less than 40 years in 32 countries.

HALE: Healthy active life expectancy measures the number of years an individual can expect to live in a healthy state.

▶ **Summary Points:**

- QALY analysis is the gold standard for most cost-effectiveness studies.

- Good CEA can yield surprising results.

- Standardizing patient care (protocols) can both improve clinical outcome (quality of care) *and* decrease cost.

Research and Discussion Questions:

- How does QALY analysis benefit the young over the old?

- Should private payers help finance technology assessment?

References

Allener, B. 2002. Cost-effectiveness modeling. *Diabetes & Metabolism* 26(2): 125–132.

Blomquist, A. 2002. QALYs. *Journal of Health Economics* 21(2): 181–194.

Blute, M. 2000. Cost-effectiveness of microwave thermotherapy. *Urology* 56(6): 981–987.

Dunn, P. 1997. Hospitals target ICUs. *AHA News* 33(20): 4.

Eastaugh, S. 1992. Hospital specialization and cost efficiency: Benefits of trimming product-lines. *Hospital and Health Services Administration* 37(2): 188–199.

Eastaugh, S. 1993. *Health economics: Efficiency, quality, and equity*. Westport, CT: Greenwood.

Eastaugh, S. 1997. Valuation of the benefits of risk-free blood. *International Journal of Technology Assessment in Health Care* 7(1): 51–59.

Eastaugh, S. 2000. Willingness-to-pay. *International Journal of Technology Assessment in Health Care* 16(2): 706–711.

Ferrucci, J. T. 2001. Colon cancer screening. *American Journal of Roentgenology* 177(5): 975–988.

Foote, A., and Erfurt, J. 1991. Benefit to cost ratio of work-site blood pressure control programs. *Journal of the American Medical Association* 265(10): 1283–1286.

Freymann, J. 1998. The public's health paradigm is shifting. *Journal of General Internal Medicine* 4(4): 319–329.

Fuchs, V. 1999. *The health economy.* Cambridge, MA: Harvard University Press.

Gold, M. 1999. *Cost-effectiveness in health and medicine.* Oxford: Oxford University Press.

Kissling, W. 2001. QM. *International Clinical Psychopharmacology.* 16 Suppl 3: S15–24.

Lightwood, J. 2000. Health and economic benefits of smoking cessation: Low birth weight. *Pediatrics* 104(6): 1312–1320.

Magid, D., Douglas, J., and Schwartz, J. 1996. Doxycycline compared with azithromycin for treating chlamydia. *Annals of Internal Medicine* 124(4): 389–399.

Mason, J. 1990. Why people are hospitalized. *Medical Care* 28(2): 147.

Meltzer, D. 2001. Medical cost-effectiveness analysis. *Journal of Health Economics* 20(1): 109–128.

Murray, C. J. L., and Lopez, A. D., (eds.). 2002. Executive summary, Volume 1. *The global burden of disease and injury.* Cambridge, MA: Harvard University Press.

Neumann, P. 2002. Are pharmaceuticals cost-effective? *Health Affairs* 21(5): 36–49.

O'Brien, B. 2002. Building uncertainty into cost-effectiveness rankings. *Medical Care* 28(5): 460–468.

Pigou, A. 1920. *The economics of welfare.* London: Macmillan.

Pollack, H. 2001. Cost-effectiveness of harm reduction in preventing Hepatitis C among injection drug users. *Medical Decision Making* 21(5) September–October.

Russell, L. 1995. *Is prevention better than cure?* Washington, DC: Brookings.

Shelton, R. 1999. Competitive contingencies in contracting. *Medical Care Review* 54(3): 571–579.

Shibuya, K., and Kunii, O. 2002. Application of cost-effectiveness analysis. *Japanese Journal of Public Health.* 47(12): 1018–1028.

Singer, M., and Younossi, Z. 2001. Cost-effectiveness of screening for Hepatitis. *Amercian Journal of Medicine* 111(8): 614–621.

Vijan, S. 2001. Which colon cancer screening test. *American Journal of Medicine* 111(8): 593–601.

Willian, A., and Lin, D. 2001. Incremental net benefit in randomized clinical trials. *Statistics in Medicine* 20(11): 1563–1574.

Chapter 7

Cost-Benefit Analysis: The Value of Life and Limb

An economist can tell you the prices of everything but the value of nothing.

– Will Rogers

American doctors should begin to build up a social ethic and behavioral practices that help them decide when medicine is bad medicine: not simply because it has absolutely no payoff or because it hurts the patient, but also because the costs are not justified by the marginal benefits. To do this we are going to have to develop and disseminate better information; some small fraction of what we now spend on healthcare could be better spent to determine limits.

– Peter Jennings, World News Tonight, December 11, 2001

▶ **Critical points in this chapter:**

- Shadow pricing
- Willingness-to-pay (WTP) and willingness-to-accept (WTA)
- Risk-assessment model

Modern medicine increasingly turns to intangible benefits for justification. Physicians are realizing the opportunity-cost implications of supporting more high-technology medicine for very rare diseases. The public also realizes that the health economy and the U.S. economy are not limitless. An opportunity for new transplant techniques will, by definition, prevent society from financing some other medical or social program. The objective of cost-benefit analysis (CBA) is to maximize net benefits (benefits minus costs, appropriately discounted).

There are fewer than a dozen topics in which careful CBA demonstrates that prevention works. The most successful preventive medicine programs in terms of dollar benefit are child immunization, smoking prevention, lead reduction, and water fluoridation. Immunization, for example, saves $8.50 in direct medical costs for every dollar spent on childhood immunization. Smoking prevention efforts over the past 30 years are estimated to have saved 33 million person-years of life. Lifetime medical expenses of smokers are put at $46,000 for men ($11,000 more than for nonsmoking men) and $68,000 for women ($13,000 more than for female nonsmokers) (Eastaugh 1993).

Lead poisoning has also been reduced as a major source of childhood disease. From 1988 to 1997 there has been a 58 percent reduction in presentation of children with high levels of lead in their blood (currently 700,000 children). The reason for this drop includes federal initiatives to end the use of lead in gasoline, lead solder in the seams of food cans, and lead-based paints in homes. It is estimated that reducing the level of environmental lead has improved cognitive function in children to the degree that it has increased lifetime earnings by $1,147 per mg/dL difference in blood-lead levels per child. And a cost analysis of removing lead from paint estimated a net benefit of $63 billion in reduced medical costs (Eastaugh 1993, 2002).

The decline in dental caries during the past 40 years as a result of water fluoridation has been such that half the children in the United States are caries-free. During an individual's lifetime, the dentistry costs of carious teeth might exceed $1,000, but water fluoridation costs about $0.12 per person per year.

To measure the benefit-cost of a specific program, it is necessary to express net value in fiscal terms so that the benefits can be weighed against the costs. The 1999 National Oceanic and Atmospheric Administration (NOAA), co-chaired by Nobel Prize winners Kenneth Arrow and Robert Solow, renewed interest in willingness-to-pay (WTP) methods for valuation of benefits. The NOAA issued new regulations promoting the use of contingent valuation studies for assessment of damage to natural resources. Eastaugh (2000) offered a contingent valuation study measuring WTP for treatment of patients with von Willebrand's disease. Median WTP for treatment of this disorder was $1,500 or $3,500, depending on how the initial bid was structured. Regression analysis shows that income, education, and a category rating scale for health status were significant in predicting WTP. The adjusted annual WTP was $2,178. WTP surveys may increasingly be useful for health technology assessment. Starting point bias in how the bids are structured must be recognized, and one can "de-bias" the results by random assignment of 10 percent of the sample to one-tenth of the starting bids. Therefore, one-tenth of the respondents would anchor an initial bid at $5,000, one-tenth at $4,500, etc., with one-tenth at the lowest initial bid of $500. There is need for further testing of the WTP and contingent valuation methods. The casual reader may incorrectly suggest that WTP is only needed for cost-benefit studies. WTP is also needed for cost-effectiveness studies to assess whether a cost per quality-adjusted life-year (QALY) is low or high, and whether a price per QALY is necessary.

In economic sectors in which competitive markets fail to exist, such as the healthcare or water resource sectors, CBA aims to do what supply and demand forces accomplish in competitive markets. The price system will not equalize marginal benefits and marginal costs if market failure exists. Another criterion of choice is maximization of the ratio of benefits to costs, discounting the numerator and denominator to present-day dollars. Alternative programs (or procedures or services) are then ranked by cost-benefit ratios, and the programs with the highest payoff ratios are selected until resources are exhausted or until the ratio equals one. This approach is equivalent to maximizing net present value in a budget constraint. A third, but outmoded, decision criterion is to support a project if the internal rate-of-return criterion exceeds the predetermined discount rate. The internal rate-of-return criterion can lead to different resource decisions from the net-present value criteria if programs are of different sizes or have varying time horizons.

If a technology is found to be the most cost-effective alternative, then the next question is whether it is cost-beneficial. For example, Acton (1973) first evaluated which of five program alternatives was most efficacious and which was most cost-effective in reducing deaths from heart attacks. He followed valuation of life and intangible benefits to assess whether the benefits made the program worth the costs to society. One obvious advantage of CBA is that it leads to a positive (go) or negative (no-go) net present value for the procedure being evaluated and does not require a cost-effectiveness cutoff level to decide whether a project can be completed within the resource constraints. However, many more complete cost-effectiveness analyses than CBA are performed, because intangible benefits pose difficulties with valuation, and the choice of a discount rate is simpler in cost-effectiveness evaluations (Eastaugh 2000).

If a technology is found to be cost-beneficial, the only question left is whether the risk is socially acceptable for public financing of the service. Society may have some preference for the social classes that are to face an unacceptable risk, even if it is known in advance that the total risk is insufficient to make the benefit-to-cost ratio less than one. Safety, as a measure by risk analysis, is a relative concept. No test or therapy that provides any benefit has ever been completely safe. Physicians, like all professionals, have learned to live comfortably with the reasonable notion that we must forgo some safety to achieve any net benefit.

The Merits of More Medicine

One may consider the efficiency of medical care in a broader context by taking output as the overall health of the nation rather than simply as days of care. Fuchs (1999) stated, "when the state of medical science and other health determining variables are held constant, the marginal contribution of medical care to health is very small in modern nations." In other words, one cannot simply add more physicians and hospitals and expect an equivalent improvement in health. Fuchs gives several reasons for this low marginal contribution. First, patients and physicians use more discretion when physicians are scarce — that is, patients seek medical care less often when it is difficult to obtain, and physicians tend to concentrate on those patients who need care the most. Second, many highly effective treatments, such as vaccinations, do not require the huge amounts of resources required by many generally less effective treatments such as heart transplants. Third, as medical care proliferates, iatrogenic disease becomes a big problem, exemplified by highly risky surgical interventions. Fourth, it is difficult to measure the output of medical care in terms of health, in that many factors other than medical care contribute to health, for example, nutrition, personal behavior (such as smoking), and environment.

Two basic truths seem apparent. First, society should not be oversold on prevention and health promotion as a strategy to slow (or reverse) the increase in national health expenditures. If health officials oversell their programs as a cost-saving vehicle, the inevitable disillusion will cause excessive additional cuts in public health programs (the backlash against such programs). Second, prevention might not save money, but such programs can often be justified in terms of worthwhile investment in improved quality of life. Keeping people happy is expensive, but in the minds of most citizens quality of life is something worth paying for.

Analogously, although many medical technologies might be cost-increasing, the public strongly supports them. Hip replacements are much more expensive than providing an elderly person with aspirin and a walker, but wouldn't most people want the quality-of-life mobility enhancment of a new hip? Some decisions by private insurance companies to include experimental therapy (such as bone marrow transplants for certain cancers) have to do with public relations. A 2002 public opinion poll listed lack of insurance coverage for experimental therapy as the number-two health problem. Cost-control was the number-one problem. There is an irony in this listing, because the number-two problem was a reaction by private insurance companies designed to combat the number-one problem (excessive costs). Medical costs are excessive for the population but not for identified individuals. Medical costs are too high, but if the money is spent on an identified person—a family member, or a nice person on the television set—then many political leaders (and followers) say, "Spend the money, even if therapy is untested and seldom successful," showing a basic difference between the individual perspective and the group perspective in making health policy. An individual with a medical condition spins the wheel of chance for treatment once or a few times, but a policy maker must play the leadership role of spinning the wheel for millions of unseen individuals and aggregate costs, risks, and benefits. Individual providers at the bedside take patients in groups of one and have a bias for action and treatment in the United States, an instinct dubbed "the rule of rescue."

Measurement of Intangible Benefits

Valuation is not a consideration in competitive markets because marginal benefit is assumed to be equal to price. However, when prices fail to exist (water resources) or price is deemed a defective measure of value (health services), an attempt is made to impute value or "shadow price." Shadow-price values can be imputed by asking individuals what they would be wiling to pay for relief from pain, grief, discomfort, and disfigurement. For example, if a year of life is valued by a willingness-to-pay measure of $28,000, and a woman would sacrifice a year of life to avoid losing her breast(s), this suggests a shadow price of $28,000 for a mastectomy (Acton 1973). In this situation Acton suggested that the additional costs for a few more drugs would bring the average shadow price, adding in the cost of grief and worry, to about $31,000. Often the analysts can only identify the need to shadow price an intangible benefit. For example, one intangible that is difficult to shadow price is the benefit of restored fertility capacity that follows a successful kidney transplant.

The shadow-price concept can also be applied to arrive at quality weights for adjusting the value of additional years of existence. One can use an analogous-disease approach to measure the willingness-to-pay value of escape from early manifestations of syphilis by the proxy disease psoriasis and from the last manifestations of syphilis by the proxy of terminal cancer cases. Direct data acquisition for "unstigmatized" medical conditions like cancer and psoriasis was more easily accomplished than working directly with syphilis victims. Economists must work with physicians to develop proxies and weighting schemes for capturing the multiplicity of dimensions of healthcare outputs. Inappropriate priorities might be set if survival probabilities are not integrated with quality-of-life factors.

A growing number of physician surveys have focused on diagnostic decisions. Two suggested approaches present evidence of how advanced a complex medical risk assessment has become. Some statisticians favored computing diagnostic probabilities by forming a control group that combines all the other diagnostic categories. This conceptual approach deals with the real-world problem in which patients might possess several diagnoses simultaneously. Alternatively, Harvard Professor Barbara McNeil (1995) suggested a decomposition in which each diagnostic group is separately treated with a baseline (normal) category as more appropriate in the absence of complex, equally critical, multiple-condition cases. Both approaches are equally valid, but the second approach might be more generalizable (and easier to explain to clinicians).

Individual physicians will not see a large number of instances of any specific rare condition in their practice but individual subjective opinion is useful. Most predictions contain an irreducible intuitive component. The intuitive threshold estimates of good clinicians contain useful information, even if they are biased in a predictable manner. Physicians often have more specific observations about the patient than can be evaluated by long-run statistical analysis. A physician friend of mine says subjective probabilities are not just the stuff we do before the statistician arrives.

The recent Harvard study offers a good assessment of quality-of-life considerations after coronary artery bypass surgery. Quality-of-life outcome measures include pain at rest, pain with minimal activity, pain with mild activity, pain with strenuous activity, and no pain. Quite predictably, a potential surgical patient places a higher utility value on no pain if he or she avoids exercise. A utility function to value outcomes was specified as a function of lifestyle and life expectancy. The data are highly subjective, but reliance on imperfect analysis provides more insights than analytical nihilism. A Rand Corporation analyst (Keeler 1999) reported that the lifetime subsidy by the average citizen to the sedentary lifestyle person is $1,900. Lifestyle choice is a critical issue for many medical decisions.

Cost-effectiveness analysis is more frequently completed when it is recognized that intangible benefits need only be estimated, not valued. Cost-effectiveness analysis requires only that all benefits be expressed in commensurate units so that the cost of achieving a specified level of benefits might be minimized. Cost-effectiveness analysis is not any simpler than cost-benefit analysis if multiple varieties of benefit are specified (in lives, years, or pain), except that in doing cost-benefit analysis one must also value intangible benefits.

Opinions on Risk Are Not Mathematical

We do not live in a safe world. Cutting one risk typically creates another. For example, if the Russian Republic were to convert the inferior 80 percent of its nuclear generating capacity to coal, over the next four decades the increased traffic from coal trucks, mining accidents, and pollution-induced disease would kill 1.8 million citizens. Many citizens fear nuclear power because unknown fears outrank familiar ones. Breathing or drinking vodka are things a person is familiar with. Consuming radiation from a nuclear accident or eating and drinking dioxin and polychlorinated biphenyls are not familiar experiences. The standard dosage of cosmic radiation at sea level is 2000 times more dangerous to human life than residing in a home 20 miles from a U.S. nuclear power plant. One round trip from New York to Los Angeles has 200 times more risk than living next to a U.S. power plant.

Risk-assessment models are typically simplistic. The U.S. Environmental Protection Agency (EPA) uses a linear standard risk-assessment model; for example, if 20 out of 1,000 rats get cancer from eating two bowls of dioxin a day, the EPA assumes that half a bowl per day would kill only 5 rats. Sliding down the dosage response curve, the EPA assumes that at 0.006 picograms per day one human in a million would die of cancer. However, the more accurate non-linear models report risk as a decaying exponential function, and government officials in Australia and Canada allow safe doses of dioxin at rates 300 to 500 times the U.S. threshold (standard). Moving to a dioxin standard that is 10 times tougher than the Australian threshold would save people in the United States $1.1 billion in cleanup costs, according to California analyst Dennis Paustenbach at McLaren Environmental Engineering. Formaldehyde has the classic "hockey-stick" dose response curve: It is safe until the dosage exceeds 10 parts per million, but at 15 parts per million 50 percent of the animals get cancer. The U.S. aversion to risk is not based on mathematics or common sense. Moderate content of PCBs in the daily diet has 90 to 98 percent less risk than eating two tablespoons of peanut butter per day. Peanut butter can contain mold-producing aflatoxin, but we do not ban peanut butter because it is an "all-American" food.

Avoiding a little risk can sometimes create a larger long-run risk. For example, 1960 data suggested that when whooping cough vaccine is given to one million children, 95 will have serious reactions (and a few will die). In the United Kingdom, parental pressure caused the National Health Service to withdraw the vaccination requirement. Whooping cough deaths soared, and the requirement was reinstated.

If small risks are often overlooked, large risks of catastrophic expense are highly unpredictable. Fuchs (1999) argued for treating catastrophic medical expenses like the demand for firefighting equipment. One does not stand outside a burning building and demand out-of-pocket payments to do the job of firefighting. Fuchs argued for collectivizing the burden of catastrophic medical expenses, either in the manner of the United Kingdom (free care) or through public insurance. Unfortunately, the U.S. catastrophic insurance bill that passed in 1988 was never implemented and was repealed in November

1989. We have Medicaid for a number of reasons: social equity, the realization that poverty erodes health status, and the knowledge that initial endowments of ill health can keep the poor in poverty.

Measurement of Willingness to Pay

The willingness-to-pay (WTP) principle in normative economics states that the value of something is simply measured by what people are willing to pay for it. Economists generally agree as a canon of faith that each person knows best his or her own interests. Cost-benefit analysis has to operate within the bounds of the individual's deficient information base, congenital optimism, or hypochondria, and to accept the expressed consumer preferences as a more relevant measure of benefits than the expert opinions of an educated elite. Experts' presumption that the public is unable to properly assess its interests may be foiled on two counts. First, the observation that people respond in a biased emotional fashion may be irrelevant for policy-making purposes if the bias is unsystematic, because the extremes will cancel each other. Second, one could make the same argument that the public cannot understand the technical details necessary to purchase calculators, cameras, cars, and stereos. The public does not have to understand all the details, as long as a free flow of information creates some small cadre of amateur consultant friends to help guide consumer choice behavior. Providers are improving their capacity to plug patient utilities into the decision analysis, survey researchers are more sensitive to elderly respondents, and development of a quality-of-well-being scale has even extended to acquired immune deficiency syndrome, arthritis, and cystic fibrosis (Eastaugh 1993).

The early WTP study most often cited was done on a sample of 100 Boston residents by Acton (1973). Acton's most publicized question involving public attitude toward risk reduction and heart attacks reads as follows:

Let's suppose that your doctor tells you that the odds are 99:1 against your having a heart attack. If you have the attack, the odds are 3:2 that you will live. The heart-attack program would mean that the odds are 4:1 that you live after a heart attack. How much are you willing to pay in taxes per year to have this heart-attack program which would cut your probability of dying from a heart attack in half (i.e., the chances are two per 1,000 you will have a heart attack and be saved by the program this year)?

The median response of $56 suggests that 200 people would chip in $28,000 to save the life of the group members in the coming year. The scenario is reasonable because most health programs are risk-reduction efforts. One might also note that a small change in the question, reducing the risk to 0.001, increases the median imputed value of a life saved to $43,000. Both of the two aforementioned questions emphasize the individual's situation. When Acton posed the question in probalistic terms, focusing on the 10,000 people living around a hypothetical respondent, the medical amounts were reduced by approximately 50 percent for equivalent risk-reduction levels.

The WTP approach can be criticized on the grounds that life is probably valued much higher for identified individuals than for members of a hypothetical population. Consumers and physicians tend to value identified individual lives more than statistical anonymous forgone lives, yet physicians are often criticized for placing a substantially higher value on identified individuals than society, with its limited resources, can afford to place on the average citizen.

The success of the WTP approach may be somewhat limited, because the methodology is fraught with problems. However, to paraphrase Winston Churchill, the approach is terrible unless you stop and compare it to the alternatives (your discounted wages are your worth). The WTP technique generates troublesome questions but not nearly so troublesome as assuming that a group is merely worth the amount its members can earn, or assuming that the political fiat is superior to economic measurements and evaluation. Those who favor political fiat over analysis may pause to count the number of times pork-barrel projects consumed resources that could have gone to education and public health.

Willingness to pay has an analogue called willingness to accept (WTA). We have asked the maximum amount that an individual is willing to pay for a program or service, but one could also ask the minimum amount that an individual is WTA to forgo the service or program. If future economic conditions prompt a contraction in the social welfare programs (such as New Zealand's did in 1992), more economists may be surveying the WTA issue. The divergence between WTP and WTA survey results may be an example of the Will Rogers rule: The public knows more about limits than the economists or the politicians. Consumers make mistakes because they are provided with imperfect information, so individuals' WTP sometimes will be underestimated (vaccinations) and other times overestimated (laetrile).

Valuation problems tend to plague many physician analysts. Subjective questions concerning valuation and effectiveness are largely a product of the values and occupation of the respondent. Young educated physicians might value a life at $10 million, but the average voter says $3.8 million. In the airline safety arena, the American Federal Aviation Administration valued a life at $4 million in 2002.

A central dilemma that economic analysts face is the unsubstantiated thesis of ever-improving technology—that is, the assumption that any evaluation will be obsolete when completed because medical science improves so fast. Yet another problem faced by the analyst attempting to do a prospective study is the refusal by physicians to pursue randomized controlled trials if any hint of inferiority among the alternatives can be raised as a red herring to prevent the experiment. Difficult decisions will need to be made more and more frequently concerning the allocation of scarce resources.

Hypothetical WTP Survey Techniques

One central research issue that Arrow (1978), Eastaugh (1993), and others have identified is the timing of a willingness-to-pay evaluation. The issue is whether respondents should be surveyed *ex ante* under a veil of ignorance concerning their future disease prognosis, or whether the survey should be done *ex post* on consumers with limited information concerning the prognosis for themselves or members of their socioeconomic group. The problem to be considered is one of response bias, since the *ex post* WTP responses will surely be highly inflated—that is, the answers will be high because the opportunity costs of those remaining dollars, given the shortened amount of time, are low to the individual about to die. Obviously, people who have a fatal disease may answer with a higher WTP response than the average citizen. However, with some chronic conditions this assertion appears to be false— that is, the general population overstates the burden of all illness more than the actual victims do. In other words, *ex post* WTP responses by victims should be adjusted downward because their WTP is based in part on their increased chances of fatality. For example, the WTP for fire protection by storeowners on the currently unaffected half of a burning city block would certainly be higher than the WTP of the average storeowner in the city. One could not plan a rational public service on the basis of the preferences of respondents undergoing a catastrophe.

Utility preferences need not be linear or independent of wealth. Risk aversion and risk preference can be observed to change over time in the same individual, or concurrently in the same person under different hypothetical situations. However, very few models of lifetime utility functions have suggested a link between individuals' earnings and their WTP for risk reduction (Bailey 1999). In valuing lifesaving activities for statistical lives, the wording of the question is a very important issue. Consider an example outside the context of health care: If the government wants to help U.S. companies with "incentives," 68 percent of the public favor the program; but if the government wants to provide "subsidies," then 60 percent are against it, even when the programs are exactly equivalent. Economists have discovered a number of elegant techniques to elicit consumer WTP preferences, but questionnaires have yet to be utilized for making substantial resource-allocation decisions. The most obvious practical problem with hypothetical WTP measures is that the questions could be considered too unreal to be treated seriously by some respondents. One way to avoid this problem is to present a plausible scenario that concerns a risky situation that has been reported on the news. The survey instruments also should be short. **Table 7-1** is an example of such a WTP questionnaire designed by the author.

As with all surveys, the best WTP questionnaires would avoid the use of value-loaded wording. For example, one would not like to ask the question "How much is your grandfather worth?" More reasonable answers will be given if 1,000 people facing a 0.002 chance of dying next year are asked, "How much would you pay to reduce your risk by 0.001?" In other words, the 1,000 individuals are willing to pay the total sum of their responses to save the one statistical life, not to be identified until next year. It is common knowledge that society places very high values on identifiable lives facing a high probability of death or disfigurement. The media frequently report a high level of psychic benefit accruing to the population following a heroic rescue attempt or an attempt to aid an identified child. For example, individuals seem to experience more psychic benefits as a group in supporting the identifiable March of Dimes Poster Child than in supporting Medicaid for multi-institutional charity hospitals. Arrow (1978) was the first to observe that individuals jump to help one six-year-old identified life, but few shed a tear or write a check if a tax shortfall causes facilities to deteriorate, thereby causing a barely perceptible statistical increase in preventable deaths.

Table 7-1 Willingness-to-Pay Preference Questionnaire

Please think for a few minutes about the following five questions and then answer them as best you can. There are no right or wrong answers.

1. By attending class today, you have been exposed to a rare, fatal form of Legionnaires disease. The disease has only been coming through the air vents for the past two hours. The probability that you have the disease is six in one thousand, (0.006). If you have the disease you will die a quick and painless death in one week. There is a cure for the disease that works 33.3% of the time, but it has to be taken now. We do not know how much it will cost. You must say now the most you would pay for this cure. If the cure ends up costing more, you won't get the medicine. If it costs less, you will pay the stated price, not the maximum you stated.

   How much will you pay? _____

2. Same story as above *except* the risk of getting the disease is now 0.002 and the cure works 100% of the time.

   How much will you pay for the cure? _____

3. Same story as question one *except* the risk of getting the disease, thanks to poor ventilation in the room, is now 0.250, and the newest cure works 100% of the time.

   How much will you pay for the cure now? _____

Assume for questions 4 and 5 that you have no prior exposure to the disease:

4. We are conducting experiments on the same disease for which we need subjects. A subject will just have to expose him or herself to the disease and risk a 0.002 chance of death. What is the minimum fee you would accept to become such a subject? _____

5. Same story as in question 4, *except* the risk of getting the disease is 0.250. What is the minimum fee you would now accept to become such a subject?

The most basic problem with WTP valuation is that the appropriate database to make estimates with any adequate range of confidence does not exist. Three subsidiary problems concern (1) lack of physician input in identification of the subtle side effects that should go into the analysis, (2) lack of appropriate behavioral-science survey instruments, and (3) lack of an appropriate populace to survey in many cases. As an example of this last problem, in doing a WTP analysis of benzene cleanup activities, how are people to be selected for the survey—workers heavily exposed to benzene, all workers, or all those who bear the burden of the cleanup? Should people with a given disease be sampled while hospitalized, or should potential candidates for the disease be surveyed, or should all citizens be queried? How is the survey instrument to be written if researchers are unsure whether benzene starts to bring about significant increases in the incidence of leukemia by x percent at prolonged exposure levels of 40 parts per million, 20 parts, or one part?

Another problem with WTP consumer-preference surveys is that the results may not be very stable over time. The public may express a lower WTP for avoiding a relatively higher and familiar risk (like automobile fatality) than for a lower but unfamiliar risk. Some individuals get alarmed over the prospect of a nuclear accident, yet tolerate much higher risks in their daily lives. Moreover, just because the public WTP to avoid uncertain risks is not in direct proportion to the nature and seriousness of some other risks does not mean that the public's preferences should be ignored.

Attempting to Improve Applications of the WTP Theory

The WTP preferences of healthy adults were tested on three groups of health professionals using the questionnaire in **Table 7–1**. The median results are presented in **Table 7–2** so as not to skew the results by overweighting the importance of the 4 to 8 percent of respondents who think that their life is worth somewhere between $1 billion and infinity. While there is nothing wrong with some people perceiving their value as infinite, it makes the mean response meaningless. The responses would undoubtedly vary across other professions. Within a given profession, the median value of life probably varies with age, sex, and income. However, even more interesting than median results across groups is the difference in response for a given individual. First, a pairwise comparison of questions one and two provides support for the certainty effect. Under the postulated certainty effect, WTP is less for a reduction in the probability from a small level (0.006) to an even smaller level (0.004) than WTP for an equivalent reduction in probability from 0.002 to zero. Of the three subject groups in **Table 7–2**, 60 to 75 percent of the respondents in each group gave a lower answer for question one relative to question two, even though the increase in survival probability was identical for each question.

Second, in **Table 7–2** pairwise comparisons of questions two and four and of questions three and five lend support for the so-called endowment effect. Of the 77 respondents, 51 percent of the sample reported fivefold higher responses for question five than for question three, and more dramatically, 92 percent of the sample reported fivefold higher responses for question four than for question two. This supports the assertion that people must be paid a substantially higher WTP bribe to risk their endowment of remaining life than to reacquire the same endowment they had already lost due to bad luck.

A third interesting result of pairwise response comparisons is the lack of clear evidence for the von Neumann-Morgenstern game-theory axiom that a person should pay more per unit of risk reduction the higher the absolute level of risk (Luce and Raiffa 1957). A respondent with no bequest motives who obeys the conventional axiom would be expected to pay more per

Table 7-2 Imputed Median Willingness-to-Pay (WTP) Value of a Life for Three Groups of Health Professionals

Sample	Second-Year Master's in Health Administration Students	Hospital Administrators in Summer HA Program	Third-Year Medical Students
Age range	22–34	30–55	24–31
Sample size	25	23	29
A. WTP to gain life expectancy (prolong survival)			
Q1, 0.333 cure rate $(0.006 \times .333)$[b]	$250,000[a] ($500)	$375,000 ($750)	$300,000 ($600)
Q2, perfect 1.0 cure rate (0.002×1.0)	$500,000 ($1,000)	$1,000,000 ($2,000)	$1,250,000 ($2,500)
Q3, perfect cure rate (0.25×1.0)	$600,000 ($150,000)	$1,000,000 ($250,000)	$1,400,000 ($350,000)
B. WTP to lose expected survival time by gambling as an experimental subject			
Q4 (exposure to a 0.002 risk)	$25 million ($50,000)	$50 million ($100,000)	$35 million ($70,000)
Q5 (exposure to a 0.25 risk)	$4 million ($1 million)	$6 million ($1.5 million)	$4 million ($1 million)

[a] Median imputed value of a life (in this case, the actual median response divided by the 0.006 x 0.333 risk).

[b] Actual response situation in parentheses.

0.0001 of risk reduction the higher the absolute risk (0.25 risk versus 0.002). This axiom is intuitive if one considers the case of how much one is willing to pay to remove one bullet in a 500-bullet gun. In the extreme case, a person pays the maximum to remove the 500th bullet and have some chance for life. Analogously, it seems plausible that a 0.002 risk reduction might mean more to a 70-year old with a 0.3 chance of dying than to a 40-year-old with a 0.01 chance of dying in the next year.

However, the scenario in **Table 7-1** may not be a fair test for this axiom, since the axiom might hold better in the high-risk section of the mortality probability curve (0.3-1.0) than in the flat of the curve (risks under 0.3). One could speculate that one of the reasons middle-aged hospital administrators in column two of **Table 7-2** have somewhat higher WTP responses than their administration-student counterparts is that they are older (and therefore more subject to risk and more in touch with their mortality). An interesting ethical issue raised by these data is whether the results should be interpreted literally. Should those who value their lives the most be saved? Under such a WTP criterion, the life of a hospital manager in his forties would be saved before the life of a health administration student in his twenties, in contrast to the discounted future earnings (DFE) higher relative valuation for the younger individual. Perhaps the WTP valuation is more indicative of the full value of individuals to their families, communities, and society.

In addition to valuing life, consumer-preference surveys can assist in the selection of an optimum therapy. Most progressive physicians have recognized, at least in theory, that treatment decisions should attempt to incorporate patient values into the decision. However, most clinicians are untrained in the disciplines of economics and behavioral decision theory and cannot scientifically survey patient preferences. The sensitive clinician attempts a "quick-and-dirty" approach to get some handle on patient values by asking, "Would you rather have short-term certain survival for, say, five years or gamble on an operation that has a low probability of death but offers an additional 20 years of life expectancy?" Physicians are increasingly coming to respect the value of asking such questions.

Targets to Study

Somewhere between 20 and 30 percent of new treatments might be prime candidates for cost-benefit studies to decide whether the benefits are worth the costs to society. A smaller percentage of established therapies might also deserve the same cost-benefit analysis. The policy issue is seldom one of cost-beneficial yes or no, but rather an issue of frequency. Obviously, if clinicians start treating more nonserious cases, the frequency of treatment skyrockets. For example, prophylactically treating slightly symptomatic conditions will dramatically decrease the cost-benefit ratio. One of the intangible benefits of doing an economic evaluation is that it may suggest to the medical community the benefits of decreasing overutilization (unnecessary care). It is good for the patient and lowers cost if we increase the degree of discrimination by improving clinical interpretation skills. This policy is good medicine and good economics. For example, decreasing the unnecessary removal rate of normal appendices can lead to slightly lower rates of perforation and other complications.

Frequently, the economic analyst is asked to perform a cost-benefit evaluation on a questionable treatment or a mandatory screening program. For example, the cost-benefit study of mandatory premarital rubella antibody screening dampened the initial enthusiasm for the program. In some cases the evaluators need only look at the touted benefits in a more scientific fashion, with a randomized controlled trial, to conclude that the treatment has zero benefits. For example, the study finding that hyperbaric oxygen provided no benefits for the elderly eliminated enthusiasm for the treatment that had been stimulated by an unscientific study published in a nationally acclaimed journal. The easy acceptance of a faulty but profitable treatment seems to be rather unprofessional if one views medicine as a science. For example, the time lag between general acceptance and proof of zero benefits was seven years in the case of gastric freezing as a cure for ulcers (1962 to 1969) and five years for internal mammary artery ligation surgery, from 1956 to 1961 (Eastaugh 1993).

Health education, which has been assailed by skeptics, is a popular current example of a new approach to improving the effectiveness of medical care. **Table 7–3** presents the results of a limited benefit-cost comparison of four approaches to increasing patient compliance to antihypertensive medications. The study sample included 402 patients randomly assigned to experimental and control groups (Eastaugh 1993). The emphasis of the study concerned the efficacy of utilizing a triage process, whereby patients were subdivided into groups more predisposed to benefit from a given health education approach. The benefits of the triage method for achieving medication compliance clearly outweigh the cost only in the case of the highly depressed patients (24.3 percent of the sample), as defined by responses to five of the seven items used in the depression-scale questionnaire. The benefit-to-cost ratio for this group (2:2) compares favorably with the average benefit-to-cost ratio of 1:24 for hypertension control for persons in the age range of 35 to 65 (option 4). In other words, triaging only the 24 percent highly depressed sub-population and providing family-member reinforcement is more cost-beneficial than giving everyone the special health education intervention. Previous studies demonstrating a cost-benefit ratio in the 1:1 to 1:3 range may not stand the test of time in claiming a statistically significant ratio above the 1:0 level when applied to a larger population or to a nonexperimental population that will be less susceptible to the Hawthorne effect. Individuals are known to change their behavior more dramatically under experimental conditions due to the mere fact of being under concerned observation. Recent work supports this approach (McAlister 2002).

In summary, the willingness-to-pay approach to cost-benefit analysis is one elixir that will not make decision making any easier, but at least the process could increase consumer input and illuminate the assumptions that currently prevail. One liberal cynic concluded that the "measurements" are

Table 7–3 Simple Benefit-to-Cost Comparisons of Triage Options versus the Option Not to Triage in Achieving Improved Medication Compliance among Hypertensives

Option	Triage	Type of Patient	IHC[a]	Education Intervention(s)	Cost-Benefit Ratio
1	Yes	High Level of Depression	65–26	Family Reinforcement (FR)	2.20[b]
2	Yes	Medium Level of Depression	58–33	FR + Message Clarification	1.15
3	Yes	No Depression	65–35	FR + Message Clarification	1.33
4	No	All Patients	60–32	FR + Message Clarification	1.24

[a] IHC = Increase in number of high compliers with treatment versus control per 100 patients.

[b] Only option 1 has a significantly better ratio for triaging in comparison to not triaging.

better described as illustrations of methodology than as serious attempts to derive representative answers. The true role of cost-benefit valuation of life resides somewhere between the pessimism of the cynic and the naïve optimism of many in the economics profession. Analysis becomes critical as the cost of new biomedical technology skyrockets beyond any recent projections.

▶ **Summary Points:**

- CBA can substitute for supply and demand forces in noncompetitive markets.

- Because unknown fears outrank familiar fears, they are often overinflated.

- WTP is the normative economics principle that states that the value of something is measured by what people are willing to pay for it.

Research and Discussion Questions:

- Does the decision to use CBA change depending on who is paying (for example, self, third-party payer, or taxpayer)?

- Will the use of CBA help public health compete for resources with other sectors (such as defense)?

References

Acton, J. 1973. *Evaluating public programs to save lives: The case of heart attacks.* Rand Corporation Report R-950-RC. Santa Monica, CA: Rand Corporation.

American Medical Association. 2002. *Cost-effective medical care.* Chicago: Resident Physicians Section, American Medical Association.

Arrow, K. 1978. Risk allocation and information: Some recent theoretical developments. *Geneva Papers on Risk and Insurance, Conference Proceedings* 8:1, Geneva, Switzerland.

Bailey, M. 1999. *Measuring the benefits of life-saving*. Washington, DC: American Enterprise Institute.

Blomquist, G. 1999. Value of life saving: Implications of consumption activity. *Journal of Political Economy* 879(3): 540–558.

Blumenschein, K. 2002. Hypothetical versus real willingness to pay. *Journal of Health Economics* 20(3): 441–457.

Donaldson, C. 2001. Eliciting patients' values by use of 'willingness to pay'. *Health Expectations* 4(3): 180–188.

Eastaugh, S. 1993. *Health economics: Efficiency, quality, and equity*. Westport, CT: Greenwood.

Eastaugh, S. 2000. Willingness to pay in treatment. *International Journal of Technology Assessment in Health Care* 16(2): 706–711.

Fuchs, V. 1999. *The health economy*. Cambridge, MA: Harvard University Press.

Keeler, E. 1999. The external cost of a sedentary lifestyle. *American Journal of Public Health* 79(8): 975–981.

Luce, R., and Raiffa, H. 1957. *Games and decisions*. New York: Wiley.

McAlister, F. 2002. Management of hypertension. *American Journal of Cardiology* 17(5): 543–559.

McNeil, B. 1995. Responses to prospective payment. *Medical Decision Making* 5(1): 15–21.

National Oceanic and Atmospheric Administration. 1999. Natural resource damage assessments: Proposed rules. *Federal Register* 59062-91.

Tufts Center for the Study of Drug Development. 2002. *Outlook 2002*. Boston: Tufts University.

Viscusi, K. 1999. *Fatal trade-offs*. New York: Oxford Press.

Chapter 8

Pricing and Market Strategy Planning

Marketing involves the identification and satisfaction of consumer needs. Marketing activity should not be regarded as an expensive, speculative drain on the resources, but rather as a planning process that can guide the allocation of these resources toward a more effective result.

– Philip Kotler

People do not care how much you know until they know how much you care. Quality work does not always mean quality service.

– David H. Maister

▶ **Critical points in this chapter:**

- Health marketing, market segment, social marketing, and demarketing

- Catchment area

- Strategic analysis

Marketing is defined operationally as the set of activities designed to satisfy consumer needs and wants, including delivery, advertising, selling, and pricing. In the past, providers seldom considered measuring and satisfying consumer needs and wants. The approach was usually linked to quality: "Buy our product (for example, open heart surgery) or our service (for example, maternity and pediatrics) and you'll have a better chance at survival, thanks to our experienced staff." Pressure on health-service providers to control costs and optimize service has stimulated interest in health marketing activities. Marketing can help firms provide better service and be more responsive to consumers' demands. Marketing improves consumer satisfaction.

Quality sells the service. In one case, the publication of differential survival rate statistics at two institutions caused the closing of the higher-mortality suburban service and the slight expansion of the previously under-utilized urban hospital's service, much to the delight of the medical school officials who needed additional patients for the education of their students and residents. Administrators who are slow to react will continue to adopt a plodder strategy to pursue "quiet" competition—for example, accepting slight changes in customer mix as a *fait accompli* that should not result in open predatory reaction among hospitals on the theory that no single competitor is strong enough to disturb the balance.

Many health professionals balk at the term *marketing* because it runs counter to their feeling that health care is special and is not to be treated like a marketable commodity or service. In fact, marketing is seldom understood by large segments of the healthcare industry, which has been criticized for having a static, limited-scope, product orientation that does not provide the consumer with the necessary information concerning the product (health services). Marketing need not involve superfluous treatments and promotional gimmicks. Real health marketing involves evaluation of consumer preference and better service delivery, with advertising playing a minor role. If health marketing is viewed in this light, the medical staff can become the service-line development group, and health maintenance organizations (HMOs) or preferred provider organizations (PPOs) can be viewed as wholesale buyers. A professional can remain a professional while adopting some of the techniques of the market. No egregious harm will be done to the professional practice of medicine if we trade a philosophy of paternalism for consumer sensitivity. The president of the Wisconsin Medical Society summarized this obvious point during his 2002 inaugural address: "Marketing is an admonition to do right by your patient; virtue is a companion of competition."

Marketing and the Nonprofit Ethos

Some nonprofit managers have the misconception that marketing is simply selling a specific product. Selling is only one aspect of the marketing process. Marketing is a process of assessing consumer wants by changing the product or the distribution channels but not a process always designed to increase demand. Marketing is meeting the needs of people and involves managing demand and improving consumer satisfaction. For example, a public utility may decide to decrease (demarket) demand for its product in the name of energy conservation. The American Marketing Association (AMA) in fact has given its highest award to four studies that have resulted in socially desirable declines in sales of a precious commodity: energy resources. In the health sector, quality and price are the attributes being marketed.

In the case of health care, a given institution or business coalition may wish to demarket nursing home care while promoting home care, or demarket inpatient surgical or psychiatric care to promote the substitute product: ambulatory care. One cold postulate is that the invisible hand and competitive pressures might induce a given firm (for example, a nursing home) to demarket its core product to some extent to promote substitute products (such as home health care). However, due to institutional inertia, the invisible hand often turns out to be all thumbs; nursing homes might prefer to maintain the status quo rather than face charges of predatory marketing behavior that pulls demand away from their neighbors. Nursing homes, hospitals, and HMOs need to observe the marketplace, experiment, and generate tangible revenue sources, discover a new niche, and remarket with more effective strategic plans.

Healthcare marketing that is designed to communicate with the public and to motivate it to consume has some unique problems in health service delivery. First, consumers frequently remember their use of health services in negative terms; pain is often a deterrent to seeking medical care. Second, even if physicians make the major consumption decisions, health managers need to regard patients as customers and potential sources of return business or word-of-mouth advertising. If the emphasis of the marketing program is to redirect the locus of care to less costly sites and to improve patient education and compliance, society will benefit.

Hospital marketing has risen steadily in popularity. Typically, the marketing budget was equal to 3.6 percent of total revenue or 14.8 percent of hospital profit in 2002. HMOs spend a little bit more on marketing. Are these figures high in normative terms? Computer stores and department stores spend a little bit more, and hotels and women's apparel shops spend a little bit less (American Hospital Association 2002). The more relevant question is what the investment is buying. Any marketing cycle should end with an evaluation of what worked and what was the cost benefit or return on investment.

No market segment is too small to overlook. For example, one Miami hospital closed 16 beds and opened a "Sniffles and Sneezes" center-day care for sick children. Working parents can leave their children for 12 hours for $30 and receive a staff pediatrician's exam for an additional $20. To minimize nursing staff reductions, nurses in the 200-bed hospital have been making "missionary marketing calls" at day care centers. Marketing in this case is giving the public a better service at more flexible hours and a lower cost. Alternatively, the superior or best hospitals can try the differentiation strategy of Nordstrom and, like the Mayo Clinic, sell premium quality at a premium price.

Marketing tailored to health care, often called *social marketing*, implies a service orientation (better health)—not a product orientation (more patient bed-days). The smart administrator considers diversification away from inpatient care to other services. The three major rationales for diversification are (1) to acquire profit-making services (such as laboratory, radiology, alcohol rehabilitation care, and inhalation therapy); (2) to increase production volume and consequently decrease unit costs by contracting with other firms to supply services (such as laboratory, laundry, and food services); and (3) to develop a feeder system into the mothership core business. Further, the product portfolio of the hospital or HMO can be diversified to include health promotion and health education activities designed to improve patient compliance. The pursuit of patient compliance and health education is a major growth area in our healthcare system. One unquestioned benefit of health marketing activities is the resulting increased sensitivity to consumer needs for amenities, information, and emotional support. Some fear that marketing health care as a commodity will ultimately demean it. In transplanting marketing techniques from the business sector, one must be careful to avoid hucksterism while pursuing competitive consumerism.

Marketing activities aimed at potential healthcare consumers are necessary for a number of reasons. First, people concerned with day-to-day living often underestimate the value of early diagnosis and preventive medicine and have to be reminded of the potential benefits of screening activities. Second, the daily news accounts of malpractice suits and second-opinion surgery studies have shaken public faith in the medical establishment. Although some skepticism is in order, unbridled skepticism can keep some people away from the healthcare system for too long. Some healthcare providers can regain public trust through customer-preference analysis and integrated market planning. For example, one HMO performed a market survey of patient preferences and concluded that people want to see a triage nurse or physician within minutes of their arrival.

Strategic Analysis

Marketing is a multistage process with many potential audiences. A hospital's marketing audience might include patients and consumers, physicians as direct customers of the institution, and physicians as middlemen. The first stage in any marketing program is the assessment of market structure, including the distinctive role the facility plays in meeting consumer demand in various market segments (marketing positioning). The existing and potential catchment area and service mix should be identified. The attractiveness and specificity of the service or product line also must be defined (market definition). The analyst should partition the market into fairly homogeneous segments, any one of which can be expanded as a primary target market with a marketing strategy tailored to it. This concept of market segmentation might imply multiple marketing efforts or marketing to only one segment area. For example, mental health has six market segments (Stone, Warren, and Stevens 1998).

The second stage in the typical marketing effort involves analysis of consumer tastes and attributes. The provider of service should assess the intensity of demand for various products, perceptions of specific services and of the entire facility, and the causal link between consumer behavior and image. Consumer satisfaction and multiattribute consumer preferences should be determined through conjoint measurement techniques (Akaah 1998, Wind and Spitz 1996). The next three stages in building a marketing approach involve assessment of the product line, presentation of differential advantages relative to the competition, and development of the initial marketing program design (integrated market plan).

Management must consider the following seven stages in evaluation and periodic reexamination before making decisions about promotion, pricing, product, and place (location):

1. *Market catchment area definition*—demographic and geographic areas that are served or could be served.

2. *Analysis of preferences of physicians*—physicians' requirements and desires for a healthcare facility.

3. *Analysis of preferences of patients as customers*—needs that potential patients seek to have fulfilled in a facility.

4. *Product-definition objectives*—assessment of the present and future product lines of the health facility.

5. *Differential advantages marketing*—defining the services and reputation that are marketable to advance facility prestige in the eyes of customers (physicians and potential patients), including providing different messages to different customers or regulatory agencies to best project the facility image.

6. *Integrated market planning and promotion*—coordinating actions resulting from assessment in Stages 1 to 5. For example, we might conclude that integration among uncoordinated hospital departments is necessary to achieve a reliable and more efficient organization. The forthcoming management ideas are often quite simple. For example, one idea is to place nuclear medicine next to the X-ray department so that patient transporters in each department can assist the others during peak demand periods. Efficient transportation and scheduling can significantly contain costs and increase consumer perception of the quality of the institution. The marketing program promotes the message to the two basic customer groups: consumers and physicians.

7. *Market activity evaluation*—assessing the costs and benefits of marketing activities and taking timely corrective action when necessary. Management and trustees must ultimately decide whether the long-run intangible benefits and discounted cash flows justify reorganizing priorities.

Market Catchment Area: Stage 1

The first stage, market catchment area definition, is a familiar process for most healthcare facilities. Hospitals have been performing this element of the marketing process under the title of "needs assessment" for more than 30 years. However, certain elements of the marketing function, such as informing the public of the availability of new services and departments, are tasks that most administrators fail to perform effectively.

Physician Customer Market Survey: Stage 2

In performing a physician customer market survey (Stage 2), the HMO or hospital must make basic decisions about the preferences it should weigh highest. If the objective function of the hospital is to maximize the patient census, then it should give highest priority to the preferences of the physicians who admit the largest numbers of patients: general surgeons and family practitioners. If the objective function is to operate the hospital as a feeder system for the hospital-based specialists, then general surgeons who require less assistance from these specialists would have a lower priority relative to internists and other specialists. Because HMOs need primary care physicians, this valuation would give them the highest weight.

Identifying Consumer Preferences: Stage 3

Historically, health planners have completed market research of consumer preferences (Stage 3). Consumers value access, but they also value amenities such as well-decorated rooms, good food, and friendly personnel. Ease of exit can also help provide the patient with an overall positive impression of the institution. A courtesy discharge policy that avoids stops at the accounts receivable department on the final day of hospitalization is one potential approach.

Physician Bonding: Don't Stop at Stage 3

Some analysts tailor the marketing approach to the physician as the ultimate client, whereas others emphasize studying the preferences of consumers. A dual approach of studying both groups is warranted. The smart HMO uses a two-pronged approach. One HMO did a market survey of consumer preferences by telephone and found that more than one-third of the families did not have a physician. The HMO published an ad in the paper stating: "If you need help finding a doctor, fill out this coupon." The consumers' referral coupons were provided only to the physicians affiliated with the HMO. As a result of the coupon referral program, the patient volume increased by 8.1 percent. The HMO assessed physician preferences by asking affiliated physicians and potential new physicians how the HMO might satisfy its physicians' needs.

Physician bonding—making medical staffs more connected to their institutions (hospitals or HMOs)—goes well beyond the old simple strategy of having an annual physician recognition dinner. Programs to enhance physician bonding to their hospital are of four basic types: (1) physician income production (joint ventures, leasing companies); (2) referral production (consumer phone referrals, appointment tracking, patient-transportation systems, and voice mail systems between physicians); (3) patient retention (patient satisfaction tracking, market research); and (4) office support systems (practice management, computer networks, bill-collection services, malpractice coverage, fax machines, and subsidized office space). Certain physicians will return the favor by acting as "product champions" and will force a reluctant board to finance their specialized product lines. The product champion can also assist in the formalized relationships necessary to build a referral system (Bruce 2002, Ecinosa 2002).

Product-Line Thinking: Stages 4 and 5

A facility should look at the product-market competencies of neighboring facilities in the process of assessing internal product-definition objectives (Stage 4). Some product lines may need to be expanded, contracted, or phased out of existence. The decisions are seldom simple. For example, maternity and emergency-room services are rarely cost-beneficial unless offsetting revenue from estimated return business and ancillary services are included. If diversification of the product line seems in order, the decision should be made in consultation with the four internal publics (trustees, physicians, volunteers, and employees) and the numerous external publics (bankers, unaffiliated physicians, philanthropists, suppliers, consumers, and regulators).

Targeting more resources to certain segments of the market in which one has a differential advantage (Stage 5) and contracting resources from other segments can reap a larger market share for facilities that previously provided a whole range of services. In the recent era of managed care carving out contracts for special services, the risk of falling behind has never been so great.

Stage 5, differential advantages marketing, should involve an honest institutional self-assessment. Poor-quality "centers of nonexcellence" must be differentiated from the ego requirements of some physicians and manage to "offer all things for all diagnosis-related groups (DRG)"—even if services are done poorly. For a hospital to underspecialize is to potentially renege on its commitment to quality and economy. To discard certain services does not deny patients access when other hospitals already offer those services. Unfortunately, petty ego-turf considerations among medical staff, managers, and trustees can slow the rate at which service-line specialization occurs.

Integrated Market Planning and Promotion: Stage 6

Stage 6, integrated market planning, includes more than the tactical in institutional decision making. After the hospital has decided on a course of action, it must inform the public, HMO, nursing home, and/or physician community via a promotional campaign. The healthcare institution must extol the virtues of its new market position plan in terms of optimal cost, service, and quality patient care. The promotional campaign should not tell consumers things that they already know (for example, that the emergency room is open 24 hours a day). Promotion should establish in the consumer's mind a point of difference between the institution and the competition. The desired target audience plus the message will determine the media of choice (magazines, newspapers, billboards, radio, television, or directories). The marketing plan should also be consumer-directed. For example, patients at the Cleveland Clinic are informed that if their physician is more than 15 minutes late, the bill gets cut in half. The message to the public is clear: We run an efficient system that respects consumers' time and money. The quality of amenities in a good hospital should not be different from the quality of amenities at a good hotel. Teaching hospitals should inform potential patients that they do not have to be referred to receive services (Town and Vistnes 2002).

If the nursing home continues to promote only general messages about "quality care," its consumer image will become indistinguishable from that of the competition. Nursing homes that promote certain special areas of excellence often improve utilization across a number of service lines, such as stroke units or Alzheimer's disease units. Facilities distinguishing their institutional comparative advantages in the minds of the consumers benefit from a halo effect across a range of services (home care).

Consumers shop more today, with a growing group of shoppers who select a new hospital or physician rather than return to the same provider, a point that institutions should capitalize on. Patients also exercise more power in selecting the services that will be purchased. Many hospitals and nursing homes educate employees in better guest relations, a point that should be included in marketing communications to customers. Highlight the areas in which standards will be met. For example, promise that nurses will respond to the call bell within 30 seconds, that food will be served hot, and that people will knock before entering a patient's room. All of these promises are merely applications of the Golden Rule: Treat the patient as you would wish to be treated. Comparison shoppers might represent a minor fraction of the institution's potential patient mix, but institutions need every possible patient (Rovinsky 2002).

Also, a marketing-promotion campaign should communicate to all employees as well as to consumers. The most irrational management decision would be to invest millions to develop a new program and then to cut the promotional campaign designed to tell the community what has been done for it without assuring that staff is fully prepared and on board with the new service standards. Some administrators might wince at investing $450,000 per 100 beds per year on marketing activities, but the greater danger comes from underinvestment.

Quality and Unit Cost by Service Product Line

Two findings that economists and physicians accept as valid lead to a third supposition of interest to both groups. First, economies of scale exist. Second, unit cost falls as volume increases. This second finding has been confirmed in numerous studies tracking post-hospital and hospital mortality and morbidity (Flood, Scott, and Ewy 1984, Eastaugh 1992, Wolfe, Roi, Flora, and Cornell 1983). The in-practice, high-volume providers do the best-quality work, and low-volume, out-of-practice providers perform poorly. Poor-quality providers receive fewer referrals and therefore cannot increase volume. **Figure 8-1** outlines both laws of scale-efficiency and quality enhancement. Part A of **Figure 8-1** is the well-known law of economies of scale. Unit cost (U) declines with a larger scale of output. In part B of **Figure 8-1**, open-heart surgery provides a classic example of curve A, cholecystectomy provides an example of curve B, and transurethral prostate resections provide an example of curve *C*. These operations (curve *C*) flatten out at a relatively low scale of 50 cases. These scale effects will shift with time and technology.

The result in part C of **Figure 8-1** is that good medicine is also good economics, with higher volume yielding better quality and lower unit costs. That facilities with lower unit costs (exclusive of their other special missions such as teaching or indigent care) also have better outcomes might seem counterintuitive, but "economies running hand-in-hand with quality" are prevalent in the market for most ordinary consumer goods. One does not need to own a Porsche to know that higher initial expense often buys higher rates of malfunction. Conversely, Whirlpool washing machines are substantially cheaper and of higher quality than General Electric.

Hospitals desiring to maximize quality might consider specialization, making fewer departments with more volume per department (and hopefully more quality per product line). Specialization of product line does not always

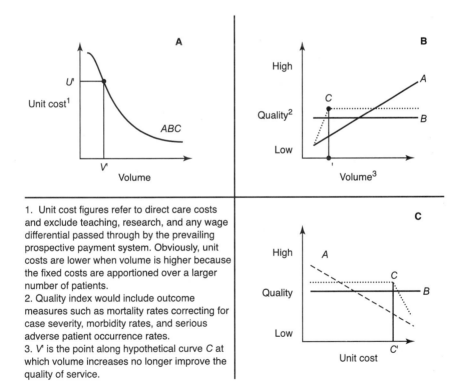

1. Unit cost figures refer to direct care costs and exclude teaching, research, and any wage differential passed through by the prevailing prospective payment system. Obviously, unit costs are lower when volume is higher because the fixed costs are apportioned over a larger number of patients.

2. Quality index would include outcome measures such as mortality rates correcting for case severity, morbidity rates, and serious adverse patient occurrence rates.

3. *V'* is the point along hypothetical curve *C* at which volume increases no longer improve the quality of service.

▲ FIGURE 8–1 Three Potential Relationships between Hospital Service Quality, Volume, and Unit Cost occur, especially in two-hospital towns with equal financial strength and equally matched medical staffs. For example, one town has a Catholic hospital in a medical arms race with a 400-bed community hospital. Each tries to maintain a prenatal center and a cardiovascular team, while the local newspaper editor argues for consolidation of the duplicated $5.1 million helicopter service and specialization of certain product lines. One hospital is better in prenatal care, whereas the other is better in cardiovascular surgery. Dysfunctional competition prevents cost control and quality enhancement. Consequently, C. Everett Koop, in his public television series, is correct in his assertion that two-hospital towns share higher costs than one-hospital towns. Increasing the HMO market share from 10 percent to 50 percent would create the incentive to close beds, cut costs, and merge the two hospitals.

Cost and Quality Scale Effects

It should be noted that scale is measured by the volume of the product-line output, not by the capacity of the total institution. Thus a large hospital with many product lines might not have enough volume to achieve sufficient scale economies, whereas each line in a smaller, more specialized hospital might achieve good volume. For instance, an 800-bed hospital offering 460 DRGs and 80 basic product lines with a net volume of 800 admissions per week would have an average scale of 10 admissions per product line. A 400-bed hospital offering 250 DRGs and 25 basic product lines might have a net volume of 500 admissions per week, or an average scale of 20 admissions per product line. The smaller hospital has double the scale per product line compared to the 800-bed facility. Scale by product line, not scale of the hospital, is the key to good medicine and economics.

One should ask whether high-volume providers make for better provider performance (the practice-makes-perfect hypothesis) or whether the better providers get more referrals and thus more volume (the best-get-more-business hypothesis). The mix of both explanations depends on the clinical condition. For some conditions, the explanation that practice makes for better performance dominates (cholecystectomy, stomach surgery, acute myocardial infarction), whereas for other conditions the explanation of selective referral is more important (cardiac bypass grafts, prostatectomy, femur fracture). Cause and effect on the quality issue are difficult to establish, given two alternative explanations: Volume is too low to maintain sufficient quality (if some hospitals closed the service, market share and volume would increase for those keeping this product line), or low-quality providers discourage referrals and keep the volume low. Irrespective of the cause-and-effect dynamic, specialization is associated with maintaining or enhancing the quality of patient care. Specialization allows nurses and physicians to develop more expertise with respect to a specific category of patients.

Strategic Product-Line Groupings (SPGs)

Hospitals need two forms of increased management control. First, line management strives for better efficiency management in the production of intermediate services, such as nursing care or lab tests. The second crucial stage of management control is effectiveness management, including utilization review and quality assurance. The goal is to enhance quality and avoid overtreating patients with costly intermediate services. From an ethical and economic viewpoint, what ultimately counts is the final product: a patient treated and returned to good health. It does little good to focus only on the intermediate components of the hospital-service production function (**Figure 8-2**). What matters from an analytical viewpoint is effectiveness and efficiency within clusters of "peer" (like) final products or SPGs. Knowing what it costs to start, expand, contract, or close an SPG is important.

Trustees and managers have a responsibility to ask what it costs to open, expand, trim, or close a given SPG, a cluster of similar DRGs performed by an identified subset of the medical staff. Consequently, profitability and growth opportunity must be determined periodically. Unlike in the business world, a hospital's service product line cannot sponsor its own autonomous marketing division. Service lines in the hospital sector are clearly more interconnected and interdependent in the provision of inpatient care. Insufficient realization of this interdependency is what caused zero-based budgeting to fail.

The definition of SPGs should be institution-specific and should involve strong input from medical staff. Allowing each hospital's medical staff to decide on their SPGs offers the following three advantages: (1) identifying SPGs would be a first step in effecting change in the organization, (2) physician partners in strategic financial planning must contribute in defining the unit of analysis if they are to gain some sense of ownership and defend the plan, and (3) medical practice habits vary considerably across regions. For a given SPG, the relevant type of physician to include in the process may vary.

For example, in one northeastern city, 85 percent of the service line of endoscopy is controlled (performed) by gastroenterologists. However, in one southern city the market share of endoscopy is evenly divided among general surgeons (35 percent), internists (35 percent), and gastroenterologists (30 percent), respectively. In the case of one western hospital, 75 percent of endoscopy is controlled by internists. Suggested changes in the medical staff composition or marketing of an SPG will have to take into account local habits and physician supply characteristics.

SPGs are based on physician peer-grouping criteria for two reasons. First, SPGs have interconnected referral patterns that require a critical mass of certain cases to make the line economically viable for all parties concerned. Second, physicians are the most important input in the delivery of patient care. SPGs are operationally useful in making physician recruitment and retention decisions. If the hospital is aggressively growing in a given area, either because the market potential is good or because profitability is high, it could experience a high return on investment in attracting or keeping clinicians in that SPG. Medical staff revenue projections by area are critical in planning.

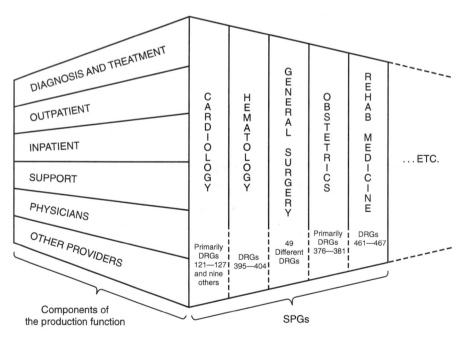

▲ FIGURE 8–2 Vertical Cost Accounting of Final Products and SPGs of DRGs

In evaluating profitability versus market opportunity potential, decision making often becomes more of an art than a management science. The language can often get quite crass, especially in the area of marketing. For example, a chief executive officer with a short-term focus might be reluctant to jettison two mediocre clinicians if they currently have fair to average profitability, even if they are "maxed out" (lack volume growth potential). To use the language of the American Marketing Association, these two physicians offering the SPG would be called cash cows because of their short-term profitability. The better hospital CEO would take the long-run perspective, consider life-cycle costing, and concentrate on safeguarding the reputation of the institution. If one factors in the malpractice expense of mediocre performers, a big loss in the courts could more than wipe out 10 years of cash-cow profits. Profitability should include some life-cycle costing adjustment for malpractice risk and facility reputation risk.

Closing an SPG will not be an easy political task because pride and egos are likely to interfere. Clinicians invest three to nine years of their lives in graduate medical training to specialize in an SPG. Even if the market for the service is saturated, they feel justified in prompting the hospital to continue offering the uneconomical SPG. Physicians must realize their part in the process. If they wish to save an SPG, they must do a better job of effectiveness management. However, hospital leaders should not feel obligated to continue providing an SPG because its providers want them to. Currently, many underutilized SPGs are incapable of achieving economies of scale or volumes sufficient to support quality care. Both efficiency and effectiveness impart net profitability, as does the payer mix. It is impossible to run a hospital or an ambulatory center if too many SPGs lose money. Hospitals will have to pick and choose among SPGs rather than choose between high- and low-cost patients. Hospitals will also face more physician unions that react with the SPG preferences of their membership (Romano 2002).

Specialization and Regionalization

Hospital trustees and managers are socially responsible individuals. One would predict, therefore, that they would choose to drop services (SPGs) rather than lower the quality of service. But the most unprofitable patients will not be left out in the cold; instead, they will be better served at regional facilities that specialize in their SPG. Patients will have longer average travel times, but unit cost to hospitals will be lower and quality of service for patients will be higher. To counteract increased travel costs, insurance plans might consider covering travel costs for patients referred to a regional center, as is done in Canada and the U.S. military.

Comparisons can be made to other sectors in which competition has bred higher quality, efficiency, and access. Hospital specialization might breed regionalization similar to the airline industry's hub-and-spoke concept. A dominant medical center might have pruned a small percentage of its SPGs to act as a keystone for inpatient care in the area, with affiliations to smaller, highly specialized, few-frills, low-cost hospitals. On occasion, the hospitals that are "spokes" might pick up SPGs that the hub hospital cannot provide as efficiently or as effectively. Two hub hospitals implicitly might trade SPG areas of specialization while avoiding antitrust litigation. This concept has been carried out in the airline sector, where maintenance and cost per mile are substantially cheaper if companies swap SPGs and service fewer product lines. For example, one airline traded fifteen DC-10s to American Airlines for eight 747s.

Specialization brings lower costs and fewer mistakes. As small hospitals back out of SPGs they never should have initiated, medical centers will inherit most intensive care unit (ICU) cases, to the benefit of quality care. Indeed, medical centers could become large ICUs. The ego-turf concerns of the professionals, whether they are physicians or pilots, will be emphasized through regionalization. For example, the "poor" 747 pilot now has to settle for flying a DC-10. As for the ego concerns of mangers and providers who have to work in hospitals on a financial diet of staff reductions and a lowered number of SPGs, financial and nonmonetary incentives have been proposed.

Deregulation and competition do raise service quality and drive costly excess capacity out of the market—witness the airline, trucking, banking, and railroad industries. Judging from the more than 130,000 empty hospital beds, short-term acute care hospitals are plagued by excess capacity (American Hospital Association 2002). Hospitals are further plagued by reregulation in the form of DRG-administered prices, but we cannot achieve pure competition by taking every citizen's insurance coverage away. The term *market competition* might sound to some as if philistine commercialism is being introduced to our medical system, but all that is really advocated in the name of competition is emphasis on concern for productivity, efficiency, and effectiveness.

No longer will many hospitals be able to function as full-service institutions offering almost every DRG. In the context of business history, an analogy can be drawn between hospitals and the urban department stores of 15 years ago. Those stores that offered a full scope of services ranging from high fashion to toasters, from soda drinks to yarn, and from hardware to silk, went bankrupt. Stores that identified and specialized in their most productive product lines prospered. Stores that maintained 500 product lines, and their poor outpost satellite locations, fell prey to the vicissitudes of the market.

Outpost clinic managers should take advantage of double-loop learning and realize after a second look at the issue that the assumptions underpinning the volume projections are overoptimistic. For example, if an urgent care center is built in a wealthy neighborhood in which everyone has a private physician, low prices and urgent care might not be a winning combination. On a second loop in the learning process, the clinic might be located in a middle-class neighborhood in which the clientele require the service and can pay their bills. However, productivity must be kept high to keep services affordable and profitable.

Farming provides another useful analogy to the healthcare sector. Farmers who shunned excessive diversification in favor of productivity enhancement have prospered. They realized that maximum portfolio scope does little if all (or some) product lines are inefficient or experiencing declining utilization. Farms saddled with debt and diversified product lines have gone under. Hospitals saddled with 50 SPGs, serving more than 400 DRGs, will soon discover that breadth and facility size do not ensure survival. In the jargon of economics, moving up the learning curve because of higher volumes in areas of specialization increases productivity, cuts costs, and improves quality.

Underspecialization and Overspecialization

Hospitals on the vanguard of product-line planning have gone through one of two basic stages of misadventure: under- or overspecialization. Both groups fall prey to what Whitehead (1932) termed the "fallacy of misplaced concreteness." Members of the first group, occupancy-maximization caretakers, place excessive faith in the slogan that "anything beats cold sheets." They will develop any SPG and underspecialize, believing that a higher occupancy rate is more important than profitability. Members of the second group, short-run profit-maximizing risk takers, place excessive faith in specialization, marketing, and the ability to attract new demand to compensate for closing other SPGs. They overtrim SPGs based on short-run profitability without careful analysis of long-run effects. Balancing the two approaches is possible, however.

The practitioners of underspecialization for occupancy maximization in the first group have a false sense of security in reasoning *a posteriori* that hospitals are like airlines in that if the hospital is filled to capacity, everything will be fine. Hospital beds are somewhat like airline seats in that they cannot be stocked as inventory, so if they are not sold today, the revenue is forgone. However, should the strategy be to offer an indiscriminately high number of SPGs in hopes of filling beds? That idea is too clever by half. Actually, a hospital can offer so many SPGs that the majority are used well below capacity, and the net profitability contribution is negative. Hence, increased volume does not prevent bankruptcy and actually might hasten closure. In finance, the ratio of volume to capacity by SPG is a critical concern. Managers should avoid the mania of declaring that all is well if census rises.

The second group, the profit maximizers, find false security in maximizing through overspecialization, believing that dropping all the unprofitable SPGs improves the long-run bottom line. These short-term managers are unimpressed with the argument that profitability of the facility next year can be damaged by excessive concern for retrospective product-line profit reports. They are misled by a shallow reading of the business literature. Hospitals are more interdependent than most organizations, whereas divisions of other types of businesses can jettison a line without much concern for the core corporation's fixed-cost burden. Unfortunately, those forgone patients in SPGs that are closed no longer make a contribution to cover fixed costs. The remaining product lines must pick up more of a burden of the fixed costs and thus may become less profitable or unprofitable. Take, for example, a "star" product line with fixed costs of $2,700 and a $25 net loss per case. The crucial task is getting compensated through increased volume in remaining SPGs after closing last year's unprofitable SPGs. In other words, enough patients must be pulled from the competition to fully compensate for the empty beds caused by discontinued SPGs. Good marketing can go only so far in improving volume. As a general proposition, these managers would do well to trim SPGs in phases and to come to understand their market better over time. Long-run profitability should be the focus of financial managers.

A hospital might close some unprofitable SPGs but not so many that the patient census erodes to the point of harming the financial health of the institution. Moreover, certain slow-developing SPGs might be misidentified as poor long-run performers. Such slow-starter SPGs can be like weak-kneed quarterbacks: They eventually might save the franchise.

Price Setting with a Purpose

Marketing strategy involves basic questions such as what services to offer (product), where to serve (place), whom to serve, how to communicate to buyers and providers (promotion), and what to charge (price). These "four Ps" of marketing strategy are often softened by health marketers: service selection (product-mix decision), access (place), public information (promotion), and "service consideration" (price). This section discusses objective functions in selecting prices in the medical context and avoids renaming well-known constructs with euphemisms, such as *service consideration.*

Hospital market planning was formerly inpatient-oriented and concerned with getting the right patient in the right bed at the right time following the right promotion and sometimes following communication of a right price. Marketing activities are more and more concerned with pricing decisions, not merely for inpatient care but also for ambulatory and alternative care. Currently, hospital leaders rely less on bed-filling and more on getting the most appropriate cost-effective channel of service distribution (including home care) to the patient so that society and the individual both get the most value for their investments. This trend is often labeled *social demarketing* (less institutional care), which should be contrasted with its antithesis, *negative demarketing* (a sleazy attempt to discourage the poor or underinsured patients from coming to the facility).

In pricing our products, three factors are critical:

1. Rivalry among existing competitors
2. Potential new entrants to the market (such as ambulatory surgery)
3. Bargaining power of buyers (such as bulk buyers eliciting discounts)

For each service product line, the institution should consider developing a tactical implementation plan. The facility may undertake nine different pricing strategies for nine product lines, depending on existing competitive conditions, the possibility of new entrants, and forecasted buyer response to price changes (price elasticity). The nine strategic pricing options are the following:

1. *Predatory penetration pricing*—short-run pricing to gain market share with no change in the product.

2. *Slash pricing*—long-run lowering of prices and changing the product to make the price slashes supportable in the long run.

3. *Follower pricing*—not an especially good strategy; it simply sets prices relative to the market leader (it avoids initiating a price war).

4. *Phaseout pricing*—setting prices high, which might only be at true cost to eliminate a seldom-used, often poor-quality service product line.

5. *Preemptive pricing*—lowering the price to make the service less attractive to potential new entrants.

6. S*kim pricing*—setting the price high for services of especially high quality or for a service for which the probability of short-term declines in market share is low.

7. *Segment pricing*—charging higher prices when so-called "snob effects" exist; that is, charging a vastly different rate for a slightly different service, such as VIP suites in hotels.

8. *Slide-down pricing*—traditional price discrimination of moving down the pricing policy to tap successive layers of consumer demand when the service is highly price-sensitive or significant economies of scale exist.

9. *Loss-leader pricing*—setting prices low relative to the average profit margin, but not below cost, to attract customer flow to complementary services.

Some mixture of these nine strategic pricing strategies is superior to the old-fashioned policy of hospital-wide pricing rules. For example, old-style cross-subsidization through public enterprise pricing was never statistically defensible (policies of markdowns for maternity care or markups for radiology or elective surgery were passed down through the generations of hospital superintendents on stone tablets). Likewise, pricing at marginal cost always made such charitable institutions appear capital-consuming, wasteful, and inefficient to the taxpayers who had to underwrite their operations by picking up all the other costs associated with the facility. Last, fair-share average-cost pricing with an equal percentage markup across all products suffers from two defects. First, it prevents the marketplace from having the opportunity to dictate a buyer-driven cross-subsidization policy—for example, accepting a higher profit markup in cosmetic surgery to support preventive medicine (as in mammography screening of high-risk groups). Second, it removes all requisite flexibility needed by management to initiate, expand, or close a service line through prudent use of different pricing strategies over time.

A specific example of how these pricing strategies might be used sequentially over the life cycle can be offered. If the hospital has no market share in starting a new product (**Table 8-1**), it might wish to attempt an aggressive pricing strategy, especially if this is a high-growth service. Strategy 1, predatory penetration pricing, is a short-run, pricing-slashing strategy to gain initial market entry and hopefully gain significant market share. The new firm on the block should not expect the dominant firms to always react. For example, Microsoft seldom reacts to a price-cutting campaign from smaller firms because it would rather take a wait-and-see attitude to observe whether the new entrant (1) can survive, (2) can pick up a significant market share, and (3) can equilibrate back to a higher price level that still might beat Microsoft's price but does not threaten to take much more market share away. Any hospital should raise its prices after short-run experimentation with predatory pricing to solidify its market position. If weaker rivals in the marketplace decide to stop offering a given service, a hospital can charge substantially higher prices (and perhaps even reap monopolists' profits). If existing firms maintain this service line but do not counterpunch or appear to be potential losers in a price war after the new firm's successful entry into the market, a hospital can attempt strategy 2: slash pricing in the long run.

Slash pricing invites a price war. In almost every case, slash pricing should involve a change in the product for the price structure to prove sustainable over time. For example, Southwest Airlines changed the product called air travel by making the public pay for certain a la carte services (such as food and checked bags) and through nonmonetary mechanisms. However, the quality of the basic product, air travel, was in no sense discounted. Indeed, the slash-pricing strategy can result in a social good by opening up the product to new users, including first-time users.

Not having a strategy is itself a strategy. Consequently, strategy 3, follower pricing, is the easiest alternative. If the service offers little potential for product differentiation and it proposes to offer a "me-too" or "copycat" entry

Table 8-1 Seven Basic Strategic Pricing Methods

Market Growth Potential	Market Share			
	Zero	Low	Moderate	High
High	Predatory penetration pricing (no change in product)	Slash pricing Predatory penetration pricing	Preemptive pricing Follower pricing	Preemptive pricing Segment pricing
Moderate	Slash pricing Predatory penetration pricing Follower pricing	Follower pricing Predatory penetration pricing	Skim pricing Follower pricing	Skim pricing Preemptive pricing
Low	Follower pricing Slash pricing	Phaseout pricing Follower pricing	Skim pricing Segment pricing	Skim pricing Segment pricing

Note: The strategies are listed according to strategic preference. Slide-down pricing and loss-leader pricing are not listed here.

(such as endoscopy), a facility can simply price relative to the industry leader. Needless to say, this is a timid strategy that invites and almost guarantees low growth. For example, one cannot name a single company that exists by offering copies of Microsoft products at Microsoft prices. (Under those circumstances, consumers would rather buy from Microsoft). To paraphrase a college basketball coach, follower pricing is a "chill-out" strategy, allowing time to mend and heal before determining a new strategy.

If all else fails and the service line has proven a financial failure, the best strategy to close out a product is strategy 4, phaseout pricing. This strategy should never be employed if any harm would come to the health of the community, as might be the case where only one hospital is offering the service. However, phaseout pricing can quickly allow the price-sensitive patients to close an existing service when flat-out withdrawal of the service would result in a negative reaction from certain trustees, physicians, or local citizens. For example, if the hospital offers inferior cardiac surgery once every three weeks at an actual cost that is 200 percent higher than that of the local teaching hospital, one can phaseout price the service at actual cost. So few customers will come to visit the hospital for inferior cardiac surgery at such a premium high cost that the hospital will have to close the service. The results of phaseout pricing are both good medicine and good economics (Brown 1999).

Strategy 5, preemptive pricing, preserves market share by preventing competitive entry or expansion and typically is used by firms with above-average market share for services with above-average market growth potential. For example, as a large, established company, United Airlines sharply reduced the prices on 11 new air routes that People's Express had moved or was about to move into. People's Express clearly underestimated United Airlines' ability to employ strategy 5, and it went bankrupt as a result. Healthcare providers need to understand People's Express' mistake: If the People's Express of the local health market catchment area is attempting to open a nearby urgent-care center or expand into coronary angioplasty, a hospital can preempt the firm's plans with pricing strategy 5. To maintain preemptive price levels that make expansion into the specific service line seem unattractive, the firm would have to trim its cost behavior in line with the reduced price or make money elsewhere in the organization to cross-subsidize the discount prices. With sufficient economies of scale, the firm may still make a profit at a price that is unprofitable for new entrants.

The public will avidly support the price wars among healthcare providers and HMOs the way they supported aggressive competition among airlines and banks. The public benefits from such activity. Managers and providers must recognize the dynamic quality of healthcare markets. All the constant change and competitive action and reaction will make any price strategy obsolete very rapidly. Failure to grasp this point and to readjust the pricing (and promotion) plan every four, six, or eight months will bankrupt some providers.

Strategy 6, skim pricing, offers the institution an opportunity to reap profits by attracting "cream buyers" to a unique product. Consumers have to perceive the product as having high value for the cost, and marketing researchers have uncovered this image in everything from lithotripsy (kidney stone treatment) to Maytag washing machines. Skim pricing is most effective for the hospital if the price elasticity of demand is low (consumers care little about price when trying to avoid chest pain or pain from kidney stones). The market barriers to entry usually are high because of the substantial fixed costs associated with acquiring the service. However, skim-pricing policies will be hard to maintain if competitors enter and achieve a comparable consumer reputation. Despite this, if a provider's brand-name reputation is so firm that it can continue to skim price indefinitely, the institution should continue to price high (such as the Cleveland Clinic in cardiac surgery). Analogously, Maytag washing machines continue to sell at very high prices because their breakdown rate is substantially lower than that of the competition. Pricing strategy 7, segment pricing, is similar. It is a mechanism to sell prestige "snob suites" to those with the ability to pay cash for amenities.

Pricing strategy 8, slide-down pricing, is a mechanism by which the facility can tap successive layers of demand at different price levels. For example, one may wish to sell mobile mammography screening to high-risk women at $111 in the three wealthy neighborhoods in Washington, D.C., but in the poor neighborhoods change the list price to $39. This strategy makes sense when there is a substantial price and income elasticity of demand. Moreover, the investment has a better net present value if the mobile mammography van is used to scale. In addition, this pricing policy does substantial social good if it brings a necessary service to new customers. Insurance plans often prevent the practice of price discrimination, but the strategy can be pursued if the service is not insured or if the provider wishes to forgo aggressive collections of cost-sharing payments from poor or elderly patients. As with any form of price discrimination, the rich can beat the system by driving to the point of service where the cost is less, but few, if any, do so.

Finally, strategy 9, loss-leader pricing, has two basic variations. Some hospitals sell loss leaders at below actual costs, which is a less-than-prudent strategy in an increasingly competitive marketplace. Other hospitals charge loss-leader prices in the sense that they charge 50 to 100 percent less than their average hospital-wide profit margin, but they never price at less-than-average cost for the service. The loss-leader approach is often rationalized as a marketing tool to pick up complementary demand. For example, one can sell infant care as a loss leader to attract parents to have adult care at the facility. Alternatively, a dentist or optometrist could sell the initial-visit charge as a loss leader in hopes of making a substantial profit on the follow-up care.

In a service industry such as health care, consumption and production typically occur in the same location. Consequently, vertical pricing decisions in distribution channels are seldom relevant except in the case of independent practice associations or other contract-service situations. Horizontal pricing decisions are made at the retail level by commercial insurance plans or Blue Cross plans paying negotiated charges. Governmental payers and half of the Blue Cross plans simply pay cost or the health industry equivalent of wholesale prices.

Demand Creation and Advertising

In principle, to inform the public is the essence of advertising. Some physicians believe that consumers are so gullible about health care that they can be duped by advertising into asking for services they do not need. A number of surveys suggest that a slim majority of Americans are well-informed about health and hygiene matters but believe that modern medicine has the miracle techniques and spare parts to fix them no matter how they live their lives. Future research should consider the question of whether the excessive faith the public has in technology makes it susceptible to misleading advertising campaigns or whether public faith is on the wane.

It should not be suggested that advertising induces consumers to suddenly shop for health plans and providers as methodically as they shop for automobiles. It is clear that many individuals opt for the protection and security of the status quo and do not shop among competing health plans. Most consumers do not immediately abandon their current providers, even after being convinced that a new health-delivery option will save the family a few dollars per week. However, over time, if the family has a "bad" experience with its physician or hospital, it will be more likely to upgrade the importance of cost considerations in its future annual enrollment decisions and move to the plan that provides the best buy with all factors considered. Consumer opinions concerning value in healthcare service delivery vary widely in U.S. society. Not all individuals agree with the average group consensus concerning medical care because care is in many ways an "experienced good"—that is, it is a good that must be experienced to value its intangible and tangible attributes.

Expanded services or new, inclusive pricing packages should be promoted in a well-managed institution. The perceived style of advertising, sometimes labeled *social marketing*, is generally more acceptable to health providers than is competitive advertising ("buy our product"). Hospitals should go beyond the product orientation of selling inpatient or hospital-based services and realize that their one chance for expansion might reside in taking a broader market orientation.

Five basic rationales for advertising include (1) public education about health care, (2) information on service availability, (3) accounting to the community, (4) seeking support, and (5) recruiting employees. The industry also lists guidelines for acceptable advertising content: truth and accuracy, "fairness" in avoiding any quality comparisons with the competition, and avoiding "claims of prominence." The hospital industry has been rather slow in recognizing the need for differential advantages marketing. In the minds of the authors of the advertising code, the public has no right to know if a competitor has less modern facilities, a less well-trained staff, or an inferior quality of care. Also, most hospital marketing campaigns should be more consumer-oriented and less physician-oriented. The management of new HMOs must frequently report to the private risk bearers who supplied the venture capital, and HMO sponsors are always putting on the pressure and searching the market for better patient-focused managers. If one assumes that the retailer controls the production channel, as in the case of an HMO, the plan can achieve maximum profits by hiring physician services at below-market prices. A second alternative is to assume that the physicians and hospitals or HMO plans pursue profit maximization while allowing a "necessary" profit margin to the other party. Prepaid group health plans are one of the few markets in which health facility managers and physicians are on a relatively equivalent bargaining basis.

Respect for the patient/consumer/customer was a marketing revolution, although a bloodless one in which Drs. Marcus Welby and Ben Casey lost. Patients are beginning to aggressively seek new alternatives and better information. During decades of cost reimbursement, with little pressure to market, the cost crisis was a byproduct of the system and the incentive structure, and not necessarily of cost. One could ignore consumers, run up a big bill, and get paid dollar-for-dollar. What a great deal! However, competition, with emphasis on purchasing on an economic basis, had to rear its head. We all like competition in what we buy, not in what we sell, and healthcare providers were no different. With the rise of competition came increasing interest in customer satisfaction, marketing, discovering what the patients wanted, cutting excess costs, and offering the service at a favorable price. Innovation occurred on five major fronts:

1. Competitive pricing and contracting (HMOs, PPOs, managed care)
2. Staffing in proportion to workload (dumping underproductive staff)
3. Financial disincentives against overhospitalizing and testing
4. Incentives to invest in aftercare and long-term care
5. Sufficient supply of both physicians and empty hospital beds

This new world might stimulate continued growth in salaried physicians. The prototype for physician groups in the next century might be the airline pilot unions. Airline pilots have experienced a drop in earnings, but the workweek is shorter and less hectic, and it allows more time for family life. The pilot unions have done an admirable job in the areas of quality assurance, statistical quality control, and customer safety. Quality improvements lead to increased volume, potential economies of scale, and competitive advantage. In health care, costs might decline because physicians will earn less individually and as a group. Enhanced quality will diminish both internal quality-maintenance (rework of faulty documents, wasted materials, and loss of morale) and external quality-maintenance costs that affect customers and include losses through malpractice judgments and negative word-of-mouth advertising. Quality gains reduce pressures for tighter oversight from the Joint Commission on Accreditation of Healthcare Organizations (JCAHO) and from the public. The increase in the quality-maintenance budget might prove that inferior care is the most costly care, and doing the job right the first time is cheaper than cleaning up mistakes (Brown 1999, Eastaugh 1992).

Statistical Techniques in Marketing

Statistical techniques frequently are directed toward causal modeling of consumer behavior (how long is a consumer willing to wait at a clinic without seeing a contact person of any sort before deciding not to return or to repeat elective service?). Path analysis, which allows the analyst to decompose the correlation between any two relevant factors into a sum of compound and simple paths, might be applied to such consumer behavior issues. The decomposition of the correlation has three basic components: direct effects, indirect effects, and spurious effects from compound paths that are not interpretable but are mathematically part of the decomposition. For example, the finding that more liberal maternity benefit packages attract more enrollees to an HMO was found to not be a spurious relation. However, in a path model, the efficacy of expanded late hour clinics might be found to be spurious if the correlation between benefits and number of enrollees vanished when the effects of income and other socioeconomic variables were controlled.

Customer preferences and objectives are multifaceted and consequently require very sophisticated methods of analysis. Customer-provided preference judgments about hypothetical questions might produce errors. In considering the percentage of error variance in the criterion variable, an inverse relationship between errors and individual involvement in the process of providing preference judgments might be expected. Lower degrees of error might be expected if the choice is among alternatives of substantial importance to the individual, for example, among potential customers for open-heart surgery or among radiologists concerning preferences toward purchasing computerized tomography (CT) scanners. High error rates probably result from situations in which decisions have minimal impact, such as patients' decisions concerning vaccination or pediatricians' preferences concerning better CT scanners.

No single technique is appropriate for all marketing problems. One technique, conjoint measurement, used to assess what combination of service or product attributes the users, consumers, or providers most prefer, is probably the most underutilized and promising technique in the health services marketing arena. It summarizes the preference-ranking information as an index that nonquantitative decision makers easily understand. Wind and Spitz (1996) were the first to use conjoint measurement techniques in a health-services market to analyze the effect of a number of independent variables on a single (response) dependent variable: consumers' hospital selection decisions. In a conjoint measurement study, the respondent is presented with a set of multi-attribute alternatives and is asked to rank or rate combinations of attributes on the basis of some desired dependent variable (such as intention to buy or use). Contrary to traditional attitude measurement approaches in psychology, the respondent is asked to provide an overall evaluation of a product basket or a combination of various attributes, rather than simply providing only the relative rating on each individual attribute. The resulting internal trade-offs that each respondent makes among the various attributes can be decomposed into internal scale-derived utility judgments of given attributes and recon-structed to impute the consumer's predicted preference for new combinations of attributes (Akaah 1998).

The early applications of conjoint measurement techniques in the health sector provided insight into what consumers value (Wind and Spitz 1996). The three most important consumer factors in evaluating a hospital were, in order of importance, proximity to home, prestige of the physician(s), and physical appearance of the hospital. It might be surprising to some that the least important factor was whether the hospital was a teaching hospital or had some affiliation with a major university. This corroborates the anecdotal testimony of many multihospital-system mangers that consumers place a small, slightly positive value on whether a hospital is a teaching facility.

Conjoint analysis has been applied to a number of new HMO market research projects. Irrespective of the institutional market segment under study, ignoring health marketing is an increasingly hazardous style of management that frequently leads to retrenchment of services or to fiscal insolvency. As increasing numbers of health services administration students are being introduced to marketing, these activities will increase, and the public and the managers will be able to assess needs and improve efficiency better. As with any management science technique, poorly applied marketing can be a disaster for the institution. The reasons health marketing is underdeveloped range from a lack of adequately trained manpower to the hesitancy of trustees to support marketing efforts due to pejorative "business-world" connotations. The health institutions that grow will be forward-looking and market-wise; these institutions will not simply react to the immediate demands of HMOs and local physicians. A good marketing program can increase consumer satisfaction, improve efficiency, and deliver better-quality health services. Above all, marketing involves creating new products and making the consumer "queen", as women make the majority of family healthcare decisions in this country.

▶ **Summary Points:**

- Marketing is an important aspect of healthcare delivery; it enhances health care by increasing patient education, compliance, and involvement.

- Real health marketing involves evaluation of consumer preference and better service delivery, with advertising playing a minor role.

- Quality care is often cost-effective care.

Research and Discussion Questions:

- What is responsible health marketing?

- Who ensures that health marketing is responsible?

References

Adams, E., Houchons, R., Wright, G., and Robbins, J. 1999. Predicting hospital choice role of severity illness. *Health Service Research* 26(5): 566–584.

Akaah, I. 1998. Integrating a consumer orientation into planning of HMO programs: An application of conjoint segmentation. *Journal of Health Care Marketing* 3(2): 9–18.

American Hospital Association. 2002. *AMA survey on marketing expenditures in the service sector.* Chicago: American Hospital Association.

Berenson, R. 2002. Medicare and choice. *Health Affairs* 21(1): 9–10.

Brown, S. 1999. *Service quality.* Lexington, MA: Lexington Books.

Bruce, D. 2002. Disease management programs. *Journal of Healthcare Finance* 29(2): 45–49.

Buchbinder, S. 2002. Managed care and primary care. *Journal of Healthcare Finance* 29(2): 35–43.

Carroll, N., and Gagnon, J. 1998. Identifying consumer segments in health services markets: An application of conjoint and cluster analysis. *Journal of Healthcare Marketing* 3(3): 22–34.

Christianson, J., and Feldman, R. 2002. Evolution in the buyers. *Health Affairs* 21(1): 11–22.

Cooper, P. 1998. Health care marketing. *Journal of Healthcare Marketing* 6(4): 12.

Draper, D. 2002. Face of managed care. *Health Affairs* 21(1): 11–22.

Eastaugh, S. 1992. Hospital specialization and cost-efficiency: Benefits of trimming product-lines. *Hospital and Health Services Administration* 37(2): 223–235.

Encinosa, W. 2002. HMO market. *Journal of Health Economics* 21(1): 85–107.

Feldman, R., and Begun, J. 1990. Does advertising of prices reduce the mean and variance of prices? *Economic Inquiry* 18(3): 483–492.

Flood, A., Scott, W., and Ewy, W. 1984. Does practice make perfect? The relationship between hospital volume and outcome for selected diagnostic categories. *Medical Care* 22(2): 98–125.

Goldfield, N., and Boland, P. 1999. *Physicians profiling and risk adjustment.* Gaithersburg, MD: Aspen.

Kanter, R. 1999. *The change masters: Innovations and entrepreneurship in the American corporation.* New York: Simon & Schuster.

Kotler, P. 1999. *Marketing for nonprofit organizations.* Englewood Cliffs, NJ: Prentice-Hall.

Romano, M. 2002. AMA's union: Physicians are employees not supervisors. *Modern Healthcare* 32(6): 14–15.

Rovinsky, M. 2002. Integrated delivery systems. *Healthcare Financial Management* 51(1): 36–39.

Siegel, M., and Doner, L. 1999. *Marketing public health.* Gaithersburg, MD: Aspen.

Stone, T., Warren, W., and Stevens, R. 1998. *Journal of Health Care Marketing* 10(1): 65–69.

Town, R., and Vistnes, G. 2002. Hospital competition in HMO networks. *Journal of Health Economics* 21(3): 733–753.

Whitehead, A. 1932. *Science and the modern world.* London: Collier-Macmillan.

Wind, Y., and Sptiz, L. K. 1996. Analytical approach to marketing decisions in health care organizations. *Operations Research* 24(5): 973–990.

Wolfe, R., Roi, L., Flora, J., and Cornell, R. 1983. Mortality differences and speed of wound closure. *Journal of the American Medical Association* 250(6): 763–766.

Chapter 9

Capital Finance

Finance is somehow both the implicit culprit and the expected savior of an industry under fiscal stress. The health field has been managed by professionals who often had a clear view of part of their external and internal environment without being able to relate these to financial realities.

– J.B. Silvers

No profit margin, no mission.

– Catholic Hospital Association

Venture capitalists look to markets in a high state of change. There is no industry in a higher state of change than health care. The medical entrepreneurs are risking more than money. They may be risking the security and effectiveness of institutions people depend on to provide services.

– James Suver

▶ Critical points in this chapter:

- Total financial requirements

- Capital costs, capital project, capital investment

- Opportunity costs

- Economic life cycle

- Financial ratio analysis

The Enron scandal placed business ethics into the public debate. Just as a homebuilder knows a yardstick has 36 inches, not 32 or 34, so investors need to know the information they receive is not inches short of the truth. Private capital has replaced government as the life blood of our healthcare sector. In the next decade the health economy needs $680 billion for renovations, additions, and replacements; $120 billion for working capital; and $80 billion for debt retirement. The advent of this era of bare-bones reimbursement does not preclude the need to allow capital to keep pace with inflation and new technology. We cannot let the biomedical capacity of the nation erode. Reimbursement for capital is critical for managers. In addition to the simple replacement concept of capital maintenance, society might wish to consider adding on a technological maintenance factor to ensure that the facility has funds for updating capital to keep pace with peer institutions. Given that medical technology is likely to be cost-increasing in the future, preservation of capital position implies capital replacement and capital improvement to keep pace with new technology. However, too generous a payment scheme fuels waste and technological cost inflation.

Ad hoc swings in the reimbursement rules have prevented many nursing homes and hospitals from preserving their capital purchasing power to anywhere near the degree that public utilities are allowed in order to ensure future operations. Health facilities have not received the same basic treatment accorded other highly regulated utility industries.

Although capital costs are a relatively small percentage of total hospital costs (roughly 6 to 12 percent in most cases), the importance of equitable capital payment policies exceeds the per-annum dollar volumes involved. Adequacy and stability are key in designing a fair payment system for financing equipment (about 38 percent of hospital capital costs annually) and plant. However, defining adequacy is not an easy task. It is probable that in the coming decade hospitals will spend $300 billion on capital. Twenty percent of this new capital will be distributed for working capital, 8 percent for debt retirement, and 72 percent for additions, renovations, and replacements. For the first time, long-term care (LTC) facilities are expected to outspend hospitals in new capital spending, with $310 billion in expenditures in the next decade.

Accurate Self-Assessment of Risk and Return

Total financial requirements, as differentiated from accounting costs, are those resources that are not only necessary to meet current operating needs but are also sufficient to permit replacement of physical plant, where appropriate, and to allow for changing community health and patient needs, education needs, research needs, and all other needs necessary to the institutional provision of healthcare services that must be recognized and supported by all purchasers of care. Given the tighter payment climate, the organization cannot be too conservative in its assumptions. Often in other business sectors the worst-case forecasts have proven far too optimistic. This was true in the case of the Stanford University debt-capacity analysis (Hopkins, Health, and Levin 1992), in which 6 percent growth became 1 percent annual decline.

Designing a Capital Project

Major capital investments should be analyzed in five basic stages:

1. Capital requirements, benefits, and opportunities
2. Project feasibility study
3. Assembly of a financing team and a project plan
4. Credit assessment (bond ratings)
5. Completion of short-term and long-term financing

Stage 1 involves identifying capital requirements to meet shifts in patient demand, clinician referral patterns, or the basic need to keep the facility state-of-the-art (replacement, renovation, modernization, and expansion). The stimulus for assessing capital position might be reactive (market share is declining because the facility is outdated) or proactive. The opportunity to be first in a new service or in a new, growing marketplace zone (location) is a proactive rationale for major new capital investment (Hammer and Champy 1999). As was pointed out in chapter 5, this process is increasingly driven by consumer preference, supplanting the "empire-building complex" of trustees and medical staff to expand simply for expansion's sake.

Stage 2, the feasibility study, involves a careful, conservative assessment of projected cash inflows, cash outflows, the opportunity costs for the resources, and the economic life cycle of the project. The intent of this stage is to develop an accurate estimate of the financial viability and logistical complexity of the various capital-project alternatives. Stage 2 requires a range of possible answers to the precise problem—not a precise answer to an ill-defined problem. When external consultants are brought in, they must realize that there is little value in refining an analysis that does not consider the most appropriate alternatives and assumptions for the hospital. The consultants can also point out unreasonable assumptions. If the hospital generates initial cash-flow estimates that are too optimistic to convince its own paid consultants, the facility will have even less success trying to convince the bond-rating agents at Moody's, Standard & Poor's, or Fitch Investor Services (all of whom are very active in LTC-facility financing). Hospital managers and trustees must resist the human temptation among their peers to overstate excessively the growth potential of any new facility or service product line.

Stage 3 involves forming a financing team (bankers and lawyers, including hospital counsel, bond counsel, and issuer's counsel) and a team of other key actors in the project plan (from the architect to the construction manager), sometimes numbering in the hundreds. Coordination is important. For example, one would not want the architects to waste time and money designing a planned facility that is much too expensive for the debt capacity of the hospital. Consequently, the fixed transaction costs of issuing debt are substantial—that is, refinancing old debt for financial reasons might not be cost-effective unless the interest rates declined 1.5 to 2.5 percent (depending on volume).

The most critical broker of the deal is the commercial banker. Commercial bankers can perform three to four jobs in a single deal, including acting as the lender, investor, debt guarantor, underwriter, and bond or master trustee. Members of the financing team might suggest purchasing bond insurance to increase the hospital's credit rating, thus decreasing the rate of interest, if the action is cost-beneficial. (Without the bond insurance the required volume could not be sold in a reasonable time). Bond insurance clearly makes sense if the decline in interest expense (in discounted dollars) is less than the cost of one-time purchase of the insurance.

Although the hospital industry is not perceived to be as risky as the nuclear power industry (rapid downgrades in credit-worthiness and no new debt financing for a decade), some recent trends are disturbing. Downgrades still exceeded upgrades by 30 percent from 1998 to 2002. Given that health care competes with other industries for scarce capital, the trends in other sectors are better than those for nonprofit health facilities. Interested readers should read Standard & Poor's quarterly *Municipal Bond Book*, or the weekly *Standard & Poor's Credit Watch*.

Stage 4, the credit-assessment stage, involves finalizing the financing documents and inviting in the bond rating agents for a review, onsite visit, and debt rating. If the issue is for more than $10 million, two independent ratings are required. Standard & Poor's Corporation (2002) described a bond rating process to measure relative credit-worthiness, using quantitative factors such as financial ratio analysis (normative time trend, past 5 years), competitive market position (market share), patient-payer mix, regulatory environment, and feasibility forecasts. To a lesser extent, qualitative factors are also considered, such as the management focus of the governing board, characteristics of the medical staff (age, faithfulness to the hospital), subjective institutional or demographic factors, and legal provisions of the indenture. Moody summarizes the same concerns under four broad subject headings: debt factors, financial factors, bond security provisions, and hospital-specific factors.

The single most important component in the credit-rating process, in addition to the obvious assessment of the nature of the project to be financed, is the financial ratio analysis of the institution. There are no hard-and-fast rules, but rating agents clearly prefer facilities with a high debt-service coverage following completion of the project (greater than 3.0) and a health ratio of case flow to total debt (greater than 1.4). Other variables considered include the fund balance per adjusted patient-day and the operating profit margin. A hospital with a poor rating (BBB speculative) is likely to have a low fund balance ratio and a debt-service-coverage ratio less than 1.7, whereas an AA-rated facility will most likely have a fund balance per diem above $700 and a debt-service-coverage ratio greater than 3.7.

Ratings are subject to appeal and might be changed even without a request from the hospital. Ratings might be improved or lowered, but in the current climate, the ratings are most frequently lowered. Rating agencies have a fiduciary responsibility to consider worst-case scenarios in the "visible" future, after the demise of capital-cost pass-through, rather than to focus solely on a hospital's current financial position. Once could nearly summarize the increasingly competitive field of capital finance as a transition from the world of Woody Allen ("90 percent of life is just showing up," often true in rating or feasibility review during the easy era of cost pass-through) to the dog-eat-dog world of Oscar Wilde, who stated that "it is not enough to succeed; you have to hope your neighbors fail." German hospital administrators refer to this attitude as *schadenfreude*, or joy in other people's failure. A capital project will no longer be viewed as financially feasible just because the local community supports it and feels a "community need"; the organization has to demonstrate that cash flow will be sufficient to make future debt-service payments (Eastaugh 1994).

In a market with many empty hospital beds, investors view financially weak hospitals as "cross-eyed javelin throwers," in that they will not win any awards but will keep the attention of their fearful audience. The president of the Voluntary Hospitals of America summarized this issue as follows: "Trustees must resist the temptation of taking off their business hats and putting on their community service hats and making totally foolish decisions on behalf of their hospitals." Grand plans for capital needs often must be scaled back. There is strength in numbers when it comes to the capital markets. Multihospital systems use master trust indentures that cover all obligated issuers (members or subsets of the system), permitting a better credit rating and borrowing at lower rates of interest.

There is a clear distinction between "making the financial deal", stages 3 and 4, and "doing the deal" in completion, stage 5. In the closing period, bonds are printed, certificates are written, bonds are escrowed with the trustee, and the financial boilerplate documents (basic language of all debt contracts—that is, obligation to pay, events of default, and indemnification) are signed. In the case of refinancing and refunding, the closing period also includes completion of legal documents to defease (pay or set-aside payment in an airtight escrow account) the prior bond issue before issuing the new debt. Defeasance is the process of removing the liens of old bond documents by escrowing sufficient funds either from proceeds of a new bond issue or from the firm's cash into a special AAA-rated secure escrow trust. This defeasance escrow fund allows debt-service payments to be made on the outstanding old bonds until they mature or can be called (redeemed prior to their stated maturity date).

Refundings are typically done with net cash defeasance (principal and related interest income in escrow is used to pay the principal and interest on the outstanding old bonds), although some hospitals have been forced by existing restrictive covenants to do either (1) full cash defeasance (principal in the escrow must pay principal plus interest on the old bonds) or (2) crossover refunding (principal amount in the escrow is used to pay outstanding bond principal, and interest income is used to reduce interest expense on the refunding bonds).

In summary, the senior managers, trustees, and hospital counsel must address four major issues:

1. Will payment methods tighten in the future such that sufficient cash flow will not materialize?
2. Will the hospital, clinic, or nursing home be in "technical default" with a future modest downturn in patient demand?
3. How can additional debt be issued?
4. How flexible are the terms of the indenture?

To expand available debt capacity, facilities must continue to develop joint venture partnerships with their most wealthy client group—the physicians. However, the partnerships are now sold on the basis of business risk versus return and not on the basis of reducing an investor's individual tax liability, as was done prior to federal tax reform.

Investment Decisions

Capital is not the same as assets, although the capital of a firm will be invested in many assets at any point in time. This is a distinction with a difference; capital management includes both liability and asset management. The focus is on the residual value to the board or owners, not on a collection of assets on the books. Capital is managed on three basic levels: (1) investment decisions (what to do); (2) financing decisions (the way to acquire it); and (3) capital-structure decisions (determining the mix of debt to equity, and determining the type of debt to incur). Investment decisions should be made based on the cash inflows and outflows, yielding a positive net present value (NPV) if the project is worth doing. Firms should attempt "what if" simulation analysis of the market reaction to a particular investment decision and consider multiplying the NPV by the probability of an event.

The return on investment (ROI) should exceed the cost of capital. For example, in one case the City Hospital of Martinsburg, West Virginia, was receiving a return on investment from its state rate commission of 3.9 percent, which was less than its cost of capital, 5.9 percent (Eastaugh 1996). This is not a good fiscal result; under good circumstances the hospital would have a return on investment, or ROI, (price-level adjusted) higher than the cost of capital, and one could label the firm a going concern. In the long run, if this result continues, the hospital's financial viability is threatened. If this were one single department with a poor ROI, one could dispose of the business segment. However, if the entire hospital experiences an obvious erosion in capital position, it must avoid new capital investment, fight to trim costs, and appeal geographic equity of such a low ROI (in this context, in a state with a rate-setting commission). The appeal can be made based on vertical equity (other types of hospitals were treated better by the rate setters) and geographic equity. In other states the hospitals received either a fair sufficient rate for a nonteaching hospital (an average 5.4 percent in the state of Maryland) or a generous price-level-adjusted ROI (8 to 9 percent in Oregon and Texas).

The several state rate-setting commissions define *capital costs* differently from the way the Medicare program does. The major question is whether hospitals should be paid depreciation for buildings and fixed equipment or for the principal payments that they are required to make. Depreciation payments are higher at the start of a facility's life cycle, whereas principal payments are higher toward the end of the life cycle. Many economic arguments can be provided against the use of depreciation for payment purposes. However, the payment for capital on a basis other than generally accepted accounting principles tends to arouse considerable ire on the part of the hospital industry. The two major options for capital payments are (1) variations on the formulas used by the Maryland rate-setting commission, which base the payments on the cash requirements of the facility for capital, or (2) the Medicare definition of capital costs, which bases the payments on the depreciation, interest, and lease costs. This issue causes a great deal of controversy because use of a basis of payment other than depreciation results in paper losses in the financial statements of hospitals. Several states (such as Maryland) pay for movable equipment on the basis of replacement-cost depreciation, whereas others (such as New Jersey and Maine) pay according to Medicare cost principles, that is, straight-line depreciation plus interest.

If investment analysis answers the question of whether this project, department, or new equipment brings economic returns (add value to the organization), the decision makers have five ways to distribute the value created: (1) keep it in reserve, (2) let it be absorbed by enhanced perks and redundancy (adding to inefficiency is not a good strategy for ethical managers), (3) enhance the subsidy for education and research done in the firm, (4) distribute the value to consumers (through lower prices), or (5) in the case of for-profit firms, pay out dividends to owners. The next section surveys how we pay for the investments selected. Capital-structure decisions are covered in chapter 10.

Financing Decisions

Financing decisions involve contracting with a set of investors or owners for a return required by the parties. For example, 6.5 percent of the project might be financed by philanthropy (the gift givers feel an implicit contract that returns a social dividend, "doing good") and 30 percent financed by an explicit contract with owners (an explicit contract with physicians seeking a fiscal dividend and capital appreciation over time). The balance of the project (63.5 percent) might be financed by some mixture of retained earnings, short-term debt, and long-term debt. On the other hand, some projects might be better leased (a topic covered later in this chapter).

Financing decisions are driven by effective cost, which itself is driven by the economy-wide pool of potential investors and investment options. Healthcare managers are typically unfamiliar with the investment community (Standard & Poor's Corporation 2002). Health care might be a $1.5-trillion industry in the year 2004, but health care will still only represent 13 to 14 percent of capital markets. On the downside, firms that are denied access to capital might close; for example, some inefficient hospitals might be viewed as being as risky as nuclear power plants. On the upside, some firms might consolidate, merge, integrate, and take advantage of resulting economies of scale and enhanced productivity. Efficiency generation, productivity gains, and the selection of a good portfolio of appropriately financed investments are the essential ingredients for success.

Financial managers have to adhere to replacement-reserve policies and limit the overexpansion of new-product-development advocates (empire-building risk). The capital budgeting process, guided by NPV and restrained by a limited supply of funds, helps to make the decisions less political. As a general rule of thumb, the hospital should try to generate $40,000 of operating revenue for every $100,000 of total assets (and $30,000 in nursing homes). Such rules of thumb are guideposts but less relevant than good financial planning. In addition, the financial manager should also support methods to offer incentive pay for those that control costs and enhance productivity.

Living Within Limits

Hospitals and LTC facilities can cope with the future limits on the availability of capital. Two strategies frequently used are sharing and leasing. The multi-hospital-system approach to health services management is potentially an effective structure if economies of scale can be captured by pooling financial resources and decreasing the duplication of services and facilities. In addition, multihospital systems can hire more sophisticated management and offer an atmosphere conducive to long-range planning. These aspects of multi-institutional systems combine to raise credit ratings, decrease interest costs, and thus make capital financing less expensive and more feasible. In the future, the competitive financial advantages of multi-institutional systems might contribute more to the regionalization of health care than will government health planning.

Leasing equipment can reduce the immediate drain on funds associated with a major purchase. Even overall costs often are reduced as the hospital takes advantage of the economies realized by the leasing firm (Eastaugh 2001). Federal tax law encourages leasing by third parties to nonprofit organizations in the following way. A vendor sells capital equipment to a proprietary intermediary. The intermediary gets the benefit of the investment tax credit and accelerated depreciation and is able to lease to the nonprofit organization at a reduced price. The nonprofit organization benefits from this reduced price, whereas otherwise it would have reaped no benefit from buying the equipment itself, as the investment tax credit was worthless to an organization that did not pay taxes. In the case of hospitals, leasing provides additional advantages in the form of (1) a hedge against technological obsolescence, (2) an alternative source of funding when debt or equity funding is available, (3) faster reimbursement, and (4) better service. Leasing has continued to grow in popularity.

The Advantages of Leasing

The rapid development of new medical products, in combination with consumer demands for more comprehensive insurance to cover the ever-expanding vista of medical technology, has pressured hospital administrators to replace their equipment more frequently and at a higher cost. Most corporate financial analysts are shocked to learn that the majority of hospitals lease less than 20 percent of their equipment. Given the nonprofit nature of more than 80 percent of the hospital industry, there are no tax incentives to discourage leasing and favor purchasing. The rule of thumb is that a small nonprofit firm should lease two-thirds of its equipment.

The main advantage of lease financing is that it allows the healthcare institution to be more flexible with regard to rapid technological changes in medical equipment. The facility can lease equipment for the duration of the equipment's useful life, which is frequently less than the item's physical life. The possibility that the cost of future obsolescence will be built into the contract price is partly offset by the higher residual value the equipment might have for the leasing company, which has greater access to national resale markets.

Leasing is also attractive to the smart health facility administrator because it allows financing to be flexible. A large initial payment is not required. Moreover, even if a project is debt financed with low annual payments, a debt contract frequently involves restrictive clauses on future borrowing. Lease financing establishes a new line of credit that is useful as a supplemental financing source in times of high interest rates and limited borrowing opportunities. One indirect advantage of leasing is that the administrator might apply leverage on the leasing company through future lease payment options to force the lessee to provide better maintenance service. For example, hospital labs with leased equipment tend to have lower downtime and lower maintenance repair costs.

Another advantage of leases is the treatment of lease costs by third-party payers. By leasing, the hospital can use the services of the asset and be reimbursed for the periodic lease payments. When equipment is bought outright, straight-line depreciation is normally required. Thus, the early large cash inflows associated with reimbursement for accelerated depreciation are not realized. Moreover, no third-party payers' reimbursement policies include full price adjustments for inflation over the economic life of the equipment. These negative effects of third-party reimbursement can be avoided when a true lease is used for financing.

One other potential reason why leasing might be financially superior to buying is that arguing whether tax concerns have favored lease or buy decisions is not debatable. Some analysts argue that the for-profit lessor benefits from the ability to use accelerated depreciation and tax advantages and consequently passes on partial benefits (in the form of slightly lower lease payments) of this asymmetry in the tax treatment to the lessees. On the other hand, some analysts have argued that the lessor simply charges an amount equal in present-value terms to the cost of buying the equipment plus whatever taxes must be paid. This last scenario suggests that it would be financially advantageous for a tax-exempt lessee to buy rather than to lease (and pay the lessor's taxes).

Capital Leases and Operating Leases

There are two types of leases from the standpoint of the lessee: operating leases and capital leases. A capital lease is viewed as a purchase agreement whereby the risks and benefits of ownership of the asset are transferred to the lessee. This type of lease cannot be cancelled and is fully amortized, so the asset and related debt must be recorded on the balance sheet.

Under an operating lease, the risks and benefits of ownership are not transferred to the lessee, and the payments under the lease contract are not sufficient to purchase the leased equipment. Thus, an operating lease is not fully amortized and does not affect the balance sheet. Operating leases usually contain cancellation clauses and might call for the lessor to maintain and service the equipment.

Two organizations have attempted to classify leases according to whether the contract entered into is more of a purchase agreement or an actual lease/rental type of agreement. The Financial Accounting Standards Board (FASB) Rule 13 distinguishes between a capital lease (purchase agreement) and an operating lease (rental agreement). On the other hand, the Internal Revenue Service (IRS) uses the terms *financial lease* to signify a purchase and *true lease* to signify a lease agreement.

The FASB standards must be used for financial statement reporting purposes. However, for third-party reimbursement purposes (Blue Cross and Medicare) the IRS standards are usually applied. If a contract qualifies as a true lease, the rental payments might be expensed on a periodic basis. If the contract is considered to be a purchase agreement (or conditional sale), the allowable expenses are interest and depreciation, as period costs.

Current reimbursement policy among third-party payers favors true leases over capital leases if revenue maximization is the objective. The capital lease is treated similarly to debt, with allowable costs determined for depreciation and interest in a fashion that might not reflect the full costs of the contract. Most third-party reimbursement schemes create a disincentive for capital leasing by not allowing the depreciation of an asset below its estimated salvage value and by limiting historical cost to the lower of fair market value or purchase at the current cost of replacement (adjusted only by straight-line depreciation and prorated over the useful life of the asset). On the other hand, a contract defined as a true lease allows full reimbursement of both operating costs and the entire lease payment. Consequently, true leases provide full reimbursement for the current costs of ownership.

What previously passed as a true lease contract allowing for transfer of ownership title at a nominal fee, in violation of FASB Criterion 2, is increasingly being appropriately labeled as a variant of the capital lease known as a *conditional sales contract* or *financial lease*. An institution that selects a capital lease should require the lessor to document explicitly the interest charges implicit in the lease. The hospital would then have a point of defense against the third-party payer that attempts to impute unfairly low interest costs.

Many smaller hospitals in financial need have opted for a type of operating lease called a *preprocedure rental*, which requires little or no fixed obligation payments but instead links fees paid by the hospital to the lessor according to the number of procedures performed. The costs per procedure are generally higher than for other forms of leasing, but small facilities would not use the equipment fully "to scale" (at 90 to 99 percent capacity) in any case. Thus preprocedure rental operating leases might be the least expensive alternative for clinics and small hospitals. One additional benefit of this form of leasing is that it avoids the problem of provider "moral hazard" among physicians who feel pressure to overorder procedures to justify the fixed expense of having the equipment (Eastaugh 2001).

Potential Changes in Reimbursement Incentives

A few states recognize replacement cost depreciation (RCD) in their state Medicaid programs (New Jersey, Minnesota, and Delaware). During the 1980's, in making the transition from historical cost depreciation to RCD, most nursing homes received higher capital payments. RCD is not universally higher in 100 percent of the situations, because when the state pays RCD, it does not pay interest expense, but when the state was paying historical cost depreciation, the interest expense was also a reimbursed cost. The Marshall and Swift index used by Cleverley (1997) and other analysts is the standard index to calculate RCD. One infrequently mentioned advantage of total replacement cost depreciation, or price-level depreciation, is that it reduces the long-term cost of services to the public. Replacement cost depreciation has been reported in a large number of corporate financial statements since FASB Statement 33 (Cleverley 1997). In basic economic terms, future capital funds are best held in the hands of the institution that can earn a higher rate of return on the investment over time. The average hospital, because it is a large, nonprofit firm, can earn a rate of return on its investments that is typically more than two percentage points higher than that of the average individual. To make this point clear, let us consider the hypothetical example of a hospital that must replace a piece of equipment in the diagnostic radiology department in five years. The original equipment costs $500,000 in 2003. The equivalent state-of-the-art replacement appreciates in value at the rate of 12 percent per year and will cost $929,000 in 2008. At the end of the time period, the hospital can finance the new equipment in one of two ways: (1) historical cost depreciation of $100,000 per year for five years with a bonus to make up the difference from the rate settlers in year five (this bonus is called the planned capital service component in some states) or (2) allowing price-level depreciation (with cash inflows of $112,000, $128,000, $146,000, $167,000, and $189,000 for the five years, to net, after adding in the accumulated interest at 5.2 percent per year from the depreciation fund, a total of over $929,000). In some states the control over the equity of the institution is effectively out of the hands of the trustees and vested under the control of the rate commission. If the hospital receives $100,000 each year for five years and earns 5.2 percent annual interest on those funds, it will accrue $286,381 at the end of the period. The differential between replacement costs and accumulated depreciation funds will have to be paid by the consumers in the form of increased rates.

Some cynics argue that local politicians support rate-setting commissions because they do apparently save money in the short term, irrespective of whether they are perhaps inflationary in the long run. Supporters of rate regulation and planning argue that society could save money in the long run if it could only force some hospitals not to purchase replacement equipment. One might advocate cost containment and still question the wisdom of a regulatory system that treats hospital management like a beggar with a tin cup, where the government rate commission has the right to determine how full the cup should be. Allowing the hospital a return on equity capital is more efficient than letting the government arbitrarily decide how much each hospital deserves and when it should receive the funds.

The Financial Cost of Leasing

Leases are not always a cost-beneficial mode of capital financing. One common misconception about leasing is that it conserves capital. But in reality, the lease payments are frequently larger than the combined principal and interest payments on debt necessary to buy equipment, especially in southern states where leasing companies have a natural monopoly. A private survey indicates that approximately 35 percent of medical equipment, or $3.8 billion, was leased in 2002. Some facilities select leases as a hedge against obsolescence, whereas other facilities are forced to accept leases because they cannot obtain sufficient tax-exempt financing to purchase necessary equipment. If the equipment becomes obsolete, most leasing companies' interest in return business will allow the hospital to trade in the old machine for the newest model for a reasonable upward adjustment in periodic fees.

Hospitals and clinics that lease should beware of hidden fees and the "fine print" in the contract (Eastaugh 2001). For example, some lessors require advance rental payments that are not credited against scheduled payments until the fifth or sixth year, or allow changes in the lease rate on 60 days' notice (unwary lessees get stuck with this). Health facilities should count each hidden expense, such as commitment fees that are not credited against future lease payments or stepped-up implicit lease rates, in the inflation adjustment provision.

Another common misconception among hospital managers is that leasing has an intrinsic cash-flow timing advantage. However, some leasing contracts require the institution to borrow a sum in advance (for security purposes), which is comparable to a loan repayable in arrears in annual installments. Consequently, there is no cash-flow advantage to such a leasing agreement if it is correctly compared to a loan of equivalent interest cost and comparable schedule for repayment. The one advantage that leasing has over purchasing is that the interest costs are typically one or two percentage points lower. Probably the most widely held misconception concerning leasing is that it represents an undetected mode of debt financing, hidden from regulatory oversight. The hidden-debt argument is at best cosmetic and at worst a zero-sum manipulation in that neither the asset nor the future liability for the lease payments appear on the balance sheet.

Another unanticipated side effect of defining true leases as capital leases is that a number of the financial ratios used to assess the credit-worthiness of the facility deteriorate. If the debt ratio or interest-coverage ratio diminishes, then the hospital's bond rating deteriorates, causing the public to pay for incrementally higher interest rates on future capital purchases. The subject of credit ratings and the limits of debt financing are reviewed in chapter 10.

Similarly, claims by lessors that leasing rates are lower than borrowing rates are not always valid. For example, miscellaneous leasing charges can significantly increase the effective interest rate over the quoted rate for the term of the lease. Leases often include hidden charges such as late-payment penalties. The calculated salvage value of the asset also affects the effective interest rate. This means that careful analysis of the net present cost (NPC) of a lease must be carried out to find the effective rate of interest, to compare this mode of financing with other alternatives.

There are no simple rules to suggest that one form of financing is uniformly superior to another. For example, leases are purported to transfer the risk of medical-equipment obsolescence to the leasing firm. However, the hospital could carry 110 percent (or 90 percent) of the risk in the form of higher (or lower) than "fair" lease-payment terms. One cannot adopt a simple decision rule, such as "purchasing is best because it adds to the hospital's asset base on the balance sheet." Capital leases also add to the asset base, and the asset base is not critical by itself (that is, increases on assets are offset by increases in long-term debt on the same balance sheet).

A complete financial analysis should include a multivariate sensitivity analysis for a range of interest rates, purchase functions, lease-cost functions, salvage values, and discount rates. The topic of capital management—the set of decisions involving financing, assets, and other resources that either improve, maintain, or erode the capital value entrusted to the firm by "investors," be they stockholders, government, a religious organization, or a community board—was reviewed briefly earlier in this book. Board members are fiduciaries with legal responsibility for the preservation of a firm's equity to accomplish the purposes for which the institution was founded. Cleverley (1997) discussed the problem of organizations that have insufficient earnings from operations to establish and maintain the equity reserves necessary for future capital needs. Some rate regulators respond by saying that the payment is not too low but inefficiency is too high. Regulators also say that there is an excess of beds and equipment per bed (a medical arms race), so they do not want all firms to "maintain the equity reserves necessary for future capital needs" (close the inefficient bed supply). On the other side, hospital managers say: Please don't underpay all of us by 10 percent; simply don't pay (contract with) some of us. In this latter sense, selective contracting can be seen as an attempt to channel payments to the more efficient providers. If the hospital or other organization is offered a contract for nonemergency service provision, it has the freedom of choice to sign or renegotiate the terms, but it cannot claim that the reimbursement formula confiscated the institution's capital.

After a decade of barebones reimbursement, hospitals have reduced capacity, often under internal programs labeled "rightsizing." The number of hospitals has declined by 17 percent in the last 12 years (AHA 2002). Nursing homes are now entering the same sort of bare-bones reimbursement environment that hospitals experienced in the 1990s. Many nursing homes may close due to financial pressures.

Payment to Nursing Homes: How Much for Capital?

Between 1997 and 2002, 593 hospital-based skilled nursing facilities (SNF) have closed. In 44 states, nursing home Medicaid payments are set on a prospective basis or some hybrid combination of prospective and retrospective systems. Considerable variation exists across states about treatment of capital costs, ranging from a single payment to a three-way payment for interest, depreciation, and a return on equity for investors. Industry representatives argue that nursing homes should have the opportunity to earn a return on Medicaid patients equal to the return earned on private-pay patients. Rate regulators counter-argue that the charges paid by private-pay patients are excessive. A few Medicaid programs have progressively offered incentives for efficiency. For example, in Maryland the difference between the Medicaid payment ceilings and the actual cost per diem is shared by the state (60 percent) and the facility (40 percent). The Medicare hospital payment system under PPS is much more generous, allowing the hospital to keep 100 percent of the cost savings below the price line. Maryland officials should not be surprised that nursing home cost behavior clusters near the maximum ceiling for payment, given that a 40 percent incentive is not sufficient to promote productivity and cost reductions among most home operators.

The effect of insufficient return-on-equity payment rates on nursing homes has long been controversial. Rate regulators argue that nursing homes are sufficiently profitable. Economists argue that nursing homes have the worst profitability and cash flow among 167 business sectors. Regulators make a mistake when they comingle issues of operating profitability with return on equity invested in the nursing home business. A few states have faced up to the obvious problems with historic cost-accounting treatment for capital payments. The so-called "fair rental" capital payment systems in West Virginia and Maryland explicitly recognize (1) the increasing value of nursing home assets over time; (2) that accounting values do not rise with inflation and thus erode (undervalue) assets over time; and (3) that no incentives should exist for property manipulation and resale merely to extract, in a "back-door" fashion, a return on equity from the payers. Under fair rental systems, a simulated rent is paid based on the current value of assets irrespective of the sales history or financing methods.

A cost-based or flat-rate-of-return payment system encourages frequent sales of nursing homes to revalue assets following sales at inflated prices and restart the depreciation "game." Depreciation payments improve as a result of each sale, and many homes have changed owners every few years. The industry has referred to this "game" as *trafficking*, with many nursing home chains buying one another's homes in addition to investing in freestanding independent homes. However, the adoption of fair-rental payment systems encourages ownership for longer periods of time and, more importantly, provides stronger incentives to invest in the quality of the physical plant and the services in the institution. Without fair-rental capital payments there is no incentive to invest in quality and upgrade the facility's reputation if the owners have to sell the facility every two to three years. Neither the West Virginia gross-rental approach nor the Maryland net-rental approach needs to increase aggregate payment levels to the industry over the life cycle of the assets, and both systems can provide acceptable (market) rates of return on equity. Fair-rental capital payments create incentives for owners to seek the most efficient financing arrangements because they reap the cost savings (and need not manipulate property ownership for maximization of reimbursement). Payers must not "rob" the homes by setting the rental rates too low, thus paying a return on equity that is below a comparable investment elsewhere in the economy. If the payment rates are too low, capital will flee the nursing home industry.

A number of studies suggest that operating risk is rising in the nursing home industry (Eastaugh 1996). This hypothesis is tested using Altman's (1998) discriminant Z model. The multivariate analysis can be retrospective (what financial ratios predict bankruptcy based on the past?), diagnostic (what areas can be improved to avoid fiscal distress?), or predictive (what is the probability of distress or failure in the future?). The secondary research question is whether risk is different in different state rate-regulatory environments. Nursing homes with more than 100 beds were surveyed in a random sample of 20 states. Over 34 percent of the sample provided financial statements for the years 1994 to 2002. The sample broke down into three basic regulatory climates for Medicaid payment of capital-related costs:

1. In tight rate-setting states, payment is based on historic cost of constructing the facility, which is the least costly basis for Medicaid payment, because change of ownership does not increase the home's value. The sample included 153 nursing homes in Washington, D.C., California, Connecticut, Florida, Iowa, Kansas, Kentucky, Louisiana, Pennsylvania, South Dakota, Utah, and Washington.

2. In fair-rental systems, payment is based on imputed rent for residential-rental services to sufficiently pay the current value of the capital assets used in providing care, yet is not so generous that it rewards frequent resale (trafficking) in nursing homes to create successively higher valuation of the facility. Facility valuation is based on assessed value, inflating historic costs. The sample included 86 homes in six states: Colorado, Illinois, Maryland, Oklahoma, Oregon, and West Virginia.

3. Generous-payment systems establish the basis of payment on the market value of the facility, thus rewarding frequent resale (trafficking in nursing homes) at higher prices to create successively higher valuation of the home. Four homes in this group had four owners in the eight-year study period from 1994 to 2002. The sample included 16 homes in Alabama and Wyoming.

Background on Models Assessing Distress or Closure

The multiple-discriminant model (MDM) attempts to measure the importance (weights, coefficients) in detecting financial distress, to establish a best-estimate equation (reduced form), and to assess how the weights can be objectively validated. MDM is used to classify and make predictions where the dependent variable is binary (bankrupt or open) or is good, questionable, or bad (open, distressed, or terminated). In this nursing home study, MDM attempts to derive a linear combination of characteristics that best discriminates between the categories (Altman 1998). If the Z score is greater than 2.6, the nursing home is financially strong; if the Z score is less than or equal to 1.1, the nursing home is very distressed (it may be closing or already be closed); and if the Z score is between 1.1 and 2.6, no information can be ascertained about the facility's financial strength.

In summary, MDM provides a single measure of the propensity of a nursing home to enter into severe financial distress within an eight-year time horizon. The reduced-form equation of unique independent variables is offered under the principle of Occam's razor: The simplest model with optimal predictive accuracy should be preferred to a more complex model that includes multiple unnecessary ratios. The estimated reduced-form equation includes only four significant unique ratios:

$$Z = 4.26X_1 + 5.63X_2 + 4.68X_3 + 1.50X_4$$

where X_1 = retained earnings or total assets; X_2 = working capital/total assets; X_3 = earnings before interest and taxes or total assets; and X_4 = book value of equity or book value of total liabilities.

A sample of 34 percent of the nursing homes in 20 states may not be large enough to yield unassailable population inferences, but the findings are suggestive. Bankruptcy rates and Z scores are presented over time in **Table 9-1** for each of the regulator payment environments. The Z model for bankruptcy prediction had a successful classification probability of 96 percent at one year prior to failure, 88 percent at two years prior to failure, and an impressive 76 percent at 6 years prior to failure. Two years prior to bankruptcy, the 34 failures had a median Z score of 1.42 compared to median Z scores of 4.12 for going concerns (still operating in 2002). Other model specifications and functional forms, including a Zeta model and a quadratic (rather than linear) equation did not improve the results.

The results in **Table 9-1** suggest a steady erosion in Z over time. The results for the 12 tight rate-setting states are particularly troubling, because the 2002 Z score is only slightly above the 2.6 threshold level for financial strength. This trend bears watching because state governments, financing 54 percent of the nursing home care in the nation, soon might get more stringent. The macroeconomic incentives are clear to any state governor: Medicaid might represent only 17 percent of the average state budget, but it represents 60 percent of every incremental new dollar in the state budget. Medicaid is crowding out other social programs, such as education, so state budget directors are planning to reduce payment levels. The etiology of this fiscal problem is demographic: Medicaid is paying more nursing home care for the expanding number of medically indigent elderly.

The tight-payment states can be expected to get tougher, and the generous-payment states are currently studying the implementation of a fair-rental system for capital payment. One potential problem with Z models is that they might be subject to Type II statistical errors, misclassifying certain firms as soon to be bankrupt. If a financial analyst claims that the nursing home deserves a going-concern exception, and suppliers of credit withhold funds based on a low Z score or other grading system, then the firm's demise

Table 9-1 Average Z Index, Probability of Distress in the Future, and Fraction Bankrupt (N= 255 Nursing Homes in 1994, N = 221 Homes Still Open in 2002)

Year	Z Mean	Probability of Distress	Cumulative Fraction Closed
Tight rate-setting states			
1994	3.12	24.8 percent	0
1996	2.86	30.7 percent	0.07
1998	2.80	32.4 percent	0.10
2000	2.75	34.2 percent	0.13
2002	2.69	36.6 percent	0.16
Fair-rental-system states			
1994	5.12	13.8 percent	0
1996	4.73	15.8 percent	0.04
1998	4.39	18.2 percent	0.07
2000	4.20	18.4 percent	0.08
2002	4.04	18.6 percent	0.09
Generous-payment states			
1994	6.42	5.7 percent	0
1996	6.28	6.4 percent	0
1998	5.96	8.5 percent	0.02
2000	5.65	10.6 percent	0.04
2002	5.32	12.7 percent	0.06

actually might be caused partially by the receipt of a low score (poor grades create a self-fulfilling prophecy).

Prescriptive Action: Seeking a Turnaround

MDM analysis can be used as an early warning system to detect problems in advance and prescribe rehabilitative action. Just because the Z for nursing homes in a region indicates that widespread distress has not permeated the nursing home business does not mean that a particular facility is in great shape. One nursing home studied had a Z score of 1.8 resulting primarily from a recent productivity bleed (erosion) that in turn eroded retained earnings. Nursing productivity and task delegation are important acute problems in institutional management (see chapter 5), and these results offered a wake-up call to the chief executive officer with the low Z score. Z scores should not be viewed as a prediction of doom, but rather as a management tool to recovery. To paraphrase Alfred Sloan's dictum: Decay is not your predetermined destiny. Poor labor productivity and other underutilized assets are often the major causes of the deterioration of a nursing home's financial ratios and these are remediable by better leadership.

As more nursing homes close under financial pressures, home health care may grow as an alternative mechanism for chronic care. The shift to prospective payment for home health care since 2001 presents a number of opportunities for investment. Some larger hospital systems invest in home health care to reduce patient length of stay, generate a more diversified revenue base, and reduce inpatient losses. Managed care plans invest in home health as a cost-effective partial substitute for inpatient hospital care or extended nursing home care. Planning is difficult without a stable reimbursement climate. CMS (The Department of Health and Human Service's Centers for Medicare and Medicaid, formally known as HCFA) should guarantee continued support for home health care and Medicare managed care. One cannot put more seniors into HMOs while pulling the sickest seniors out of home health care. However, home health care currently has a good NPV under a wide range of assumptions (see **Table 9-2**). Home care is cost-beneficial for the elderly, with a 1.5 to 2.7 ratio, if it substitutes for expensive inpatient hospitalizations. Home care is also a cost-beneficial substitute for some nursing home care and enables the patient to enjoy the independence of living in familiar, friendly surroundings. Home care is also cost-beneficial for AIDS patients.

The AIDS patient can receive $400 a day of home infusion antibiotics and nursing, rather than $800 per day of hospitalization (Eastaugh 2001).

Innovation and Profits

The concept of profitless health care is moribund. A tax-exempt hospital must earn a profit to render future patient service and stay modern. The Catholic Hospital Association recognized the financial imperative with the poignant slogan: "No profit margin, no mission." An example of the old-style paternalistic view that deplores both finance and marketing was provided by Dr. Cecil Shepps at the annual meeting of the American Public Health Association. Dr. Shepps stated that "nonprofit hospitals should be in the business of doing good, expanding a money-losing department because it is the right thing to do; not breaking the rules and making big profits" (personal communication). There are many potential areas for argument with those who are (1) quick to label all business concerns corrupt and unethical; (2) quick to treat patients as supplicants rather than as valued customers; and (3) quick to reject the hypothesis that departments often lose money because consumers and local physicians steer clear of low-quality facilities (which in turn become unprofitable because they are empty, not because they are providing any better social goods). Managers in for-profit and nonprofit organizations are equally anxious about generating capital to secure a better future for their institutions. Managers and clinicians view capital as the lifeblood for rebuilding, modernization, and remaining state-of-the-art as an institution.

Table 9-2 Net Present Value of Home Health Care as a Function of Hospital Days Saved, Home Health Costs, and Cost Savings per Bed Day

		Annual Hospital Days Saved		
		13 Days	15 Days	17 Days
	$3000	$3,136	$4,080	$5,024[a]
Annual Home Healthcare Costs	$3500	$2,636	$3,580	$4,524
	$4000	$2,136 [b]	$3,080	$4,024

[a] Best-Case Scenario

[b] Worst-Case Scenario

Source: Eastaugh (2001)

Indeed, it seems realistic to view private capital as a better bet than national health insurance, given our current politics.

There are still unique features in the investor-owned sector. Such hospital chains have to pay dividends to their shareholders. They have more of a growth imperative to satisfy stockholders' desire for a long-term capital gain. Students unfamiliar with finance are often surprised to learn that investor-owned capital is also more expensive than tax-exempt revenue bonds.

Investor-owned firms have the mixed blessing of access to a unique and flexible but more costly source of capital (investor equity). In the best-case scenario, the chain might use $1 million in current earnings to attract an extra $14 million in financing but at an average cost of capital of 11 percent. If the investor-owned chain were to breach its past promises to shareholders, the cost of equity capital and cost of debt could rise significantly. Indeed, broken promises to institutional investors could do more to reverse the growth of for-profit hospitals than anything else on the policy front. In contrast, a tax-exempt hospital with a modest to good credit rating will be capable of parlaying $1 million in current earnings into $3 to $4 million in financing (by borrowing $2 to $3 million at low interest rates and receiving tax-exempt philanthropy). Shift in federal payment policies is the number-one risk issue for nonprofits to monitor.

Risk and Return

A successful firm knows that its success depends on its knowledge of risk—that is, what it knows and how quickly it can learn new approaches. If we apply knowledge to tasks we already know how to do, we call it productivity. If we apply knowledge to tasks that are new and different, we call it innovation. Achieving these twin goals with risk analysis and risk adjustment is good economics and good medicine. Yet the popularity of capitation managed care plans is in doubt in many areas because the rate of innovation in risk adjustment is very slow. Many integrated delivery systems (IDS) managers fear that implementation of the initial severity adjustment by Medicare could slash their Medicare risk rates by 5 to 15 percent. Capitation should encourage the appropriate supply of beneficial services by the right level of care provider ("right care," avoiding the 10 to 25 percent of care that is ineffective or unnecessary). Methods to predict insurance risk must be retooled to prevent "cream skimming" discrimination against the sick and to reward quality providers. The irony of the current marketplace is that if a plan is "blessed" with an above-average quality reputation for treating AIDS or diabetes, a financial crisis can develop. If all the high-cost patients in an area enroll in a high-quality managed care plan, the plan will go bankrupt unless it begins to pay more prospectively per member per month for these sicker patients. High-cost, sicker patients are the most aggressive value shoppers in finding the HMOs that deliver the best service for their specific condition. Therefore, one finds the most acquired immunodeficiency syndrome (AIDS) patients in the HMO that treats AIDS cases the best and the most diabetics in the HMO that treats diabetes most effectively and generously (lower cost-sharing burden to the patient).

Until a more refined severity adjustment is implemented, the risk of adverse selection makes HMOs averse to advertising above-average quality performance for specific types of patients. Why? Because the business risk of attracting high-cost sick patients must be hedged. If patient severity measures can be refined, payers could pay a high per member per month (PMPM) premium for the predicted high-cost sick patients. If done accurately, this risk adjustment will increase access to services, reduce the bias to demarket the sickest Americans, and set appropriate reinsurance rates. Without this payment risk adjustment, the ethical HMO receives substandard reimbursement for quality service, and the unethical HMO reduces quality and/or service delivery to the high-cost patients. Basing some payment for very sick enrollees on their individual cost experience will reduce the twin problems of selection bias and stinting (underuse by some managed care plans). For example, ceding some cases to traditional cost reimbursed Medicare in advance will protect very sick patients (Newhouse 1999).

"Countervailing power" is becoming a common phrase in the physician community. Specialist physicians who feel pushed around by payers and managed care plans are striking back with a specialist empowerment movement. In this context, specialists are the new gatekeepers for the specialty services. These newly empowered specialists dislike having some generalist physician assume the traditional gatekeeper role in referring the patient to each and every specialist. Capitated specialists have been capitated for special carve-out contracts in cardiac surgery, cardiology, AIDS/human immunodeficiency virus (HIV) medicine, and 39 other specialty areas. Specialty empowerment forces managed care plans and hospital managers to sign up preferred specialty partners.

Shifting risk will be risky business for some. Income will be reduced for providers with relatively low-risk patient loads. If you treat healthier-than-normal individuals, your revenues will decline. Confidentiality issues may arise from employers' realization that they are paying higher premiums for certain individuals with poor health status.

Winners and losers emerge from a new risk adjustment system that shifts payments from plans and providers that do not have much risk to those that are carrying above-average amounts of risk. With the new system, higher payments will flow to urban and teaching hospitals—those that are currently overworked treating the sickest cases. Risk fairness will allow eight million more Americans to afford health insurance. Employers can offer a broader array of insurance alternatives without fear of selection bias. Benefit packages can be enriched with more coverage for drugs, hospice care, and home health care. The ultimate benefit of risk adjustment is that it allows a much fairer risk-sharing formula between primary physicians and health plans.

In the short run, consultants will be the biggest beneficiaries because of the industry concern for data reliability and validity. The small hospital that sees its revenues decline 10 percent might have seen only revenue declines of 2 to 4 percent if they had invested in better information systems. We all need better data management systems to encode, collect, and analyze information regarding patient services, health status, and conditions. In summary, institutions must improve their information systems or lose money.

Conclusions

Risk cannot be eliminated, but it can be prospectively analyzed, assessed, and hedged. In the coming world we must convince all concerned parties to spread the risks. Payers must take on some risk by paying for the research and development of valid and reliable severity-adjustment systems, and they must pay a higher capitated amount for high-cost patients (they must not sweep the problem under the rug and say reinsurance can solve all problems).

Specialists wanting to free themselves from the heavy hand of gatekeepers will assume more risk and take on capitated contracts for their specialty services. Managed care plans must be more willing to implement independent second opinion programs for their patients who were denied treatment. This last point was the most constructive byproduct of the 2002 Congressional debate over the Patient Bill of Rights. In summary, a new mixed payment system of pure capitation plus prospective payment for high-risk, high-cost patients, plus traditional reinsurance, will create the most fair and equitable marketplace in the future. If an HMO does a great high-quality job of treating diabetes, AIDS, or heart disease, it could advertise this fact and not be harmed financially by the resulting influx of high-cost patients. Quality service should never again be rewarded by substandard payment, and quality should never again be ignored as a "non-refundable expense." Under a new mixed-payment system, the public should increasingly demand valid and reliable report cards for managed care plans. Finally, unethical "quick-buck" plans could no longer profit by underserving the sick and enrolling only the healthy. These outcomes would represent good economics and good medicine for all.

▶ Summary Points:

- Health care competes with other industries for scarce capital.

- Health care is subject to the same financial rules as other businesses.

- Leasing is a hedge against obsolescence.

Research and Discussion Questions:

- If a capital lease is viewed as a purchase agreement whereby the risks and benefits of ownership of the asset are transferred to the lessee, how does a capital lease differ from a purchase?

- How well does retrospective financial ratio analysis predict future problems?

References

American Hospital Association. 2002. *Annual Survey of Hospitals*. Chicago, IL: American Hospital Association.

Altman, E. 1998. *Corporate financial distress: A complete guide to predicting, avoiding and dealing with bankruptcy*. New York: Wiley.

Altman, E. 1999. Financial ratios, MDA and prediction. *Journal of Finance* 23(4): 589–607.

Baker, L. 2002. Managed care and technology adoption. *Journal of Health Economics* 20(2): 395–421.

Bayless, M. 1996. Strategies reducing cost. *Healthcare Financial Management* 49(10): 38.

Bolton, P. 2001. Blocks, liquidity and control. *Journal of Finance* 53(1): 1–26.

Cleverly, W. 1997. *Essentials of health care financing* (4th ed.). Gaithersburg, MD: Aspen.

Eastaugh, S. 1992. *Health care finance: Economic incentives and productivity enhancement*. Westport, CT: Greenwood.

Eastaugh, S. 1994. Hospital diversification and financial management. *Medical Care* 22(8): 704–723.

Eastaugh, S. 1996. *Facing tough choices: Balancing fiscal and social deficits*. Westport, CT: Praeger Presss.

Eastaugh, S. 2001. Costeffective potential of home health care. *Managed Care Quarterly* 9(1): 20–26.

Feinstein, A., and Rasking, J. 2002. *Health care facilities outlook and guidebook*. New York: Lehman Brothers Global Equity Research.

Graham, J. 2001. Debt leases and taxes. *Journal of Finance* 53(1): 131–161.

Greene, J., and Metwalli, A. 2002. Cost accounting on capital investment decisions. *Journal of Health Care Finance* 28(2): 50–63.

Hammer, M., and Champy, J. 1999. *Reengineering the corporation: A manifesto for business revolution*. New York: HarperCollins.

Hopkins, D., Health, D., and Levin, P. 1998. A financial planning model for estimating hospital debt capacity. *Public Health Reports* 97(4): 363–372.

Lee, D. 2002. *Rating methodology: For-profit hospitals versus not-for-profit hospitals: Explaining the gap*. New York: Moody's.

McKeever, W., and Fide, S. 2002. *Managed care industry X-ray: Outlook for 2002 and 2003*. New York: UBS Warburg Equity Research.

Newhouse, J. 1999. Risk adjustment and medicare: Taking a closer look. *Health Affairs* 16(5): 26–43.

Reinhardt, U. 2001. Hippocrates and the "securitization" of patients. *Journal of the American Medical Association* 277(23): 1850–1851.

Robinson, J. 2000. *The corporate practice of medicine.* Berkeley: University of California Press.

Robinson, J. 2002. Bond market skepticism and stock market exuberance. *Health Affairs* 21(1): 104–117.

Silvers, J. 2001. Role of capital markets in restructuring health care. *Journal of Health Politics, Policy and Law* 26(5): 1019–1030.

Silvers, J. 1997. How do limits affect your financial status? *Healthcare Financial Management* 51(2): 32–41.

Standard & Poor's Corporation. 2002. *Debt ratings criteria (municipal overview).* New York: NY, Standard & Poors.

Taylor, G., and Kam, M. 2002. *Hospital industry commentary.* New York: Bank of America Securities Equity Research.

Wheeler, J., and Smith, D. 2002. Health care capital market. *Journal of Health Care Finance* 28(2): 13–24.

Younis, M. 2002. Hospital profitability. *Journal of Health Care Finance* 28(2): 65–74.

Chapter 10

Debt Financing and Capital Structure

Health facilities no longer have government as a "Sugar Daddy" paying the interest on their debt coupon by coupon. Many will close. We view such firms as "cross-eyed javelin throwers" in that they will not win any awards, but they will keep the attention on their fearful audience.

> – Investment banker

The penalty for a "wrong" decision 15 years ago was usually no more than the effort of persuading some donor to make good a relatively small financial loss. The decisions were private affairs, usually made intuitively. Now they are public affairs involving large sums of borrowed money. Intuition has been replaced by discounted cash flows and debt capacity analysis.

> – Walsh McDermott

▶ Critical Points in this Chapter:

- Risk analysis

- *Ceteris paribus* — all else equal (what is the contribution of one factor?)

- Commensurate gain

For new business ventures to succeed, healthcare executives need to conduct robust risk analyses and develop new approaches to balance risk and return. Risk analysis involves examination of both objective risks and subjective risks. Mathematical principles applied to investment portfolios also can be applied to a portfolio of departments or strategic business units within an organization. The ideal business investment would have a high expected return and a low standard deviation of risk. Nonetheless, both conservative and speculative strategies should be considered in determining an organization's optimal service line and helping the organization manage risk.

Successful business ventures typically occur in five stages: develop a good idea, write a coherent business plan for expansion, attract capital, improve the efficiency of the production process, and reap the productivity benefits and economies of scale of the new consolidated organization. Healthcare executives know that the success of these ventures depends on their knowledge of risk: what they know (risk analysis) and how quickly they can learn new approaches (risk adjustment).

Risk analysis involves examination of objective risks and harder-to-quantify subjective risks. If projections suggest that under a wide range of possible assumptions the venture will have good profitability and a positive net present value (NPV), the feasibility analysis is robust, and confidence in the venture will be high. The better the feasibility results, the better the risk classification for the venture.

Capital Structure Decisions

Capital structure fixed rules of thumb, even when price and age are adjusted, are seldom useful guideposts. In this context, Silvers and Kauer (1996) have been long-time advocates of taking a more aggressive financial approach rather than an accounting approach. They have concluded that the risk taking of medical researchers is seldom matched by managerial imagination and aggressiveness. Having covered investment analysis and financing decisions in chapter 9, two basic questions remain concerning capital structure decisions: (1) What is the appropriate balance between debt and equity financing? (2) Given the level of debt, what is the best mix of long-term and short-term debt?

Modigliani and Miller (1963) provided the standard answer to the first question. They suggested that the optimal capital structure occurs when the marginal costs of debt financing equal the marginal benefits. Marginal benefits, depending on ownership type, include access to lower-cost, tax-exempt debt or the tax deductibility of interest payments. Why do the marginal cost and marginal benefit curves intersect? The benefits increase at a constant rate because each additional dollar of debt reaps approximately the same marginal benefit, but the marginal costs start low and increase at an accelerating rate as the debt-to-assets ratio increases (0.4 to 0.6) and faster still for ratios greater than 0.6. Very few hospitals would try to defend an optimal mix of debt in excess of 0.7 (even in financially tough markets, such as New York and Boston). More and more payers are opting for a unilateral or bilateral selective contracting system that includes no specific guaranteed payment for interest payments. Government tax policy stimulates debt financing, but within the constraint that very high debt levels are too costly. Borrowing becomes more expensive as fewer and fewer firms lend to hospitals, the hospital's creditworthiness erodes, and interest rates are higher. With greater reliance on debt, the probability of default increases, and investors demand higher interest payments to compensate for this risk.

An Alternative for For-Profits

For-profit firms sometimes employ an alternative to trade-off theory called "pecking-order" theory in addressing the debt-level issue. This less popular pecking-order theory departs from the well-balanced trade-off theory, given that equity funds are pegged at the bottom of the pecking order (by retained earnings). When for-profit managers think that their stock is undervalued, they will be motivated to use debt financing, but if the stock is overvalued, they will issue new common stock. In the finance professor's ideal world, investors fully recognize the bias of managers to issue new common stock when it is overvalued because it helps to maximize the wealth of the current shareholders. Therefore, stock prices typically dip 3 to 5 percent after the announcement of a forthcoming new stock issue, and managers try to make debt their first choice. New common stock is the last choice in the pecking order of alternatives.

Small fast-growth companies that have large capital demands have little choice but to issue new stock (selling a large piece of the company). By contrast, some mature companies have had to go private and stop selling common stock because the price is so undervalued on the market. It is better to go private than to continue selling the stock at a low price.

Many mature for-profit firms with too much debt (overleveraged) issue new stock and use the money to refund debt in order to get the debt-to-assets ratio below some target (0.52). A few mature companies that are using too little debt (underleveraged) acquire more debt financing and use the funds to repurchase stock. As is demonstrated with the example in this chapter, tax-exempt firms have less flexibility in their capital-structure options. Tax-exempt organizations have access to tax-exempt long-term debt, but access to short-term debt is restricted to taxable bank credit. However, the flexibility attributed to for-profit firms is somewhat overstated if nobody will buy their stock at a sufficient price.

Short-Term or Long-Term Debt?

The second capital structure question is: Given the level of debt, what is the best mix of long-term debt and short-term debt? Gapenski (1998) outlined three general approaches to the short-term/long-term debt mix issue. The first approach, the aggressive approach relying the most on short-term debt, allows some fraction of the firm's permanent assets to be financed with short-term borrowing. This contrasts with the traditional approach, which is to finance all permanent assets with permanent capital. Why prefer short-term debt? Short-term debt is normally less costly than long-term taxable debt, and short-term debt is sometimes a little less costly than long-term tax-exempt debt. What is the downside in comparison to variable-rate long-term borrowing? There is a risk that downturns in financial ratios could result in lenders refusing to renew the credit. However, if the borrowing is long-run, there is no risk that the renewal can be turned down over the next nine to 12 months.

The second approach Gapenski outlines is the conservative approach, centering on the maximum use of long-term debt. Advocates of this approach emphasize the reduced fixed costs (legal fees and so on) of borrowing over the life cycle of the institution. Interest rates might be a bit higher, or much higher for taxable long-term debt, but the facility does not face a renewal risk each year. The third approach is a middle-of-the-road alternative between the two extremes, the maturity-matching method, under which the manager matches the maturities of the liabilities with the maturities of the assets being financed, resulting in a moderate level of reliance on each type of debt.

In the past two decades, there was an explosion in hospitals' use of debt financing to help support and expand their operations. Later in this chapter the reasons for an explosion in debt, the constraints on future increases in the debt ratio, and the implications of debt ratios for hospitals in a state of expansion or decline are identified. In addition, the often-neglected reimbursement issue concerning definition of an adequate rate of return on equity to ensure sufficient private market financing of hospital capital needs is discussed.

Regardless of ownership type, responsibility for protection of assets, quality of care, and facility reputation rests with the governing board. Hospital trustees have a fiduciary responsibility for the preservation or enhancement of a facility's equity. When the equity capital of an institution is eroded as a result of insufficient reimbursement, inflation, and poor profitability, the ability of that facility to continue meeting community needs will be reduced or eliminated. Some combination of insufficient payment rates and suboptimal financial management can create a shortfall in the retained earnings necessary to maintain sufficient replacement reserves.

Philanthropy has declined dramatically in the last two decades, so charitable contributions will not solve our future problems of access to capital. Lenders do respect a successful fund-raising effort, as it might provide a proxy measure of community support and cash flow for the institution; however, the sum total of charitable contributions and grants was only a very small portion of the average tax-exempt hospital's revenues in 1997. Excessive reliance on debt is viewed by many hospital administrators as a critical problem. In the past few years, debt-to-equity ratios have increased dramatically. A facility's ability to issue debt depends strongly on both the degree to which it is already leveraged and the capital market's estimation of the default risk of the firm. Capital management is becoming increasingly important.

Internal Capital Planning: Long-Run Plans and Short-Run Investments

A basic tenet for fiscal managers is that the capital process must be managed to properly operate the institution. A comprehensive approach must be considered for the long-run issues: strategic capital planning; basics of credit ratings; basic corporate financial tools for investment decisions; and an outline of fixed-rate, insured-rate, and variable-rate financing. Facility managers need guidelines for working effectively with investment managers and benchmarks for evaluating their results.

Many published studies suggest that hospitals make capital investment in identifiable life cycles (Eastaugh 1992). More basic research is needed concerning the length of these investment cycles, timing, and negative ramifications to deferred investment. A number of professional estimates of the capital needs of the healthcare industry have been made. These estimates strongly depend on the assumptions concerning the number of facilities that should survive, capacity utilization (occupancy), facility size, growth in technology, scope of services, and expansion of different services. Even with health expenditure growth at 5 to 6 percent per annum and technology growth at 1 to 2 percent per annum, capital needs could vary widely.

Will the healthcare sector receive its estimated capital needs? Will capital suppliers satisfy capital needs? As with every industry, capital demands inevitability will be some fraction of capital "needs." However, it might be important to the future health of the population that this fraction of demand-to-need be closer to 0.8 than to 0.4 or 0.5. Capital-financing availability will shape the structure, access, quality, and cost of our healthcare system significantly in the twenty-first century. Hospitals at the end of the investment cycle mostly need capital for physical plant and modernization. At the level of individual programs, certain "orphan investments" would be undercapitalized, such as preventive, social, and rehabilitative services, and urban teaching hospitals. All through the investment cycle, hospitals require capital for new program development, working capital, and debt service. Hospital managers might have to lengthen the investment life cycle.

The degree to which hospitals adjust their investment cycles might vary according to size, ownership, membership in a multihospital system, and the amount of retained earnings on hand. The capital investment cycle is crudely captured by the hospitalwide accounting age (younger than nine years representing the "early stage" and older than 24 years representing the "late stage"). Accounting age is calculated as the ratio of accumulated depreciation to the original value of plant and equipment. In simulation models, the most critical issue has been assigning an equitable capital add-on payment (CAPPAY), expressed as a percentage of operating revenues. A simple model would include the ratio of the first year's operating revenue to project cost R (ranging from 0.4 to 0.55); the life of the asset T (ranging from 28 to 35 years); the percentage of the capital investment debt financed B (0.85); and the present value of capital reimbursement less principal and interest payments over the life of the asset expressed as a percentage of project cost CF (cash flow CF = 0.22). If $T = 28$ and $R = 0.47$, solve for CAPPAY:

$$CAPPAY = (B + CF) \div (T \times R) = 0.081$$

The facilities with better financial position are clearly more likely, ceteris paribus (all else being equal), to make major capital investments. Investment behavior also depends on accounting age, profit margin, plant fund, retained earnings, fully funded depreciation accounts, and occupancy rate. These variables are interrelated, and it is difficult to associate empirically the unique contribution of each factor. For example, it is more difficult to achieve higher occupancy rates in smaller hospitals. If one assumes that half of the admissions are nonscheduled, both a 68 percent occupied 65-bed hospital and an 88 percent occupied 500-bed hospital are at 100 percent occupancy three days a year (model assumes half of the inpatients are scheduled admissions). Physicians and patients prefer newer facilities (lower accounting age). This preference will in turn affect profitability and occupancy. It is assumed that for every year of decrease in accounting age, a hospital's admission rate will increase by 0.5 percent. The model's critical assumptions for investment probability are presented in **Table 10–1**. Current and projected profit margins are increasingly critical factors in whether a facility initiates a major capital project.

The smaller and less profitable hospitals in the 8- to 16-year age category are not likely to make major capital investments in the coming decade (see **Table 10–1**). Typically, hospitals with recent large capital investments have higher capital expenses and lower operating profit margins. However, hospitals that avoid replacement and modernization decisions also tend to have lower profit margins. This problem of underinvestment or delayed investment can be either involuntary (the facility is financially distressed) or voluntary (the trustees and managers are overly timid about the potential for new assets generating sufficient income). Organizations with moderate-range capital expenses are usually the hospitals that have made major capital investments but not in the immediate past.

Health facilities in a poor financial position are older and less capable of spending the average amount of funds on equipment and plant improvement. Profitability erodes if a facility does not invest. Multihospital systems are better able to adapt because they are capable of risk spreading. For example, systems could smooth out the "lumpiness" of investments by spacing them over time among chain members. Chains can allocate expensive new investments to member facilities that currently operate under the capital cap (the payment add-on) and increasingly share such capital-intensive departments (such as magnetic resonance imaging). As long as the new investment is fully accounted for on a member facility's balance sheet, this trend will not lead to abuse.

Table 10-1 Capital Investment Probability as a Function of Hospital Accounting Age, Occupancy, Size, and Probability (GT Denotes Greater Than)

Accounting Age	Occupancy	Size (Beds)	Operating Margin	Probability of Investment per Annum
25+	GT 50%	20–100	GT 0.015	0.010
*	GT 60%	GT 100	GT 0.012	0.012
*	any	any	GT 0.040	0.020
*	other combinations		—	0.005
17–24	GT 50%	20–100	GT 0.025	0.011
*	GT 60%	101–300	GT 0.020	0.014
*	GT 70%	101–300	GT 0.050	0.090
*	GT 70%	GT 300	GT 0.040	0.088
*	GT 80%	GT 300	GT 0.060	0.170
*	other combinations		GT 0.035	0.050
*	other combinations		0.0–0.034	0.010
8–16	GT 50%	20–100	GT 0.025	0.007
*	GT 60%	101–300	GT 0.020	0.009
*	GT 70%	101–300	GT 0.050	0.040
*	GT 70%	GT 300	GT 0.040	0.035
*	GT 80%	GT 300	GT 0.060	0.070
*	other combinations		GT 0.035	0.010
*	other combinations		0.0–0.034	0.001
4–7	GT 80%	GT 300	GT 0.080	0.015
	other combinations			0.000

Capital replenishment is a long-range issue that should not be subject strictly to short-run cost-cutting goals. Policy makers should consider the proverb of the old man who, in the interest of cost cutting, decided not to feed his ox. The ox did fine, so the man did not feed him for nine more days. The ox dropped dead on the tenth day. Do we as a society want the medical technology that promotes quality patient care to drop dead? Like most analogies, this one is imperfect. Quality care is more likely to erode slowly, almost imperceptibly, rather than to drop dead suddenly. More critically, the hospital sector might be overcapitalized on average, but certain poor hospitals in poor neighborhoods are less well-positioned to survive.

A formula cannot ensure that all hospital closings will be nonharmful. Future developments in capital spending, the quality of service, and the health status of certain populations are difficult to foresee, and the need for monitoring change is apparent. To be flexible, we could allow hospitals with high capital costs (defined as greater than 10 percent of total costs) to select a one-time capital-adjustment option patterned on accelerated depreciation.

Analysts should draw a distinction between return of capital and return on capital. Return of capital is embodied by the returns generated from the assets for the institution. Whether an equitable return of capital would be based on the original cost or on the state-of-the-art-replacement cost of the capital asset is irrelevant. Price-level depreciation obviously keeps pace with advances in medicine but does not encourage better productivity among providers or manufacturers of hospital assets. Too generous a level of price-level depreciation obviously would be highly inflationary. However, historical cost depreciation erodes capital stock if inflation is greater than zero.

The return on capital is the effective cost of capital. In a for-profit firm, the cost of capital is the average rate per annum a company must pay for its equities. This figure changes over time with economic circumstances and shifts in perceived risk from investment in the facility (it might be 8 percent this year and 10 percent next year). The cost of capital is the discount rate that equates the expected present value of all future cash flows to common stockholders with the market value of common stock at a given time. The problem of calculating a cost of capital for tax-exempt hospitals is more difficult.

The cost of capital for tax-exempt organizations is shadow-priced by focusing on the motivation of donors. Lenders clearly value parting with their capital at the interest rate negotiated in the deal. But donors and certain generous third-party payers might have other motivations. The key issue is whether the donors or quasi-donors want simply a tax deduction or a tax deduction plus social dividends (the joy of seeing better health care delivered in their community). One could carry the argument to the extreme and suggest that if the donor is forgoing the dollar return from investing in the business world, then the donor does bear an opportunity cost equal to the competitive rate of return of for-profit equity capital.

Unfortunately for hospital managers, as a matter of public policy the government and other payers have not made reimbursement a level playing field by granting tax-exempt organizations a return on equity to match that of for-profit chains. Silvers and Kauer (1996) effectively dismissed the regulators' traditional argument that paying hospitals a return on equity is a "forced" contribution to capital stock. Restoration of a return-on-equity (ROE) payment, with a higher rate for for-profit hospitals and a lower rate for tax-exempt firms, represents an ex post payment for a return on ex ante donated capital of contributors. To shadow-price contributions in a weighted average cost of capital at zero assumes that the capital has no worth and will be equally easy to access each year in the future in perpetuity. In this last respect, federal tax reform, by reducing the tax benefits of giving, makes it more difficult for hospitals to attract donations.

Marketing the Debt

Financing authorities organized by state governments have aided hospitals greatly in issuing tax-free debt. The need for a debt-service reserve fund has been eliminated in many cases. These securities typically offer high yields and have proven to be very attractive to fire and casualty companies, banks, and mutual funds. The Federal National Mortgage Association has similarly enabled hospitals to issue debt at reduced interest costs by reducing the riskiness of the security.

For the last two decades, a larger number of private security brokers have been offering hospital securities. They have also helped hospitals to better tailor their debt to the needs of both the hospital and the lender. If the issue is large enough ($10 million or more), it attracts secondary-market interest, which increases its liquidity and lowers its cost enough to make it competitive with other high-volume tax-exempt bonds (such as municipal bonds). The increased demand for debt financing has been matched by an enlarged infrastructure for the issuing of that debt.

Federal issuing agencies, institutional lenders, and bond-rating agencies must evaluate the creditworthiness of the institution through quantitative measures (financial ratio analysis) and qualitative criteria (such as community support volunteers). Ratio analysis should not be univariate. The superior alternative is to consider simultaneously the patterns in changes of a number of ratios over time. Altman (1968) labeled this approach a *multidiscriminant-analysis methodology*. This method of multidiscriminant profile analysis reduces a number of problems of misclassification encountered in simple comparisons of single ratios. The obvious objective of the credit analysis is to establish whether the borrower can generate sufficient cash flows to service its debt requirements and meet other financial obligations.

Financial Constraints on Hospitals Issuing Debt

As a hospital becomes highly leveraged, it becomes increasingly susceptible to default. To protect themselves, lenders look at many financial indicators to determine the riskiness of a debt issue. Increasingly, hospitals find lenders placing restrictions on hospital finances to insure against the possibility of default. Constraints are often placed on financial ratios such as those mentioned earlier. Even if the constraints are not explicit in the loan agreement, hospitals find that if their leverage position deteriorates, the cost of new debt increases. Eventually, lenders will refuse to purchase any debt when the investment becomes too risky.

Hospitals must maintain financial stability, as reflected in their leverage and coverage ratios, if they are to continue to finance growth through debt. If other sources of capital remain scarce, maintaining ceilings on financial ratios can severely limit a healthcare facility's ability to grow. Such ceilings might be the only way to ensure the solvency of weak facilities.

Once a hospital has reached the limit of one of the constraints, it is possible to determine the maximum growth rate a hospital can maintain and still be within the constraint. This has been done before under some very limiting assumptions, but equations can be derived to solve for the maximum growth rate under more relaxed assumptions. Net income is assumed to be used to help meet capital requirements in the year it is earned. Additionally, we assume straight-line relationships between revenue and the capital needed to generate that revenue and between net income and revenue. Under these two assumptions, and to maintain a reasonable rate of capital expansion, hospitals must rely on external sources of funds. The extent of this reliance on debt is determined largely by the hospital's ability to generate profits internally. The sensitivity of the key financial ratios to net income margin is demonstrated in the next section.

How Financial Ratios Might Restrict Hospital Growth

To demonstrate how a ceiling on the ratio of debt-to-total-capital can restrict growth, consider the case of Community General Hospital (CGH), currently operating with a debt-to-total-capital ratio ceiling of 50 percent. CGH has a net income margin of 2 percent of revenues and requires $1.15 of capital investment (plant and equipment) and working capital to support each dollar of revenue. Under these conditions, the hospital is constrained in the next year to a maximum growth rate in real dollar terms of 3.6 percent.

To see that this is so, let us say that CGH generates $1,000,000 in total revenues this year. Next year the hospital will generate total revenues of $1,036,000 (see **Figure 10–1**). Net income is $20,720, which can be matched by $20,720 in new debt, maintaining the 50 percent debt-to-total-capital ratio. The sum $41,440 is exactly equal to the additional working capital and capital investment required to generate the $36,000 of additional revenue (except for rounding off the growth rate). At higher growth rates the capital requirements exceed the total funds that can be obtained from debt and equity. The hospital

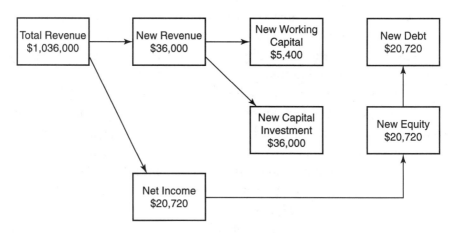

▲ FIGURE 10–1 Capital Growth under the Debt-to-Total-Capital Restriction

would have to become more highly leveraged (issue more debt) to maintain a higher growth rate. At lower growth rates the required new capital can be generated without reaching the debt-financing limit.

A formal equation can be derived to calculate the maximum growth rate for any debt-to-capital ratio, which can be used to see the effects each variable has on the growth rate.

G = maximum growth rate

CI = $ of capital investment required to support $1 of revenues

WC = $ of working capital required to support $1 of revenues

$X = \dfrac{\text{debt} \div \text{total capital}}{1 - \text{debt} \div \text{total capital}}$ = maximum debt/equity ratio

M = net income margin

Funds generated by growth = funds required to support growth

$(1 + X)(M + G)(M) = (CI + WC)G$

$$G = \frac{(X + 1)(M)}{(CI + WC) - M - (X)(M)}$$

Table 10–2 represents the maximum allowable growth rates for various values of debt-to-total-capital. For the purposes of these calculations, $M \times CI + WC$ is assumed to equal 1.15. Higher values of CI and WC would result in lower maximum growth rates.

Table 10–2 Maximum Growth Rates under Debt-to-Total-Capital Restriction					
	Net Income Margin				
Debt-to-Total Capital	0 percent	1 percent	2 percent	3 percent	4 percent
0.50	0	2	4	6	8
0.67	0	3	6	9	12
0.70	0	3	7	10	13
0.75	0	4	8	12	16
0.80	0	5	10	15	21
0.90	0	9	21	35	23

Debt-to-Plant Ratio

If CGH was at its debt-to-plant limit of 0.67, it would be restricted to a maximum growth of 4.35 next year (see **Figure 10-2**). Here, CGH generates $43,000 in new revenues and requires $43,000 in new plant and equipment and $6,450 in new working capital to support this growth—a total cash requirement of $49,450. Net income of $20,860 is generated during the year, leaving the debt requirement at $28,590. This maintains exactly the 0.67 debt-to-plant ratio.

If the growth rate exceeded 4.3 percent, the additional debt required to support operations would exceed 0.67 times the additional plant and equipment. A lower growth rate would reduce the debt requirement below the maximum allowable level. Again, we can derive an equation to determine the maximum growth rate for a hospital that has reached the limit of its debt/plant constraint.

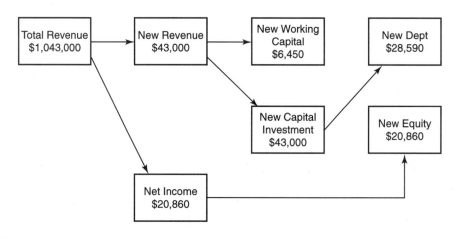

▲ FIGURE 10-2 Hospital Growth under the Debt-to-Plant Restriction

G = maximum growth rate

CI = $ of capital investment required to support $1 of revenues

WC = $ of working capital required to support $1 of revenues

X = maximum allowable debt/equity ratio

M = net income margin

Funds generated by growth = funds required to support growth

$(CI)(X)(G) + (M)(1 + G) = (CI + WC)G$

$$G = \frac{M}{(CI + WC) - (CI)(X) - (M)}$$

Table 10-3 presents the maximum growth rates for values of X. Again, $M \times CI + WC$ is assumed to equal 1.15.

Debt-Service-Coverage

It is reasonable to expect a lender to want some guarantee that a hospital will generate enough income during the year to repay principal and interest. The ability to repay principal and interest is reflected in the debt-service-coverage ratio. This is the ratio of the cash flow available to repay debt to the required debt payments. Specifically, the debt-service-coverage ratio equals:

$$\frac{\text{Net Income} + \text{Depreciation} + \text{Interest}}{\text{Interest} + \text{Principal Payments}}$$

Depreciation is added because it is a noncash charge on the income statement. Typically, this ratio is required to be at least 1.0 to 1.5, with higher coverage ratios being more restrictive to the use of debt. Suppose that CGH has a required margin of 1.50. Depreciable life on new capital investments at CGH averages 20 years, and any new debt would be paid back in equal principal payments over 20 years. If the current interest rate on debt is 10

Table 10-3 Maximum Growth Rates under Debt-to-Plant Restriction

	Net Income Margin				
Level of Constraint: Debt/Total	0 percent	1 percent	2 percent	3 percent	4 percent
0.67	0	2	4	7	9
0.70	0	2	5	7	10
0.75	0	3	5	8	11
0.80	0	3	5	8	13
0.90	0	4	9	14	19

percent, then it can be shown that the maximum allowable growth rate is just under 3.4 percent.

In this case, CGH would generate $34,000 in new revenues. This growth would require additional plant and equipment of $34,000, to be depreciated over 20 years at $1,700 per year. Additional working capital of $5,000 is needed as well. Net income for next year would be $30,680. Additional debt of $18,420 is required to support operations. The debt will be paid back in annual installments of $921. The first year's interest due is $1,842, and the total interest plus principal due in the first year is $2,763. We can now see that the coverage ratio will be maintained at 1.5.

Additional net income is $680. Depreciation is $1,700. Interest is $1,842. The sum is $4,222, which, except for rounding errors, is exactly 1.5 times the required interest and principal payments. **Table 10–4** summarizes these figures. Again, faster growth would require additional debt, and CGH would be unable to maintain its coverage ratio.

Deriving an equation to determine the maximum growth rate under various situations is a simple task. The final equation is presented below.

G = maximum allowable growth rate

CI = $ of capital investment required to support $1 of revenue

WC = $ of working capital required to support $1 of revenue

C = required coverage ratio

I = rate of interest on debt

RP = repayment of interest on debt

M = net income margin

DL = depreciable life of new plant equipment

$$G = [(C \times M) \div RP + (C \times I \times M) - (I \times M)] \div [(((WC + CI) \times C) \div RP + ((WC + CI) \times C \times I) - M - (CI \div DL) - ((WC + CI) \times I)]$$

Table 10–4 How CGH Meets Its Debt-Service-Coverage Ratio			
Cash Inflow	=	1.5 x Required Payments	
Additional Net Income	$ 680	Principal	$ 920
Additional Depreciation	$1,700	Interest	$1,842
			$2,762
Interest	$1,842		
	$4,222 – 1.5 x $2,762		

Table 10-5 presents the maximum growth rates for coverage ratios of 1.25 and 1.5. As the coverage ratio approaches one, the maximum allowable growth rate approaches infinity.

Table 10-5 Maximum Growth Rates under Debt-Service Constraint								
	1.25 Coverage				1.50 Coverage			
Prevailing Interest	Net Income Margin				Net Income Margin			
Rates	0%	1%	2%	3%	0%	1%	2%	3%
6%	0%/yr	3%/yr	10%/yr	23%/yr	0%/yr	2%/yr	4%/yr	8%/yr
8%	0	2	7	24	0	1	3	7
10%	0	2	6	15	0	1	3	6
12%	0	2	5	11	0	1	3	5
14%	0	2	4	9	0	1	3	5
16%	0	2	4	8	0	1	3	5

For the purposes of calculations for **Table 10-6**, working capital and capital investment needs are assumed to be $1.15 for each dollar of revenue. The repayment period on new debt is 30 years, and the average depreciable life of new capital investment is 25 years. These are typical figures for most hospitals, although depreciable life in proprietary hospitals tends to be a bit shorter (20 years), and depreciable life in voluntary hospitals tends to be longer— 25 years (unpublished data provided by the Capital Finance Division of the American Hospital Association).

Table 10-6 Maximum Growth of Different Capital Investment Requirements	
Capital Investment	Maximum Growth
0.8	12 %/year
0.9	10
1.0	8
1.1	7
1.2	6

As fewer patients are covered under a health plan that recognizes interest expense as an allowable expense for cost-based reimbursement, the coverage ratio as normally calculated in business increasingly neglects a hospital's ability to repay its debt. The figures used to calculate the coverage ratio should be the unreimbursable portion of the interest expense. Assume that CGH has cash flows (which include interest expense) of $20,000 and interest and principal payments of $15,000, or a coverage ratio of 1.33. If 50 percent of CGH's $5,000 in interest expense is reimbursed (because 50 percent of CGH's volume is reimbursed on a cost basis), then these figures should be adjusted to $17,500 [$20,000 − 0.5($5,000)] in cash inflow and $12,500 [$15,000 − 0.5($5,000)] in required debt service. The coverage ratio increased to 1.40. To calculate a maximum growth rate, one can simply use I' instead of I in the given equation, where $I' = I \times V$ and V is the percentage volume not cost-based.

Under typical conditions, a hospital that has reached its debt ceiling and has a small net income margin often is limited to an annual growth rate of 4 percent or less. For hospitals with a high percentage of revenues coming from uninsured indigent-care patients, the net income margin is often 1 percent or less. In the future, these hospitals will find it increasingly difficult to generate new funds from any source.

Hospitals that are not presently near their debt capacity might find their leverage positions weakening quickly as growth continues unabated. For example, if CGH has a debt-to-capital ratio of 0.5, an annual revenue growth of 10 percent per year, and a net income margin of 2 percent, the debt-to-total-capital ratio would increase to 0.67 in just nine years. If the debt-to-plant ratio is 0.5, then under these conditions this ratio would increase to 0.67 in just six years.

We have surveyed capital-structure decisions facing the healthcare industry. Hospitals unable to maintain a reasonable income margin lose their autonomy. To insure against this, payers should allow for a small but significant profit margin. Three equations are derived in this chapter to measure the impact that private-sector financing authorities could have on hospital growth as a function of various suggested financial ratio ceiling requirements. After a sensitivity analysis, it is concluded that a 3 percent operating margin would be barely sufficient to reduce the case study hospital's high dependence on debt. The definition of an adequate operating margin will vary among different-size hospitals and different ownership arrangements. Teaching hospitals might require a 4 percent to 6 percent margin, yet they are the least likely group to achieve their target. Payment formulas fixed in this manner would not only remove the incentives for excessive reliance on debt financing but also allow new capital to be equally equity-financed (47 percent equity and 47 percent debt). Philanthropy will continue to have a minor role to play (6 percent of new capital stock).

The hospital sector might reach the limits of its debt capacity in a decade. Progressive Democrats have suggested a coordinated intervention into the capital process. To allocate capital irrespective of wealth of the patient mix, Congress could create a local Federal Reserve-style capital bank to correct or subsidize hospitals that emphasize research or indigent care. Unfortunately, a capital bank might be as inefficient in distributing equity as investment in the ideal of equity as community-based hospital planning. The "cure-all of regulation" does appeal to hospitals that are desperate for access to capital. Hospitals turned to debt financing because it was cheap and because other sources of funding (grants and gifts) had declined. As hospitals become more and more highly leveraged, new debt issues will be perceived as being more and more risky. Interest rates will rise, increasing the cost of hospital debt. Some of this increase will be passed along to consumers through reimbursement mechanisms, but hospitals will increasingly have to shoulder much of the burden themselves. Payers want hospitals to earn an ROE by improving productivity.

The emerging healthcare marketplace is risky, because there is a widening spread of possible outcomes. The measure of spread is the standard deviation (or variances). Risk has two components: unique risk (specific to the individual firm), and market risk of the industry (which is affected by marketwide shocks and changes, such as change in federal Medicare payment policies). Investors can eliminate unique risk by having a widely diversified portfolio of holdings, but they cannot eliminate market risk. In other words, all the risk of a fully diversified portfolio consists of market risk. A firm's sensitivity to changes in the value of the market portfolio is the beta.

How Much Risk Can You Take?

Contrary to the popular view, gambling is not speculation. A gamble is the assumption of risk for enjoyment of the risk itself. By contrast, speculation is undertaken in spite of the risk involved, because a favorable risk-return relationship is perceived. Speculation is the assumption of considerable financial risk in obtaining commensurate gain. Commensurate gain means a positive expected profit beyond the risk-free alternative (a Treasury bill). Considerable risk means the risk is sufficient to affect the acquisition decision. You might reject the venture that has a positive risk premium because the added gain is insufficient to the risk involved. In today's rapidly changing healthcare marketplace, risk aversion and speculation are consistent strategies in the evolution of an optimal portfolio for your preference. You might be risk-averse in some areas, and speculative in other ventures.

In some situations, adding a seemingly risky asset to a portfolio actually reduces the risk of the entire portfolio. Investing to balance a portfolio and reduce net risk is called *hedging*. If you are overinvested in nursing home care, then investing in a more risky high-tech home healthcare business is a hedge for your overall portfolio. The hedge works because home healthcare is a partial substitute for nursing home care, and any new payment system to reduce nursing home lengths of stay hurts your nursing home business and strongly helps your new home healthcare business. I live 14 miles from Ocean City, New Jersey, and my hedge for suntan lotion investments is rain umbrellas (this hedge worked well in the wet early summer of 1998).

A number of large hospitals own nursing homes. One should avoid the fallacy of evaluating the risk of an asset (such as a nursing home) separately from the other assets owned by the "mothership" investor (for example, the hospital). Joint risks are difficult to assess in a complex organization with joint products. Nursing homes can produce profits and reduce inpatient hospital losses with good discharge planning. To reduce the volatility of the overall mothership portfolio, you will accept higher risk in individual components of the portfolio (such as buying a home healthcare agency and a teaching nursing home).

Diversification and Structure

Another method used to manage portfolio risk is diversification. In designing a diversification plan, one must consider all relevant factors. A robust analysis of rivalry determinants includes product differences, brand identity, intermittent overcapacity, diversity of competitors, and exit barriers. Entry barriers to consider involve capital requirements, cost advantages and economies of scale, switching costs, and expected retaliation. Determinants of supplier power to consider include market concentration, importance of a critical mass level of volume, impact of inputs on cost and quality differentiation, threats of forward integration, and the risk of backward integration. Most critical are the determinants of buyer power: buyer propensity to substitute, switching costs, bargaining leverage, product differences, price sensitivity, and the perceived value of service quality.

Healthcare firms must diversify, hedge, and restructure in order to survive. In times of stress we seek out new partners. In evaluating new partnerships, each party must assess risk and return and weigh the chances for mutual benefit. Benefits may include greater access to capital, new markets, and enhanced professional management expertise. We must better train managers to assess risk. This task was easier in the past. In the "old days," when there were few objective risks, students could be trained in processes (not strategy and subjective risk estimation). However, future generations of managers must work on strategy selection, forecasting, and subjective risk estimation.

Cost Reports, Mergers, and Competition

Cost report scandals are often reported in the media. Categories of costs that have no hope for acceptance should be eliminated, and those possessing only a small probability of approval should be identified on the face of the report "protested items." These protested items would not have to be included in taxable income because they are identified clearly as improbable occurrences. If a more accurate cost report is filed, "phantom" tax liabilities can be avoided. One West Coast firm experienced a $59 million difference between net-of-discount cost-based revenues reported for financial purposes and amounts requested per the cost report. Assuming a dubious cost report, the company paid approximately $18 million in taxes on revenues it can reasonably expect never to realize. Although the company will be able to take a deduction when the cost report is settled and recoup the tax already paid, it generally takes three years to reconcile. In terms of present value (assuming a conservative 6 percent discount rate), the company will lose approximately $2.7 million as a result of its artificially inflated tax liability.

Recent evaluations of mergers suggest that cost control for society, in terms of lower costs for the community, will not be primary benefits of the organizational marriage. Surveys of Health Care Investment Analysts (HCIA, 2002) data suggest that mergers slightly improved profitability by reducing expenses and increasing gross and net patient revenues. The results contradict any claim that mergers save patients money because the increase in billed charges more than makes up for any cost cuts; that is, cost reductions are not partially passed on to consumers through reduced patient expenses. Most of the merging facilities realized that one cannot merge a little bit; a merger is all or nothing. Some hospitals also experience marginal cost increases in overhead due to the Noah's Ark effect, or the urge to keep two of everything, such as two department heads, in too many areas of each hospital after the merger. Such lack of cost cutting does not make sense, unless one thinks that the hospital exists as an employment program for hospital employees. In a competitive world, cost control and product enhancement (quality) are keys to success. Merger participants must also consider Department of Justice antitrust concerns (Eastaugh 2000).

Some hospitals might prefer to stand alone. The remaining investor-owned freestanding hospitals might offer a fiscal example of economic Darwinism: They must be very strong to avoid being absorbed by the for-profit chains. Some for-profit systems have problems with high overhead and a high ratio of debt-to-total assets. Half the big chains have action plans to cut overhead. In one case, the two top layers of administration were eliminated, so individual hospital CEOs now report to group presidents, who report to chain system presidents.

For the traditional economist, nonprice competition is to competition what computer football is to full-contact football, a poor approximation at best. The price competition for the health maintenance organization (HMO) business kicked in during the 1990s. Robinson (2002) reported from a sample of 5,090 hospitals that the average inflation-adjusted cost per nonelderly patient declined 0.71 percent in high-competition markets and increased 2.82 percent in low-competition markets. Market failure might be prevalent in the hospital industry, but competition does have the expected impact on hospital costs (lower cost).

Hybridization and Joint Ventures

The treacherous and complex payment climate demands creative joint venturing among chains, autonomous hospitals, insurance companies, HMOs, and consortia groups. Some of this competitive activity led to very noncompetitive monopoly or oligopoly markets. HMOs and hospitals must soon realize that they are not facing a minor dip, but rather are dealing with an old-fashioned dog-eat-dog shakeout. For-profit firms are considering several strategies for improving their attractiveness to investors. Interdependent strategies range from tighter operations (such as reduced overhead and better productivity) to converting long-term debt and improving earnings per share by trading existing shares for a real estate investment trust (REIT) on company property. The REIT is a business organization that combines two concepts. First, it is an investment vehicle whereby individual and institutional investors can pool their resources and participate in a professionally managed real estate portfolio. Second, a qualified REIT is exempt from any corporate income taxes, provided it complies with certain Internal Revenue Code requirements. The ability of a qualified REIT to distribute its income to shareholders in the form of dividends free of corporate income taxes obviously enhances its ability to generate an attractive yield to its outside investors. The REIT was used by one mid-Atlantic chain. Earnings per share became more attractive because the number of shares outstanding were cut in half, but the balance sheet erodes. Investors in the REIT own the bricks and mortar of 20 hospitals, and the chain continues to own the equipment.

Ultimately, investor-owned firms emphasizing cost control and debt reduction will shrink or expand according to their price competitiveness (especially as they enter more price-competitive markets, such as psychiatric care). Continued attempts to offer a capitation product present a two-edged sword: The risk of financial failure but the possible benefit of revitalization of this mature industry. Hybridization is becoming a two-way street. Tax-exempt firms were the first to travel the road to multiple for-profit taxable subsidiaries, and investor-owned firms might donate failed ventures to the tax-exempt. (If one cannot make a business profit or a tax profit from a failure, one might as well label it a "nonprofit" concern).

Hospital chains will continue to reduce exposure to the declining inpatient sector in order to reduce corporate overhead. But if they fail to raise earnings, they will become ripe takeover candidates. In theory, the pooling of complementary strengths represents the hope behind the hybridization and joint-venture trend. Many weaker chains, insurance firms, and hospitals might be swallowed up by the large surviving chains. Restraints on autonomy will be especially difficult for the acquired firm if the parent firm instinctively overmanages its new "teammate."

Although this chapter has been operations oriented, it appears most appropriate to end with a few observations concerning business ethics. The pursuit of a nonmonetary ethos has been paradoxical: The more it is pursued, the more elusive it becomes. An obsession with the ownership issue produces a narrowness of vision and ignores basic issues such as survival and access to sufficient capital to promote quality care. Our search for capital and joint ventures might reap some unfortunate results (given imperfect payment formulas) if socially irresponsible firms fail to provide community access to the poor. The solution is to not kill the "golden goose" and rail against non-physician profit-taking. Rather, the solution is to enforce a social contract to force all concerned to bear their fair share of the burden of charity care.

▶ Summary Points:

- The return on capital is the effective cost of capital.

- Cutting overhead, particularly senior management, is an effective way to reduce costs without reducing quality.

- Assumptions concerning risk and return should be conservative.

Research and Discussion Questions:

- How do we operate in the real business world and provide a social good?

References

Altman, E. 1968. Financial ratios, discriminant analysis and the prediction of corporate bankruptcy. *Journal of Finance* 23(4): 589–609.

American Hospital Association. 2002. *Panel survey of hospitals*. Chicago: American Hospital Association.

Blue Cross and Blue Shield Association. 2002. *State legislative health care and insurance issues*. Chicago: National Blue Cross and Blue Shield.

Carpenter, C., and McCue, M. 2002. System bond issue. *Journal of Health Care Finance* 29(2): 26–33.

Conrad, D. 1999. *Integrated delivery systems: Creation, management, and governance*. Ann Arbor, MI: Health Administration Press.

Cyert, R. 1998. *Academic strategy: The management revolution*. Baltimore: Johns Hopkins Press.

Eastaugh, S. 1992. Effectiveness of community-based hospital planning: Some recent evidence. *Applied Economics* 14(5): 475–490.

Eastaugh, S. 1998. *Health care finance: Cost, production and strategy design*. Gaithersburg, MD: Aspen.

Eastaugh, S. 2000. Managing risk in a risky world. *Journal of Health Care Finance* 18(4): 10–17.

Gapenski, L. 1998. *Understanding health care financial management*. Ann Arbor, MI: AUPHA Press/Health Administration Press.

Goldstein, L. 2002. *Not-for-profit health care: Access to capital and debt capacity: Alternative debt financing strategies and their credit implications*. New York: Moody's.

Health Care Investment Analysts. 2002. *Trends in health care spending*. Annapolis, MD: Author: Health Care Investment Analysts.

Johnson, R. 1999. Nonprofit hospitals: Bargain prices. *Health Affairs* 16(4): 284–285.

Kidder-Peabody and Company. 2001. *Tax-exempt hospital revenue bonds: A data base*. New York: Kidder-Peabody.

Lawson, D., and Barrai, B. 2002. *Hospital industry handbook*. New York: Salomon Smith Barney Equity Research.

McDermott, W. 1998. Technology's consort. *American Journal of Medicine* 74(3): 353.

Modigliani, F., and Miller, M. 1963. Taxes and the cost of capital. *American Economic Review* 53(3): 433–443.

Robinson, J. 2002. Bond market skepticism and stock market exuberance. *Health Affairs* 21(1): 104–117.

Silver, J., and Kauer, R. 1996. Return on equity for not-for-profit hospitals. *Health Services Research* 21(1): 21–25.

Smith, D., and Wheeler, J. 2002. Finance strategy relationship. *Journal of Health Care Finance* 29(2): 1–11.

Standard & Poor's Public Finance. 2002. *2002 median health care ratios*. New York: Standard & Poor's.

Taylor, G., and Kam, M. 2002. *Hospital industry commentary*. New York: Bank of America Securities Equity Research.

Zuckerman, L. 2002. *Health system ratios: Then and now*. New York: Standard & Poor's.

Chapter 11

Future Issues and Alternatives

Americans utter general words about how everybody should have adequate health care, and create 47 overlapping arrangements to deal with the question of access. Our American tradition is to not do anything with a comprehensive single system, although it may be very expensive and duplicative.

– John T. Dunlop

Epidemiology is the practice of medicine without the tears. Evidence based medico-statistics is not better than standard wise clinical judgment.

– Arthur Holleb, M.D.

▶ **Critical Points in this Chapter:**

- National health insurance

- Universal access

- There is a delicate balance to maintain between health care as a social good and health care as a consumer good.

In 1978, when Arthur Holleb, medical director of the American Cancer Society, spoke the words above, we were startled to find out how poor the level of medical knowledge is at times. Effective cost control should not mean remote control medicine by utilization review from a distance. We now have three decades of experience with evidence-based medicine, improved policy guidelines, and cost-effective clinical decision making. Providers see the need to improve both quality and efficiency, but managed care patients report many problems. For these patients, the system is increasingly corporate-run, rationed, NC (no choice), RT (red tape), SL (severely limited), and offers LP (loss of privacy). The corporate-run system has been worse than the proposed government-oversight managed competition Clinton health plan. The ironic twist is that the managed care system has grown as fast as predicted under the 1993 Clinton plan. All the blame for dislocating changes (NC, RT, SL, LP) rests on the marketplace. For patients, the invisible hand of market forces is all thumbs. Government is the good guy, with 80 percent less red tape, fewer limits, enhanced privacy, and a new patient bill of rights. Market ideologues are wounded and in full retreat.

We can expand quality and access to necessary medical care. Political forces for national health insurance resemble dammed-up rivers. The pressure on the dams is enormous but unseen; it is only when the public issue attention cycle peaks because healthcare providers dump poor patients (or go bankrupt) that the strain is realized. Are we ready for a systematic healthcare system that offers (1) universal coverage, (2) universal access, (3) cost control, and (4) flexibility for steady quality-of-care improvements? Previous studies suggest that a regulatory approach to national health insurance simply expands bureaucracy and administrative costs. Pessimists argue that the United States is simply passing through its eighth issue attention cycle favoring, but not initiating, national health insurance. Passage of some national plan seemed forever imminent during certain periods in the past: 1917 to 1919, 1933 to 1934, 1947 to 1948, 1964 to 1966, 1973 to 1974, 1979, and 1993. The inertia on the issue is the product of a long U.S. tradition of equivocation on health policy. Equivocation "triumphs" each decade because the public is willing to pay to maximize the diversity of health plans available and fears that government intervention will result in choice being constrained. The lack of widespread discontent with our expensive medical systems seems to ensure slow marginal change in existing programs. On the other hand, optimists point out that Congress passed progressive reforms despite a diffuse mood of skepticism and bare-bones reimbursement. Yet, government remains central to healthcare delivery. According to conservative estimates, the United States will spend $2.8 trillion on health care in 2009, and 69 percent of this total will be government dollars. One-tenth of this 69 percent figure will come from tax subsidies (Office of National Cost Estimates, 2002).

Fans of the Canadian healthcare system have advocated abolishing all private and public insurance plans to create a one-payer plan to cover everyone, financed entirely by taxes, with a system of state and regional boards negotiating with providers on compensation. The benefits of such a one-payer system are obvious to many: less paperwork, less administrative expense, and fewer financial barriers to access. The problem with the Canadian approach is that the local government can ration care through inconvenience: long waits for elective surgery, tests, and checkup visits. Many managed care health plans have been cited for having these same problems but to a lesser degree. Rather than copy the Canadian model, Enthoven (1999) advocated preserving an employer-based approach, offering tax incentives, and mandating "universal coverage for all" through a competition healthcare plan approach. The many health plans, contracting with both employers and statewide "public sponsors," would compete for enrollees based on price and quality. A third alternative, advocated by the National Leadership Commission on Health Care, would keep Medicare and the present health insurance system but spend an additional $38 billion in public funds to guarantee a basic adequate benefits package. To avoid the unpopular word *taxes*, the commission advocated premiums and fees in the form of income tax surcharges.

Lack of insurance and poor access to care are the forgotten stepchildren of our increasingly competitive medical marketplace. Hospitals compete for market share of the paying-patient business, but no one competes for nonpaying patients. The debate over indigent care will lead nowhere until some consensus is gained on whether our top priority is institutional financial support or provision of access to a minimum standard of care for underinsured and uninsured citizens. Institutional managers try to minimize uncompensated care and mainstream the poor to other hospitals, no matter that this is costly and inefficient. The tenet of faith among managers and some researchers that equity, efficiency, and access are zero-sum propositions is certainly open to question. On the other hand, one could question whether we can promote affordable managed care systems for the uninsured and still maintain the dream of mainstreaming all people into "best quality" service-delivery systems. We hear reports on how the poor are dumped from hospitals. Policy makers insist that indigent care is a vexing problem and demand that providers do "it" better—with hardly any consideration of the "it" we want improved. Good care for our population is the answer. But what is the question?

Wanted: Stable Financing

Most healthcare professionals are familiar with statistics that demonstrate the paradox of deprivation amid excess (excess acute care beds and almost $3.8 billion per day spent on health services). Roughly 32 million adult Americans lack health insurance, even when the unemployment rate dips below 5.0 percent. According to the Department of Health and Human Services (DHHS), about 80 percent of the uninsured had jobs or were dependents of those who worked (ONCE 2002). Point-in-time data on the uninsured population are skewed toward the demographic traits of those individuals who have periods of being temporarily uninsured. Over half of the uninsured periods last less than five months. If only uninsured spells are reported in a point-in-time survey, 59 percent last longer than two years, and only 13 percent end within four months. From the more realistic longitudinal viewpoint, observing people over time, only 15 percent of uninsured periods last longer than two years. Employed people and people with higher income are more likely to experience uninsured spells than point-in-time data on the uninsured indicate. One in every five uninsured individuals has family income exceeding $5,000 per month. Two-thirds of the people who lose employer coverage, but do not lose employment, have uninsured spells that end in four months (ONCE 2002). The majority of this employed/uninsured group lack insurance while serving as probationary employees on new jobs. The hard-core uninsured/unemployed population, lacking insurance for over two years and not eligible for Medicaid, might represent fewer than 5.4 million Americans. An expanded Medicaid program could help these 5.4 million citizens. Can we afford to allow one in seven nonelderly Americans to lack health insurance? Are we our brothers' and sisters' keepers with respect to health care?

What should come between a family and the health care they need? Nothing is more important than the peace of mind that comes from knowing a family's health coverage will stay with them. Coverage to the working poor can be expanded without destroying the profits of the insurance industry. Why should we care? Simply consider the effectiveness of insurance industry television ads against the Clinton Reform Plan of 1993, the famous Harry and Louise television ads, for which the Health Insurance Association of America paid $28 million. Misinformation campaigns can continue to stop healthcare system reform.

Innovation or Inequity

The United States has one of the most inconsistent policies toward health services delivery: We produce it as a consumer good, finance it as a public good, and let the private sector un-insure or underinsure one-third of the population. As we debate system reform to cover the uninsured, greater attention is being paid to other national systems. The OECD survey (2002) suggests that the reciprocal problems of patient access and cost control can be addressed by implementing flexible global budgets and guaranteeing coverage for all citizens. Higher investments in health education and health promotion happen only after budget caps are placed on acute medical care expenditures. To avoid the special interest group impact of lobbyists, a U.S. global budget board would have to be independent and modeled after the Federal Reserve Board.

Policy trends in U.S. health care currently point in all different directions, like a pile of jackstraws. Support can be found in Congress for deregulation, reregulation, national health insurance, managed competition, planned competition, and free competition. U.S. health care is plagued by underinsurance, overuse, underuse, and misuse. Currently 39 million Americans, 15 percent of the population, have no health insurance. For the working poor, it is harder to get a prescription than to buy a gun. The problem is described as "deprivation amidst plenty" (Reinhardt 2001). Safety is increasingly a major concern in floaters' minds. "If not now, when?" could be the slogan for those who want to make health care a right for all citizens. Good economic times are optimal for enacting a new social program. Passing national health insurance would enhance national productivity and reduce the dead weight loss in the economy that comes from $320 billion in annual medical administration paperwork from 1,520 different insurance forms. Every other nation has no more than three forms and spends 80 percent less per capita on administration and paperwork (Eastaugh 2001).

Reform: Forever Imminent

The old saying that necessity is the mother of invention has a corollary: Lack of necessity impedes innovation. The working poor have no political power, and special interest groups like the insurance industry are against change. Since 1962, nine U.S. presidents and 21 sessions of Congress have considered the issue of national health insurance, but reform remained forever imminent. Physician provider groups began to separate from their natural ally for the status quo, the insurance industry, in the late 1990's. Various physician groups began to call for national health insurance and systems reform as patient complaints and bad debts increased. Most physicians sided with consumerists, and against insurance lobbyists, in the Congressional debate over the Patient Bill of Rights.

Lessons from Two Nations

As policy makers debate national healthcare reform options, greater attention is being paid to other national systems. Important lessons can be learned from the last nation (South Korea, 1989) and the first nation (Germany, 1883) to pass national health insurance. The reciprocal problems of access and cost control can be addressed by implementing three initiatives: global budgets, promotion of primary care, and improving health education. Any plan that does not pursue all three initiatives (BCE: budgets, care, and education) will fail to achieve the two bedrock objectives of reform: universal access and cost containment.

Nations with national health insurance or a national health service use a global budget to contain the size and the scope of the healthcare sector. Global budgets provide an annual cap on total national healthcare spending. The global budget forces providers to contain costs and make explicit budget choices. The American College of Physicians and the American College of Surgeons have endorsed implementation of a global budget by an independent national commission that reports to Congress. This proposed national commission would cover public and private operating budgets and capital outlays for the healthcare industry. Why would U.S. providers move to such a major reform measure? Because physicians view global budgets as the lesser evil, in contrast to managed care systems that provide meddlesome micromanagement of individual patient care decisions. Physician autonomy is better with global budgets.

Rather than look, as many have, to Canada or England as a prototype for reform, we might do better to look at South Korea. Similarities between South Korea and the United States are striking: Each nation has a history of fee-for-service medicine, a high ratio of specialists and surgeons, four beds per 1,000 citizens, and a bias for the best "microquality" for the injured patient by running them through a tunnel of technology. In 1989 compassionate conservatives running the South Korean government passed a national health insurance plan. How long did it take Koreans to sign up the 24 percent of the population that was uninsured? Four months. One-fourth of the population signed up for the same insurance plan that government employees received. How long was the national health insurance bill? Four pages.

A U.S. humorist like Dave Barry or P.J. O'Rourke could offer up a good synopsis of U.S. policymaking: (1) U.S. laws have to be piecemeal and take 10 years to do so very little; (2) since 1997 our Child Health Insurance Program (CHIP) signs up to 1.2 million children per year—in the United States you cannot cover one-sixth or one-fourth of the population in four months (or 40 years); (3) our bills must be 1,600 pages long, not four pages like the 1965 Medicare Act. The South Korean push for primary care has doubled the number of medical students going into primary care in the last decade. Many U.S. policymakers and analysts have listened to the South Korean experience and advocate abolishing Medicaid in favor of giving the uninsured access to the insurance programs for federal employees, requiring parents to insure and bring their children in for annual checkups, offering a prescription benefit, subsidizing insurance premiums for poor families, and giving tax breaks to those with modest incomes.

There are three basic lessons from the German experience with 12 decades of national health insurance. The first is that cost control is important but global budgets can be too tight—so tight that it might, in the long-run, erode the biomedical capacity of the nation (therefore the global budgets are being liberalized over the next five years). The second lesson is that a trim, administratively efficient national system can maximize consumer by choice offering 1,100 different insurance options. Germans have three claims forms (not 1,520, like the United States), but they offer a wide variety of benefit plans (1,100, not five like Korea, or one like the Canadian single-payer approach). The Germans offer variety and consumer choice, yet they spend only 5.1 percent of the health economy on administration and paperwork (Reinhardt 2001). The United States spends over 20 percent on administration and paperwork. Thirdly, the Germans are strikingly efficient at promoting primary care and health education through their general internists and pediatricians. Germans do not have the U.S. problem of a gross oversupply of specialists.

National Spending Comparisons

Drawing an analogy between nations over time is a hazardous undertaking. One German minister asked the author, "Who will be the Otto von Bismark of American health care?" An equally interesting question is whether the United States can expand access half as effectively as South Korea, while containing cost half as effectively as Germany. South Koreans experienced the same demand-pull inflation in newly insured citizens that the United States experienced from 1966 to 1971 (prior to implementation of price controls by Republican President Nixon in 1971). Rather than rigid price controls, current South Korean leaders are looking to the new global budgeting system of Germany. The German system of Global Budgets by Consensus (GBBC) has kept the healthcare sector at 10 percent of GDP (**Table 11-1**). In the new German system, fee negotiations between providers and sickness funds require final approval from the local government, and the flexible process is typified by compromise and consensus building. Every six months federal and state governments, sickness funds, labor unions, hospitals, and physician associations agree on fees and annual expense targets in each sector of the health economy. If physician fees exceed their target in one time period, they subsequently are reduced in future periods to penalize the providers for cost overruns. In the jargon of accounting, this political process is a variance analysis under a limited budget (the global pie of dollars for local health care). If the budget variance is unfavorable (over budget) the prices are deflated in proportion to the unnecessary portion of the volume growth. Therefore, in action the global budget is effectively a flexible spending cap.

There are two types of global budgets: global budgets by formulae, and GBBC, utilizing a national board or commission. Global budgeting offers the equitable distribution of dissatisfaction; that is, no segment of the health economy is left satiated with unlimited growth in funding. Global budgeting is not a bloodless technical exercise whereby provider payment rates are automatically set according to a multiyear rolling average growth economic equation. Global budgets have a strong capitalist tradition in many U.S. cities

Table 11-1 Health Care Costs in Selected Countries, 2003

	Health Expenditures Per Capita (US$PPPa)	Percent Gross Domestic Product (GDP)	Government Fraction of Health Expenditures
1. USA	$5,698	13.5 percent	0.465[b]
2. Germany	2,998	10.6	0.778
3. Canada	2,883	9.8	0.721
4. France	2,584	9.8	0.788
5. Denmark	2,504	8.6	0.698
6. Netherlands	2,489	8.3	0.739
7. Norway	2,488	7.8	0.828
8. Australia	2,368	8.6	0.698
9. Japan	2,254	7.8	0.796
10. Sweden	2,186	8.0	0.839
11. Italy	2,138	8.3	0.729
12. United Kingdom	2,092	7.5	0.848
13. Ireland	2,089	7.3	0.765
14. Spain	1,839	7.6	0.795
15. Greece	1,587	8.2	0.754
16. South Korea	1,034	5.9	0.718
17. Mexico	612	5.5	0.808

[a] Purchasing Power Parties (PPP) are used to convert expenditures to $US. PPPs convert the rate of currency from one country into a common currency, in order to purchase the same quantity of a given item in all nations (OECD 2002).

[b] 0.542 if you do not exclude the $84 billion tax subsidy to purchase private insurance.

and towns. For example, the budgets for eight Rochester, New York hospitals are set by global budgeting (two corporate CEOs representing 79 percent of insured patients sit at the budget roundtable) (Eastaugh 1999).

The generosity of the global budget process depends on local economic conditions. When the Canadian government tried to implement harsh expenditure limits from 1966 to1999, political pressure forced the government to add an additional $16 billion to the annual budget in 2002 (Sullivan 2001). In the South Korean context, the budget pie is not so large because the economy was in tough shape in the 1990s, and the benefit plan was never as generous (Germans get four weeks of full reimbursement for going to a spa). The share of GDP going to health care has doubled in South Korea, to 5.9 percent of GDP since the passage of national healthcare insurance in 1990.

Results in **Table 11–1** suggest that countries with national health insurance are more effective at containing costs. Each of the countries listed below the United States in **Table 11–1** have private sector spending that varies from 15 to 30 percent of total health expenditures. There probably is a link between economic growth and expansion of the healthcare sector (Bhargava 2002).

Growth in the health economy is best measured against the yardstick of growth in the general economy. As we observe in **Table 11–2**, the three nations with the lowest rate of growth in real elasticity (Germany, United Kingdom, and Canada) all have stringent programs for setting global budgets on the healthcare sector. Each of these three countries operates with a unique

Table 11–2 Elasticity of Per Capita Health Care Costs Relative to Per Capita Gross Domestic Product (GDP), 1980–2002	
	Real Elasticity[*]
1. South Korea	1.56
2. Japan	1.45
3. USA	1.29
4. France	1.28
5. Sweden	1.08
6. Netherlands	1.08
7. Canada	0.94
8. Denmark	1.00
9. Italy	1.02
10. Norway	1.01
11. Ireland	0.98
12. Spain	0.98
13. Australia	0.97
14. Greece	0.96
15. United Kingdom	0.93
16. Germany	0.91

[*] Health price-deflated per capita costs relative to GDP-deflator-adjusted per capita GDP (OECD 2002)

political context. The labor government is attempting to reverse 18 years of tight Tory budgets for the British National Health Service. Canadian providers are lobbying to create more flexible caps in each of the 10 provincial health plans. The most stringent country for using a global budget system to contain the health sector at 10 percent of GDP, Germany, has announced it will reform all three global budgets in the year 2004. First, German hospitals' fixed budgets are becoming flexible negotiated target budgets (with teaching hospitals receiving DRG adjusted casemix budgets). Second, pharmaceutical expenditures that were set under fixed budget caps are being replaced by flexible regionally negotiated spending caps. Third, legally fixed ambulatory care budgets are being replaced by regional negotiated flexible budgets (Wismar 2002).

If these three nations are rolling back their systems of global budgets, two nations in **Table 11-2**, South Korea and Japan, are forced by slow economic growth to implement flexible global budgets for the healthcare sector. The Japanese have one interesting policy custom. The premiums are kept affordable in Japan because the law requires that the premium be based on a percentage of income rather than on actuarial risks. Perhaps Bill Gates should pay $4,000 per month for healthcare insurance, and you and I should pay $40?

Lessons for the United States

The United States has the best high-tech medical system in the world. While we are number one for high costs, we rank twenty-third in infant mortality and sixteenth in adult life expectancy (OECD 2002). U.S. health care is delivered within a web of fragmented systems. For superior quality to occur, the twenty-first century U.S. health sector must offer coverage for all and be designed to function effectively and efficiently with minimum variation and high reliability. A patchwork system of managed care rules, bad debts, illegal patients, and cost-shifting games does not do the job. Americans want one-stop shopping in an integrated delivery system that delivers measurable quality and consistency, without unnecessary and costly variation. We can get a better system if we demand it. South Korea passed national health insurance despite facing the same barriers to action that we face: distrust of government, a robust private sector opposed to change, conservative politicians, and heterogeneity of the population.

For ethical and economic reasons, the United States should be concerned that short-shifting 39 million uninsured Americans only makes their own care more expensive in the long run. If health care is a necessary basic commodity like food, society should underwrite a minimum basic needs policy for all, as the American Hospital Association advocates. Currently, the uninsured poor suffer from "reverse targeting" of preventive care. The population at the highest risk is least likely to be screened or treated. This often results in higher costs of care later on.

Policymakers should pay attention to how other nations implemented the concept of a right to health care. After an initial flood of new patients and new funds came the need for global budgets (either a rigid fixed cap or a flexible cap). By placing all competing needs on the global budget table, we can begin to overcome the U.S. habit of thinking that our healthcare problems are a list of discrete, unconnected defects in the marketplace. Congress is familiar with these issues, and has already set up a Medicare Volume Performance Standard Budget that operates much like a global budget for Medicare.

A flexible global budgeting process should yield a more efficient, effective, and equitable healthcare system. Public healthcare efforts like health promotion and health education will begin to get a larger share of the budget pie. To avoid the special interest group impact of fatcat lobbyists with the biggest budgets, a U.S. global budget board would have to be independent and modeled after the Federal Reserve Board. An ideal U.S. GBBC would have the consensus-building style of the German system with a focus on evidence-based medicine and patient outcomes.

A U.S. GBBC process could use continuous quality improvement to allocate capital and operating funds to local regional funds to enhance the efficiency and quality of service delivery. We could pay in proportion to service quality, and reimbursement could stimulate more investment in health promotion and health education. The results would be good economics and good medicine. Budget discipline constrains the Qs (quantity or volume of service) to cap the Es (expenditures). Global budgets are superior to price controls because they manage both P (price) and Q. One last positive impact of global budgets is the impact on administrative costs and paperwork. Global budgets do not allow administrative waste to eat up necessary funds to provide health benefits to the entire population. Nations with global budgets spend 3.6 to 4.4 percent on administration. By contrast, the United States spends 22 percent on administration and paperwork.

The United States can also do more to help global health care in third-world nations. Investing $34 annually per capita would cover anti-retroviral therapy for AIDS, bed nets for malaria, monitored drug therapy for tuberculosis, vaccines, oral rehydration solutions for life-threatening diarrhea, antibiotics for acute respiratory infection, and midwives in attendance at childbirth. Such a program could save 12 million lives per year, with all the attendant economic benefits.

Equity and Quality

Federal policy making has always operated on the "big-wheel principle": those who are first now later will be last, and those who are last will be first. Consequently, the winds of change might make the egalitarians powerful again in a few years. Then we might have an equitable federal indigent care policy, even if national health insurance is judged too expensive. Americans have the highest aspirations for the right of access to the best care for everyone, but we never have the necessary amount of resources to do this on a fee-for-service basis. Managed care is one strategy whereby we institutionalize the right to care with an efficient mode of service delivery. Aggressive bidding systems, which pay more for a better quality service, might be the major innovation for the next decade.

Among providers, the first two strategies in **Exhibit 11-1** appear to be the most effective. Price might begin to take an equal seat with quality in negotiations with payers.

We must stop vacillating around the issue of quality. We cannot have the best healthcare organizations going under because they are good at helping the sickest patients. A better healthcare system would identify when health risks are inequitably distributed among health plans and develop a means for fairly redistributing dollars to those plans that are best serving the sickest patients. Public and private sources can combine forces in buying only from high-quality health plans that report their quality data outcomes to the public and establish a better risk-adjustment mechanism.

The popularity of capitation managed care plans is in doubt in many areas because the rate of innovation in risk adjustment is very slow. Managed care firms fear that implementation of severity adjustments by Medicare will slash their Medicare rates. Methods to predict insurance risk must be retooled to prevent "cream skimming" discrimination against the sick, reduce stinting

Group 1: Productivity defender specialist

Major strategy: Improve productivity, improve managerial cost accounting, reduce excess variable costs, and achieve cost leadership of specialized quality products.

Minor strategies: Pay incentive compensation on productivity gainsharing, slowly diversify following divestment of poor product lines (inferior quality and poor profitability).

Group 2: Selective analyzer, Type 1

Major strategy: Diversify a limited way into related (health) services, and pay incentive compensation based on revenue gains.

Minor strategies: Demonstrate moderate interest in improving productivity.

Group 3: Selective analyzer, Type 2

Major strategy: Diversify moderately into unrelated lines of business (nonhealth) and related (health) services.

Minor strategies: Use good information systems to assess synergies between clinical departments and outposts.

Group 4: Diversifier/prospector

Major strategy: Diversify strongly into unrelated lines of business (nonhealth) and related (health) services.

Minor strategies: Create opportunities in a constant search for new and better investment opportunities.

Group 5: Reactor

Nonstrategy, reaction to local competition.

▲ EXHIBIT 11–1 Five Basic Management Strategies

(undercare), and reward quality providers. Risk cannot be eliminated, but it can be prospectively analyzed, assessed, and hedged. In the coming world, we must convince all concerned parties to spread the risks. Payers must take on some risk by paying for the research and development of valid and reliable severity adjustment systems, and they must pay a higher capitated amount for high-cost patients. A new mixed payment system of pure capitation plus prospective payment for high-risk, high-cost patients will create a more equitable marketplace. If a health maintenance organization (HMO) does a great high-quality job of treating diabetes, acquired immunodeficiency syndrome (AIDS), or heart disease, it could advertise this fact and not be harmed financially by the resulting influx of high-cost patients.

Alternatively, we might be ready to pay in proportion to service quality.

We must pay the high casemix severity providers more for giving better quality care. Some analysts have suggested patching up the system of hospital price controls (diagnosis-related groups, or DRGs) by including a severity-adjustment factor. This new and improved prospective payment system (PPS) would make for a fair "prudent buyer" and help preserve the biomedical capacity of the nation. In theory, this approach could save money, and the savings could be redistributed to finance the rising demand for long-term care. Ways to design a PPS scheme that better protects the four basic dimensions of equity should be considered:

1. Vertical equity, ensuring that different types of hospitals, such as specialty hospitals or teaching facilities, are treated equally.

2. Horizontal equity, ensuring that within a peer category, facilities with equivalent case mixes are paid equally.

3. Financial equity, ensuring that pay is for performance, considering service quality and volume, and not just in proportion to the number of cases.

4. Geographic equity, ensuring that national DRG rates do not let "windfall profits" accrue beyond what is judged to be fair, given operating efficiency and effectiveness.

Quality of service is the one major element missing in the current analysis. Ideally, one would want a payment system that fosters improvement in quality of care, pays lower-than-average price for lower-than-average quality, and stimulates closure of unnecessary inferior hospitals. A reform in the current PPS should offer incentives for inferior performers to improve and should provide punishment for those who do not improve their quality and efficiency. A quality-enhancing bidding (QEB) system could achieve these stated goals, minimize extra administrative costs, and address the issues of geographic inequity and windfall profits. Under a QEB system, Medicare could receive annual sealed competitive bids. QEB would differ from California's MediCal Medicaid contracting in three crucial ways:

1. The sealed bids would not involve catchall per diems, but rather average payments per DRG with a cost weight equal to 1 (if the bid were $4,000 and the DRG weight for that condition equaled 1.25, the payment would be $5,000).

2. Hospitals would be required to bid if they were judged to have below-average quality by their local peer-review organization (PRO) and in the pilot-test phase of QEB if they were located in a windfall-profit state.

3. Retrospective incentive compensation for quality improvements would be offered one to two years later (if a hospital bid $4,100 in a market where the national price would have been $4,900 and it improved its quality rating by 10 percent relative to the PRO moving average, the hospital would receive a retrospective 10 percent kicker bonus for quality improvement). The total payment would not exceed national DRG prices, so this provision is budget-neutral.

Some representatives of the hospital industry are likely to object to QEBs by claiming that capping the most costly institutions always erodes quality, based on the false premise that the most costly hospitals are the best and serve the most severely ill. However, equitable compensation for severity can be incorporated into the bidding system either (1) directly, by continuous measurement of severity as a new sight-digit code or (2) indirectly, on a sampling basis by factoring a reasonable incidence of retrospectively measured case severity into each class of hospital (university medical center, major teaching, moderate teaching, minor teaching, and nonteaching). Quality does not increase cost as a general rule, but rather decreases cost: The skilled and adroit are more cost-efficient than the slow and clumsy users of excess procedures or inappropriate therapeutic adjuvants. It is necessary to invest in quality by designing a bidding system that constrains costs and encourages better service and convenience. The quality-oriented preferred provider organizations and HMOs already aggressively seek competitive bids for referral hospital care based on the cost/quality/convenience mix their enrollees desire. The elderly and poor should be equally protected, with government defining a floor on quality and the DHSS managing the bidding process.

Quality-enhancement payments would give physicians more leverage to go to trustees and management and say, "Do not forgo this quality-improvement investment." If an investment helps patient care, the facility will get paid for it. To avoid the liar's dice dilemma, QEB would encourage the development of quality and efficiency in tandem. Restricting the biggest QEB gains to low-quality hospitals is important because these hospitals have the greatest potential for improvement, much as the worst-run companies are often the easiest to turn around. At least until QEB is judged cost-beneficial, incentive pay to improve quality (IPIQ) should be restricted to those hospitals in which the investment is most likely to change behavior. Wringing the windfall profits out of suboptimal hospitals and redistributing the resources to more efficient, quality-enhancing providers represents financial equity at its best. A QEB program would help inject the Smith Barney slogan into medicine: "We earn patients the old-fashioned way: We treat them better." IPIQ should be a major cause for physicians.

Chapter 6 surveyed cost-effectiveness studies. As a doctor of public health and a health economist, the author has seen politicians misuse cost-effectiveness studies. For example, Harvard School of Public Health articles attributed a greater share of the dramatic drop in U.S. heart disease mortality from 1980 to 2000 to improved treatment. The statistical analysis indicated that prevention (diet, exercise, less smoking) was half as important as treatment. Some politicians have suggested that acute cardiac treatment is a better bargain than prevention. But the data actually suggested that the healthcare system: (1) did not work enough to reduce risk factors and (2) overallocated too many resources to acute care and reduced funds available to prevention and public health programs. We can only begin to imagine the sort of low-tech strategies that can change behavior and improve the public health in the next century. We must do a much better job cost-justifying the public health programs of the future.

Quality enhancement is cost-saving. According to the Department of Health and Human Services, misuse of prescription drugs costs taxpayers more than $13 billion annually. Given the annual costs of $28 billion due to strokes, use of a new clot-dissolving drug in the initial hour after a stroke could save $4 billion. Better service and alternative treatment sites have reduced disability rates for older adults by 1.3 percent per year since 1983. If the annual 1.3 percent decline in disability can increase up to 1.6 percent per year, enough would be saved to eliminate all proposed fee hikes and Medicare tax hikes in the next decade (Office of National Cost Estimates 2002 and U.S. House of Representatives 2002).

More research needs to be done on severity measures and patient values. On the patient side, patients can compare health plans with the Health Plan Employer Data and Information Set (HEDIS), a standardized report on health plan performance developed and disseminated through the National Committee for Quality Assurance (NCQA), an independent organization whose board is composed of purchaser, health plan, and consumer representatives. CMS (formally HCFA) also works closely with NCQA to develop HEDIS measures explicitly for Medicare and Medicaid enrollees (NCQA 2002). The new HEDIS version included new process-driven performance measures such as immunization rates for childhood infections, influenza vaccinations for high-risk adults, screening for cervical cancer, eye exams for persons with diabetes mellitus, and appropriate treatment of otitis media in children. One outcome measure—the fraction of elderly enrollees reporting a change in their health status—will be adjusted appropriately using accepted mathematical models controlling for demographics and chronic conditions.

Try to Manage Change, or It Will Manage You

Politicians frequently seek headlines by claiming that the bulk of the medical cost problem is caused by the fraud and abuse of a few providers. This contributes to piecemeal attention being given to such infrequent problems as Medicaid kickbacks and HMO scandals, rather than the more insidious problem of inflationary or quality-eroding incentive structures. A quality-enhancing bidding system would go a long way toward promoting good medicine and good economics.

In visiting Chinese hospitals and medical schools, I was interested to discover that the ancient proverb, "May you live in interesting times," was often misinterpreted by Western visitors as a curse. The opportunity for substantial reform is best in just such times of stress and strain. In fact, the Chinese term *wei ji* has a simultaneous dual interpretation: opportunity and danger. Over the next few years, our health system faces immense opportunity and danger in reformation on four fronts: access, efficiency, effectiveness, and *quality of life*. The challenge for providers and managers during this period of unparalleled opportunity is to win a clear victory on all four fronts and not erode either access or quality in the name of efficiency. This is a clear challenge for both managers and policy makers. The job is doubly tough for our physicians. The challenge to physicians will be to carry on one shoulder lifesaving technology and the concomitant financial burden and, on the other shoulder, the will and imagination to apply modern management techniques to the practice of medicine.

How well physicians and managers work together will determine whether we experience the bad or the good side of the "invisible hand." Bad competition will result in overemphasis on a narrow business focus and an attempt to avoid providers' social obligations. For example, consider the lawsuits against Columbia and HCA in 1998. Any balanced view of health care should consider it both a social good and a consumer good. Good competition can invoke a broader business focus and health-delivery orientation. Good competition can stimulate neighboring providers to offer better services at more reasonable expense through specialization, economies of scale, and quality assurance. This process can improve, or erode, patient access to quality services throughout all market segments.

The nature of health services delivery is changing. We can no longer deny that health care is a blend of art, business, lifestyle, and science. Providers' traditional objectives have been expanded to include consumer-sensitive service in a more economical style, advocating patient compliance and health promotion while offering the best technical quality of care. Overemphasis on any one aspect might spell disaster for the provider and those who pursue only business interests will be no more protected or respected than used-car dealers. Likewise, those who disrespect business skills, marketing, and consumers' shifting tastes might face an early retirement. Changes in payment systems occur so rapidly that providers and medical suppliers are hard-put to keep pace and react, much less plan proactively. There is still room for improved efficiency in a health sector that spends $1 billion every five hours. Some of the resources do little good, but the majority of care averts death, pain, and erosion of functional health status. However, we must be careful not to discount quality or access in the name of economic efficiency. There is a delicate balance to maintain between health care as a social good and health care as a consumer good.

> ### ▶ Summary Points:
>
> - Government is central to the delivery of health care in the United States, primarily as a financier.
>
> - Americans spend more on health care per capita than any other nation, and yet have poor population health statistics when compared to other OECD nations.
>
> - Health care is both a social good and a consumer good.

> ### *Research and Discussion Questions:*
>
> - If we are to increase access to health care in the United States on par with Europe, will it be necessary to make U.S. physicians' salaries comparable to those of European physicians?
>
> - What effects will government-directed health care have on healthcare innovation?
>
> - How can we ensure universal access to health care without losing our edge in medical research and education?

References

Bhargava, A. 2002. The effects of health on economic growth. *Journal of Health Economics* 20(4): 423–440.

Dunlop, J. 1990. *Business and public policy*. Cambridge, MA: Harvard University Press.

Eastaugh, S. 2001. International comparisons of 15 countries. *Hospital Topics* 79(3): 10–21.

Eastaugh, S. 1999. *Health care finance*. Gaithersburg, MD: Aspen.

Eastaugh, S. 1995. *Facing tough choices: Balancing fiscal and social deficits*. Westport, CT: Greenwood.

Enthoven, A. 1999. Markets and collective action in regulating managed care. *Health Affairs* 18(6): 26–31.

Handy, C. 2002. *Beyond certainty*. Boston: Harvard Business Review.

Iezzoni, L. 1999. *Risk adjustment for measuring health care outcomes*. Ann Arbor, MI: Health Administration Press/Association for Health Service Research.

Institute of Medicine. 2002. *The quality chasm: A new health care system*. Washington, DC: National Academy Press.

Issacs, S., and Khichman, J. 2003. *To improve health and health care*. San Francisco: Jossey-Bass.

Lyles, A. 2002. Cost and quality in direct contracting. *Health Affairs* 21(1): 89–101.

Marquis, M., and Long, S. 2002. Role of price in health insurance decisions. *Health Services Research* 36(2): 935-951.

National Committee for Quality Assurance. 2002. *A road map for information systems: Evolving systems to support performance measurement.* Washington, DC: National Committee for Quality Assurance.

OECD. 2002. Organization for Economic Cooperation and Development. *Health data 2002 Paris: OECD.* Korean data from Ministry of Health and Social Affairs, Seoul.

Office of National Cost Estimates. 2002. *Trends in health care spending.* Washington, DC: U.S. Government Printing Office.

Reinhardt, U. 2001. Can efficiency in health care be left to the market? *Journal of Health Politics, Policy & Law* 26(5): 967–992.

Studnicki, J., and Murphy, F. 2002. Toward a population health delivery system. *Health Care Management Review* 27(1): 76–88.

Sullivan, A. 2001. $16 million more for Canadian health care. *New York Times,* September 3.

U.S. House of Representatives. 2002. Overview of health insurance coverage. *Green Book,* 22nd Edition, U.S. Government Printing Office.

WHO. 2002. *World health report 2002.* Available at *www.who.com,* World Health Organization, Geneva.

Wismar, M. 2002. *Health care reform in Germany.* Hannover, Germany: European Health Policy Research Institute.

Glossary

A

Access is an individual's ability to obtain appropriate health care services.

Activities of daily living, ADL, is an index or scale which measures a patient's degree of independence in bathing, dressing, using the toilet, eating, and moving from one place to another.

Adjusted average per capita cost, AAPCC, is the basis for HMO or CMP reimbursement under Medicare-risk contracts. The average monthly amount received per enrollee is currently calculated as 95 percent of the average costs to deliver medical care in the fee-for-service sector.

Allowable costs are items or elements of an institution's costs which are reimbursable under a payment formula. Both Medicare and Medicaid reimburse hospitals on the basis of certain costs only.

Antiselection or adverse selection is a tendency for utilization of health services in a population group to be higher than average.

B

Balance billing in Medicare and other federal health programs, (TRICARE) private fee-for-service health insurance is the practice of billing patients for charges that exceed the amount that the health plan will pay. Under Medicare and TRICARE, the excess amount cannot be more than 15 percent above the approved charge.

C

Capacity utilization is the extent to which a productive facility is utilized.

Capital is fixed or durable non-labor input or factors used in the production of goods and services, the value of such factors, or the money specifically allocated for their acquisition or development.

Capitation is a method of payment for health services in which an individual or institutional provider is paid a fixed amount for each person served without regard to the actual number or nature of services provided to each person in a set period of time.

Certainty equivalent is a sure outcome (10 years of life) that a decision maker deems equivalent in value to an uncertain proposition.

Case-mix index is a measure of the mix of cases being treated by a particular healthcare provider that is intended to reflect the patients' different needs for resources.

Compensation test is an economic gauge of the desirability of a program. A program is considered to be welfare enhancing if those who gain from it are willing to pay enough for their gains to compensate the losers (also *potential Pareto improvement*).

Community rating is a method of calculating health plan premiums using the average cost of actual or anticipated health services for all subscribers within a specific geographic area.

Coordination of benefits (COB) are procedures used by insurers to avoid duplicate payment for losses insured under more than one insurance policy.

Contingent valuation is a method of placing a monetary value on a good or service that is not available in the marketplace.

Cost benefit analysis (CBA) is the ratio of the discounted costs to benefits of a program or action expressed as the net present value or NPV. All costs and benefits are monetized.

Cost effectiveness analysis (CEA) is a comparison of costs and outcomes between alternative programs or interventions with a common effect.

Cost identification is the first step in performing a CBA or CEA.

Cost of illness is the total costs (direct, indirect, opportunity, and intangible) incurred.

Cost of illness study is an analysis of the total costs incurred by a society due to a specific disease.

Cost per cure is the true cost per cure. Includes the marginal costs for successes and failures.

Cost minimization analysis is the search for the least costly alternative.

Cost utility analysis is a good tool to provide a common unit of comparison. Not all of the benefits are quantified in monetary terms. For example, QALYs, states of health associated with the outcomes are valued relative to one another. Most appropriate if the important outcome is multidimensional. Uses final output data — adjusting survival for the quality of the survival; lives saved, disability day averted.

Crowd-out is a phenomenon whereby new public programs or expansions of existing public programs designed to extend coverage to the uninsured prompt some privately insured persons to drop their private coverage and take advantage of the expanded public subsidy.

D

DALE, disability-adjusted life expectancy, separates life expectancy into good-health years and years lived with the disability. While DALE is estimated to exceed 60 years in half the countries in the WHO, it is less than 40 years in 32 countries.

DALY, disability-adjusted life years lost, combines years of life lost (YLL) through premature death (before 82.5 years for a woman and before 80 years for a man) plus years lived with the disability (YLD).

Decision analysis is an explicit, quantitative, systematic approach to decision making under conditions of uncertainty in which probabilities of each possible event, along with the consequences of those events, are stated explicitly.

Direct medical costs is the value of healthcare resources consumed in the provision of an intervention or in dealing with the side effects of other current and future consequences linked to it.

Discounting is the process of converting future dollars and (health) outcomes to their present value. Allows for present value comparisons of programs with different time horizons.

Discount rate is the interest rate used to compute present value.

DRG, diagnosis related group, is a method of reimbursement established under Medicare to pay hospitals based upon a fixed price per admission according to diagnostic related groupings, not the amount of time in the hospital.

E

Economics is the study of the allocation of scarce resources.

Economies of scale are savings that are acquired through increases in quantities produced.

ERISA, the employee retirement income security act is a Federal act passed in 1974 that established new standards and reporting/disclosure requirements for employer-funded pension and health benefit programs.

Expected utility theory is a framework for analyzing decisions under uncertainty positing that alternative actions are characterized by a set of possible outcomes and a set of probabilities corresponding to each outcome. The sum of the products of the probability of each outcome and the utility of that outcome is the expected value of utility.

Externalities are the positive (beneficial) or negative (harmful) effects that market exchanges have on people who do not participate directly in those exchanges. Also called "spillover" effects.

F

Federal employees health benefits program, FEHBP, is the voluntary health insurance subsidy program administered by the Office of Personnel Management for civilian employees (including retirees and dependents) of the federal government.

Fixed costs are those held at a constant or fixed level, independent of the level of production and the time frame of the analysis (building costs).

Frictional costs are incurred as a result of a transaction (administrative costs).

Functional status is an individual's effective performance of or ability to perform roles, tasks, or activities.

G

Global budgeting is a method of hospital cost containment in which participating hospitals must share a prospectively set budget. Global budgeting may also be mandated under a universal health insurance system.

H

HALE, healthy active life expectancy, measures the number of years an individual can expect to live in a healthy state.

Health is the state of complete physical, mental, and social well-being and not merely the absence of disease or infirmity.

Health plan employer data and information set, HEDIS, a set of performance measures for health plans developed for the National Committee for Quality Assurance (NCQA) that provides purchasers with information on effectiveness of care, plan finances and costs, and other measures of plan performance and quality.

Herfindahl index, HHI, is a commonly accepted measure of market concentration. It is calculated by squaring the market share of each firm competing in the market and then summing the resulting numbers. For example, for a market consisting of four firms with shares of thirty, thirty, twenty, and twenty percent, the HHI is 2600 ($30^2 + 30^2 + 20^2 + 20^2 = 2600$). The index takes into account the relative size and distribution of the firms in a market and approaches zero when a market consists of a large number of firms of relatively equal size. The Herfindahl index increases both as the number of firms in the market decreases and as the disparity in size between those firms increases.

HIPAA, is the Health Insurance Portability and Accountability Act of 1996.

I

Indifference curve is a line showing various combinations of goods (usually two) that yield a constant level of satisfaction or utility.

L

LOS, length of stay, (usually measured in days).

M

Marginal cost is the cost to produce one additional unit of good or service.

Marginal utility is the additional satisfaction or utility received by consuming one additional unit of good or service.

Medical savings account, MSA, is an account in which individuals can accumulate contributions to pay for medical care or insurance. Some states give tax-preferred status to MSA contributions, but such contributions are still subject to federal income taxation. MSAs differ from Medical reimbursement accounts, sometimes called flexible benefits or Section 115 accounts, in that they need not be associated with an employer. Authorized under HIPAA.

Monopoly is one seller or supplier.

Monopsony is one buyer.

O

Oligopoly is a few suppliers.

P

Pharmaco-economics compares the cost of drugs against their effectiveness. Looks for the most cost-effective drug for a particular condition.

Q

QALY, quality-adjusted life years, calculate life expectancy adjusted for quality of life, where quality of life is measured on a scale from 1 (full health) to 0 (dead). The product of the Probability x Utility x Life Expectancy.

R

Risk is the responsibility of paying for or otherwise providing a level of health care services based on an unpredictable need for these services.

Risk adjustment is a process by which premium dollars are shifted from a plan with relatively healthy enrollees to another with sicker members.

S

SCHIP, the State Children's Health Insurance Program, was enacted as part of the Balanced Budget Act of 1997, which established Title XXI of the Social Security Act to provide states with $24 billion in federal funds for 1998-2002, targeting children in families with incomes up to 200 percent of the federal poverty level.

Small-group market is the insurance market for products sold to groups that are smaller than a specified size, typically employer groups. The size of groups included usually depends on state insurance laws and thus varies from state to state, with 50 employees the most common size.

U

UCR, usual, customary and reasonable fees are(1) the physician's usual charge for a given procedure; (2) the amount customarily charged for the service by other physicians in the area (often defined as a specific percentile of all charges in the community); and (3) the reasonable cost of services for a given patient after medical review of the case.

Underwriting is the process of identifying and classifying risk.

Utility (value), or valuation of heath outcomes, is a subjective value of a health outcome.

W

Willingness-to-pay, WTP, is a model to assign a price that individuals and society are willing to pay for a program, intervention, or to accept a risk.

Index